Critical Perspectives on Culture and Globalisation: The Intellectual Legacy of Ali Mazrui

Edited by
Kimani Njogu
Seifudein Adem

TWAWEZA
COMMUNICATIONS
Working Towards a Better World

Published in 2017 by:
Twaweza Communications Ltd.
P.O. Box 66872 - 00800 Westlands
Twaweza House, Parklands Road
Mpesi Lane, Nairobi Kenya
website: www.twawezacommunications.org
Tel: +(254) 020 269 4409

Design and Layout: Catherine Bosire
Cover Photo: Victor Gitonga

The 2016 Nairobi Symposium on the Intellectual Legacy of Professor Ali Mazrui and the publication of this book were supported by Open Society Initiative for Eastern Africa (OSIEA) and the Ford Foundation

ISBN: 978-9966-028-67-9

Printed by: Don Bosco Printing School
Email: boscoprint@donbosco.or.ke

Contents

Acknowledgments

This book results from a symposium entitled "Critical Perspectives on Culture and Globalization: The Intellectual Legacy of Ali A. Mazrui" held in Nairobi, Kenya, from the 15–16 July, 2016, in honor of Ali Mazrui (1933-2014), the globally acclaimed Kenyan. The symposium was organized by the Institute of Global Cultural Studies at Binghamton University, New York, and Twaweza Communications, Nairobi; it was funded by the Ford Foundation and Open Society Institute of Eastern Africa (OSIEA). We are immensely grateful to the two institutions for their support for the symposium and publication of this book. Indeed, Maurice Makoloo (Regional Director, The Ford Foundation) and Mburu Gitu (Regional Director, OSIEA) worked with the symposium steering committee to ensure that we had a very successful event.

We owe a debt of gratitude to the many scholars who came from all over the world to share their insights about the life and scholarship of the global Kenyan known as Ali Mazrui. Chief Justice (Rtd) and President of the Supreme Court of Kenya, Dr. Willy Mutunga, and Professor Alamin Mazrui worked hard before, during and after the symposium to ensure that the intellectual legacy of Mwalimu Ali Mazrui was institutionalized. Their thoughtfulness is much appreciated. We are also thankful to the media houses in Kenya and abroad who ensured that the intellectual conversations in the symposium reached wider audiences.

Another outcome of the symposium was the setting up of a Working Group to explore how the intellectual legacy of Professor Ali A. Mazrui could be solidified and incorporated in higher education in Africa. The signs are now encouraging that the Professor Ali A. Mazrui Centre/ Institute of Global Cultural Studies will be established at the Nairobi-based United States International University (USIU) – Africa. We are grateful to the Working Group and the USIU-Africa management for moving the process forward.

We also acknowledge and deeply appreciate the editorial and technical assistance we received in preparing this manuscript for publication from David Aduda (Nation Media Group), Victor Gitonga and Catherine Bosire.

Notes on Contributors

Abdul Samed Bemath is a South African based freelance library consultant, bibliographer and indexer. He has compiled three annotated bibliographies of the works of Professor Ali A. Mazrui covering the period 1962-2016.

Ahmed Ali Salem is Associate Professor, Department of Islamic World Studies, Zayed University, United Arab Emirates.

Chris Wanjala is Professor of Literature at the University of Nairobi. He is the author of two critical books: *The Season of Harvest* (1978) and *For Home and Freedom* (1980); edited *Memories We Lost and Other Stories* (2017) and a novel, *Drums of Death* (2005). His forthcoming autobiography, *Yearnings Beyond Mount Elgon,* will be published soon.

Hamdy A. Hassan is Professor of Political Science, College of Humanities and Social Sciences, Zayed University, Dubai.

Horace G.Campbell is the Kwame Nkrumah Chair of African Studies at the Institute of African Studies, University of Legon, Ghana. He is on leave from Syracuse University where he holds a joint Professorship in the Department of African American Studies and the Department of Political Science, Maxwell School in the United States.

Jideofor Adibe is Associate Professor of Political Science at Naarawa State University, Keffi, Nigeria.

Kimani Njogu holds a Ph.D (1994) in Linguistics from Yale University. He is an indipendent scholar and Director of Twaweza Communications, Nairobi, Kenya.

Munene Macharia is a UN recognized *Expert* on *Decolonisation.* He is Professor of History and International Relations at USIU-Africa, Nairobi, Kenya.

Mohamed Bakari retired from Istanbul University, in June, 2016, and is currently winding up his affairs in Istanbul to return to Kenya, where he hopes to teach in one of the universities in his country of birth.

Paul Tiyambe Zeleza holds a Ph.D (1982) in African history from Dalhousie University and is the Vice Chancellor and Professor of Humanities and Social Science, USIU-Africa, Nairobi, Kenya.

P. Anyang' Nyong'o is currently part-time Professor at the University of Nairobi Department of Political Science and Public Administration, Nairobi, Kenya.

Samuel M. Makinda is Professor of Security Studies and International Relations in the School of Business and Governance at Murdoch University in Perth, Australia.

Seifudein Adem is a former Research Associate Professor and Associate Director of the Institute of Global Cultural Studies at Binghamton University, New York, where he also served as a full-time faculty member from 2006 to 2016.

Timothy M. Shaw was a graduate student of Professor Mazrui's at Makerere University in the late-1960s. He is now visiting professor at UMass Boston & Adjunct Professor at Aalborg, Carleton, Ottawa & Stellenbosch univerisites.

Foreword

A Tribute to an Intellectual Griot

This book explores the intellectual legacy of Professor Ali Mazrui who died on October 12, 2014, at the age of 81. He was one of Africa's greatest intellectuals of the 20th century and a prominent architect of postcolonial scholarship, an indefatigable voice for Africa's intellectual rebirth and empowerment. Mazrui's stature rests on several extraordinary achievements, three of which can be singled out.

First, there was his prodigious volume of scholarship. He published more than 30 books, hundreds of essays, commentaries, and film documentaries. Second, the range, probity, and impact of his intellectual analyses, interventions, and debates were extraordinary. Mazrui embodied the life of the public intellectual par excellence. He was a towering intellectual who moved seamlessly between the classroom, conference circuit, popular media, and corporate boardroom, to the corridors of political power. He relished intellectual debate and combat because he believed in the power of ideas as a dynamic force in human history. Third, his commitment to repositioning Africa's global standing and the place of African scholarship in global scholarship was unfaltering. He did this by unapologetically remapping and inserting Africa in global history, developments, and discourses, and through scholarship that was capacious in its interdisciplinarity, internationalism, and interculturalism.

I first met Professor Mazrui in 1978 when he came as a guest speaker at my MA class at the London School of Economics and Political Science. Over the years I got to know him personally through my friendship with his nephew, Alamin Mazrui, as well as through our encounters at the annual meetings of the US African Studies Association, and many other forums and contexts. My generation of African intellectuals admired his exceptional brilliance, infectious love of ideas and debate, passion for Africa's regeneration and generosity as a mentor. He was a man my generation of African academics admired, a scholar we sought to emulate.

His contributions to African studies were intellectual, ideological, and institutional. Intellectually, against prevailing notions that sought to simplify and homogenize Africa, he insisted on the continent's diversities, complexities, and contradictions of African histories and societies, of its multiple dimensions and trajectories. This was captured brilliantly in his BBC Reith Lectures, *The African Condition*, and most memorably in the 1986 television series and accompanying book, *Africa: A Triple Heritage* in which he built on Edward Blyden and Kwame Nkrumah's ideas that Africa represented a complex confluence of three civilizational forces: the indigenous, Islamic, and Western.

His trenchant critiques of Eurocentrism remained a permanent feature of his work. A methodological subversion of Eurocentric historiography was most evident in two books, *Nationalism and New States in Africa: From about 1935 to the Present* published in 1984 and Vol. 8 of the *Unesco General History of Africa* that he edited and was published in 1993. In both books decolonization and contemporary African history were dated to 1935, not 1945, to the Italian invasion of Ethiopia rather than the end of the Second World War.

His attack on the authoritarian propensities of nationalism, the assault on democratic aspirations and ideals of what has come to be called "the first independence" by the African postcolonial leaders was perceptively captured in a series of his early books on post-colonial African politics. They include two books he published in 1967, *On Heroes and Uhuru-Worship: Essays on Independent Africa* and *Towards a Pax Africana: A Study of Ideology and Ambition*.

Another major intellectual contribution centered on his work on Pan-Africanism to which he brought his multilayered analytical perspective. He distinguished between five versions of Pan-Africanism: the Trans-Atlantic, continental, sub-Saharan, Pan-Arab, and global. He underscored the complex interconnections between them as an essential part of understanding African liberation movements and ideologies. This also allowed him to complicate conventional conceptions of Pan-Africanism and advance the notion of "Afrabia" that challenged imperial constructs of Africa and the Middle East.

Mazrui's historically and culturally expansive and more accurate understanding of Pan-Africanism reflected and reinforced a broader conception of African Diasporas that is evident in his later work, including *The African Diaspora: African Origins and New World Identities* that he co-edited in 1999.

Equally remarkable is Mazrui's work on the globalization of Africa. He believed passionately that Africa was a global civilization, that it was central, not peripheral, to the development of world history, both as a victim and a player. This is powerfully articulated in a series of publications including his 1990 book, *Cultural Forces in World Politics* and *Africa and other Civilizations: Conquest and Counter-Conquest, The Collected Essays of Ali A. Mazrui* published in 2002.

Mazrui's ideological contributions to African scholarship and politics are similarly broad and remarkable. He was the epitome of liberal thought. He engaged in spirited attacks on both the rigidities of Marxism and African socialism. This was evident at the famous Dar es Salaam debate with Walter Rodney, the Guyanese Marxist scholar activist.

Mazrui's relocation from Idi Amin's Uganda to the United States in the early 1970s refocused and sharpened his scholarship into an expansive humanism. His work was increasingly marked by a deep concern and commitment to human rights, agency, and freedom. He wrote copiously on struggles for social justice for marginalized communities based on race, gender, and religion. He became a fierce critic of postcolonial tyrannies, apartheid, and racial oppression in the diaspora, and of women's exploitation, Islamic fundamentalist intolerance and Euroamerican demonization of Muslims.

The eclectic works of Mazrui from the late 1970s to the time of his death reflect a mind increasingly agitated by oppression in all its forms, scholarship animated by moral passion and fearlessness, an abiding faith in the indomitability of human agency. He ruffled many feathers among western intellectuals some of whom had lauded him while he was in Uganda as a paragon of liberalism. The National Endowment for the Humanities withdrew its name from the credits of his acclaimed television series.

He entered the fray of the fraught debate for reparations against slavery when he was appointed to the Eminent Persons Group by the OAU on the subject. In 2002 published *Black Reparations in the Era of Globalization*. His commitment to gender was articulated in a series of interventions both intellectual and political. Writing on the African Renaissance he argued that it needed three major revolutions in skills, values, and gender relations. Thus he saw women's emancipation and empowerment as an ethical, cultural, political, and economic necessity, as a developmental and democratic imperative.

Mazrui's scholarship also increasingly focused on the ferocious debates about trends in Islam and the rising Islamophobic post-cold war West looking for new a eternal enemy to feed the insatiable hate machine of the military industrial complex. This is reflected in series of publications including *Islam: Between Globalization & Counter-Terrorism* published in 2006 and the co-edited collection *Islam in Africa's Experience* published in 2008.

As for his institutional contributions, space only allows the listing of a few highlights. He was instrumental in the development of the field of African political science beginning at Makerere University where he became the first African professor of political science. The topics he dealt with helped set terms of debate in the field of African politics, and Africa's international relations. Moreover, he mentored generations of African students.

Mazrui was also an influential figure in the development of the field of African and African American American studies first as Director of the Center for Afro-American and African Studies at the University of Michigan from 1978 to 1981. Later when he relocated to Binghampton University he served as Director of the Institute of Global Cultural Studies. It is also important to mention that he was elected President of the US African Studies Association.

In addition to his role as an institutional builder of African, African American, and global studies, he left an indelible legacy on the development of African of higher education both as a scholar and as an academic leader. His prodigious scholarship on African universities and intellectuals include his two books *Political Values and the Educated Class in Africa* published in 1978 on the problematic colonial legacies of African universities and ambiguous identities of the educated class; and *The Power of Babel: Language and Governance in the African Experience* published in 1998 on the disempowering effects of the dominance of European languages in African scholarly knowledge production and governance

He also held a series of administrative and consultative positions. They include serving as Chancellor of Jomo Kenyatta University of Agriculture and Technology; member of the Pan-African Advisory

Council to the United Nations' Children's Fund; Vice-President, World Congress of Black Intellectuals; member of the United Nations Commission on Transnational Corporations; member of the World Bank's Council of African Advisors; and Vice-President, International African Institute.

For me Professor Mazrui was one of Africa's most important intellectual griots, a fierce guardian of African memory and dignity, a seer of our present condition, who fervently believed in our future possibilities. He was a giant of the first postcolonial generation of African scholars to whom my generation and the generations coming after us owe tremendous debt and gratitude for giving us the permission to think big, critically, and confidently about our history and humanity in the past, present, and future.

This book, which results from a Symposium held on 15th - 16th July 2016 and organized by Twaweza Communications and the University of Binghamton, Centre for Global Cultural Studies is a worth tribute to this intellectual griot.

Paul Tiyambe Zeleza

Vice Chancellor, and Professor of the Humanities and the Social Sciences, USIU-Africa, Nairobi.

Culture and Globalization: A Contextual Essay

Kimani Njogu

Writing about language policies in Africa and the continuities of the colonial experience, Mazrui (1988: 22) has correctly observed that the colonial governments had two major considerations in determining their language policies on the continent: language as a vehicle for cultural transmission, and language as a carrier of knowledge, at times subversive to the *status quo*. The colonial government recognized that language can be used to transmit a content that could transform the consciousness of the colonialized so that it consents and supports the colonial status quo. Language would be a tool of legitimizing the state and its operations in the colony. Equally, language as a bearer of knowledge could imbue the African with counter-consciousness dangerous to the very survival of colonialism. In this second sense, language could be used in a tool of subversion, mobilization, resistance, liberation and freedom. It could undermine an oppressive state and citizens affirm their humanity.

In the case of Kenya, the British colonial government attempted to create a balance between these considerations by allowing limited access to the English language; the critical factor being the extent to which the language served the interests of the colonial government in its labor needs and the extraction of natural resources. African languages continued to play a peripheral role in the affairs of government and education, except in cases where urbanization, militarization, and commercialization brought together people from a range of ethno-linguistic groups. In such cases, languages such as Kiswahili created a place for themselves as *lingua franca* especially among workers, traders and police officers. It was also, as Ali Mazrui & Alamin Mazrui

(1995) have observed associated with Islam and Christianity in Kenya and Tanzania. They observe:

> "Kiswahili facilitated social intercourse among Muslims from different ethnic groups and regions, an d gradually built up a comprehensive culture of its own over and above language as a mere medium of communication. Swahili culture was born with its own form of Islam, its own world-view, its own dress culture, its own cuisine, its own ethics and aesthetics." (1995: 2-3)

Under colonialism, Kiswahili clearly had a major role as a language of inter-ethnic interaction and evangelization. But in general African languages continued to be marginalized and to serve as indicators of low socio-economic status, with English marking itself as the language of prestige, high status and upward socio-economic mobility. A disconnect between content carried by local languages and that of English and Kiswahili emerged: English was viewed as the language of generating and transmitting international and national knowledge and community languages were seen as instruments of cultural expression at the local level. Restricted in their use, community languages became tools for ethnic solidarity and expression.

During the liberation struggle, Kiswahili was used by Kenyan nationalists to reach out across ethnic groups and to subvert the colonial agenda of ethnic stereotyping and divisiveness. After independence, the role of Kiswahili as the language of inter-ethnic solidarity at the political arena declined because the colonial state was not dismantled and with rural-urban migration African languages were de-emphasized, especially by the emerging middle-class. Instruments of power and the psychology that was dominant at the colonial period found continuity on the attainment of political independence. There was no expression of linguistic nationalism. Indeed whereas there has been a strong sense of linguistic nationalism in Asian countries, the same cannot be said of many African countries (Mazrui and Tidy 1984: 299; Mazrui and Mazrui 1998:154). In certain cases, the push has been for the acquisition of more Western languages such as German and French, especially among the middle-class.

But there have been significant moments in East Africa when nationalists have urged that the central role occupied by English be re-considered. For example, immediately after Kenya became a Republic (1964) Prime Minister Mzee Jomo Kenyatta delivered his speech to the first parliament in English and then concluded by speaking in Kiswahili after declaring English "a colonialistic language." He urged that the country releases itself from linguistic chains by adopting Kiswahili as the nation's official language (Republic of Kenya, 1965: Column 8). In all his public speeches Kenyatta spoke in Kiswahili, even if briefly. In 1974 he declared it a national language, as well as the language of parliamentary proceedings. Unfortunately, this declaration did not receive enough support from the political elite and English was in case the language of status and prestige. Moreover, despite these nationalistic proclamations, motions debated in Kiswahili ended up in bills written in English because the language of the judiciary remains English. The executive, the legislature and the judiciary did not harmonize the vision of Kiswahili as the language of national cohesion and popular participation in public affairs. No real energies were expended to promote African languages, including Kiswahili in educational institutions by the Kenyatta government. It was left to the Presidential Working Party appointed in 1981 and adopted by the government in 1984 to have Kiswahili recognized as a tool for national development. The party noted that "Although Kiswahili is the national language, there are many university graduates who cannot communicate in Kiswahili" (p. 443). Thereafter, the educational system in Kenya changed in order to follow the American system: eight years of primary education, four years of secondary education and four years of university education.

The entry of 8:4:4 system of education made Kiswahili a compulsory and examinable subject in all schools in the mid-1980s. This action has ensured that the youth in Kenya get a strong mastery of the language, to the extent that the language is now likely to be an official language, together with English and Sign language, in addition to its role as the language of national identity and cohesion. All public universities now encourage post-graduate students from Kiswahili Departments to write their dissertations in Kiswahili, and a number of theoretically rigorous studies are currently undertaken in the language (Chimerah 2000). More work needs to be done to consciously bring Kiswahili into professional organizations and training institutions, such as the Kenya School of Law and the Kenya Medical School. The inclusion of Kiswahili as a service course in these institutions will help professionals serve the public more effectively. The course could be designed as a PASS/FAIL unit and professionals required to pass before they can serve the public. At another level, politicians would be required to show proficiency at a higher level that is currently the case. These actions would ensure that the language gains the status and prestige it deserves as and the national and regional *lingua franca*.

Unlike Kenya, Tanzania has done much to anchor Kiswahili in national affairs through political action and the setting up of institutions for the development of the language (Abdulaziz 1971). Between 1940 and 1961, English was the dominant language of Tanganyika in the educational system. The medium of instruction in rural primary schools was Kiswahili during the first five years. But after those initial years all subjects, except Kiswahili, were taught in English. English was taught as a subject from the third year of primary education and was a medium of instruction in many urban schools. But Mwalimu Julius Nyerere in consolidating the nation-state entrenched Kiswahili in the national psyche. At independence in 1961, Kiswahili became the national language and the tool for interethnic unity. With the 1967 Arusha Declaration and the introduction of Education for Self-Reliance, a linguistic shift became eminent. Primary education was supposed to be complete by itself and to prepare the youth for life and Kiswahili would be the tool to deliver this goal. Consequently, in May 1967, soon after the inauguration of Education for Self-Reliance, Kiswahili was officially declared the medium of instruction in all primary schools in mainland Tanzania, except in selected private schools in Dar-es-Salaam. Through the publication of books to meet curriculum needs, translation of existing materials, writing of dictionaries and supplementary texts, the language was given the opportunity to flourish. Until now, it is the medium of instruction in all government primary schools.

Language instruments such as the National Kiswahili Council (BAKITA) and the Institute of Kiswahili Research (IKR) at the University of Dar-es-Salaam are contributing in the standardization of Kiswahili and the expansion of its lexicon. But the language is also developing at the expense of other Tanzanian languages and the phenomenon of language loss is real. Moreover, certain segments of the leadership in Tanzania are pushing for the reintroduction of English as a medium of instruction in all schools. In the recent past, a few private schools have started using English as the medium of instruction in the belief that doing so will open up opportunities for Tanzanians which are currently denied them through emphasizing Kiswahili in the education system. The earlier dream of making Kiswahili the only medium of instruction at all levels of education in Tanzania seems to be waning and may require a new push by language activists in the region.

Tanzania might want to consider improving the teaching of English as a language for purposes of interaction but it would be a tragedy if it forfeited the use of Kiswahili. It is vital that Swahiliphone Africa consolidates the regional language so that it can guide the rest of the continent. The balancing and consolidation would need to start at the national level.

There is no doubt that a major linguistic challenge facing African countries today is how to develop a language policy that would both accommodate languages inherited from the colonial experience, such as English and French, while at the same time creating an important space for the development and promotion of indigenous languages, such as Kiswahili (Okombo 2001). Colonialism presented two scenarios for Africa vis-à-vis the language question: Whereas the British system of indirect rule made use of traditional systems of knowledge and governance, whenever possible, by making local languages important for the colonial administrator, the French policy of assimilation gave very little regard to indigenous languages, prioritizing instead the French language and culture. The British colonial regimes introduced English, even if to a limited degree, but allowed at least in the initial stages, the growth of indigenous languages. This is not to suggest, of course, that British colonialism had an interest in developing African languages *per se*. The support was provided only to the extent that they served colonial interests. Towards the end of the colonial era, the British government in the colonies seems to have accelerated the use of English among the people as a way of preparing the local elite to take over and to perpetuate and protect British interests.

The presence of languages that are in competition with each other in Africa – with some occupying a more prestigious and powerful space than others – creates a situation of tension and contestation. But would the tensions lead to a deliberate erasure of some languages and a re-inscription of others? I see the questioning we are engaged in as an attempt to allow for the co-existence of multiple languages but with a rigorous effort to develop African languages in their various forms and manifestations following the 2000 Asmara Declaration. At the center of these initiatives would be, of course, the development of national and regional languages. Linguistic diversity as a way of maintaining biological and environmental diversity is the most viable for Africa. In addition, the promotion and development of African languages is a necessary prerequisite to political, economic, social and cultural emancipation.

Indigenous language development is part of the decolonization of the African continent in all domains of life. There are, naturally, pedagogical and instrumental constraints and facilitations to the proposal of anchoring African languages; some of which may be located in the colonial experience as well as the phenomenon of globalization, information technology and economic constraints. Considering the limited resources in Africa, for instance, how can we pointedly develop a set of regional languages while keeping linguistic diversity alive? An important starting point in the case of East African countries is the unambiguous, deliberate and rigorous development of Kiswahili at the national and regional level.

It is broadly recognized that a key feature of Eastern African countries is their triglossic nature; a consequence of the colonial encounter, sketched above, which also assigned prestige and status to the acquisition of foreign languages and deliberately discouraged the teaching and learning of African languages, except for evangelical purposes and basic functions of interpersonal communication. Although most missionary work was undertaken in indigenous languages, the colonial government did occasionally seek to suppress this process of Christianization. And that did not just happen in East Africa. When German missionaries arrived in Cameroon at the onset of the German colonial period they used local languages for education and evangelization. However, in 1897 the colonial administration put a ban on the use of indigenous languages in schools. Only the German language was to be used for teaching and learning. Moreover, in 1900 the 'Schutzgebietgesetz' law gave missionaries the right to only carry out their evangelization mission in local languages. Despite these prohibitions, indigenous languages continued to play a critical role in evangelization – through translation of the Bible, hymns and other religious texts – as well as in popular communication in homes, cultural production, commercial activities and so on.

But as the reins of power changed hands at independence, one would have expected that there would be a reversal of the language policy and practice and that indigenous and national languages would receive greater emphasis and visibility in governance, law, economic engagement and education. This is especially so because schools and other spaces where education takes place are prime arenas for language reclamation. But that was not to be, at least in Kenya. In Kenya, the national language and other indigenous forms of expression have not received sufficient attention and have continued to play a marginal role in national affairs and educational institutions. Moreover, they are not deliberately developed and promoted. Indeed, because of the uneven relations between languages, certain indigenous languages are in jeopardy and are in danger of being lost especially within the context of ethno-linguistic expansion, technologization and homogenization.

Although globalization – a process of cultural interconnectedness, homogeneity, integration, and disintegration – (Tomlinson 1999), is contributing to language loss, there are other factors that might also accelerate to the loss of some Kenyan languages, such as Suba, Ogiek, Il Chamus and El Molo. One factor is that languages which do not have a systematic and vibrant writing and reading tradition and which rely heavily on orality, are likely to die out if one generation fails to learn them. Current generations are not learning, reading or working in the languages of their parents. Hence the urgent need to carry out descriptive and sociolinguistic action on all languages, as well as linguistic classifications, including distribution patterns, standardized orthography, and the development of dictionaries and printed materials. There is need to develop reading materials for children in local languages. Also, within the context of language loss, Kenyan linguists are urging the government to rigorously and consistently support the development of indigenous languages and the Ministry of Culture and National Heritage has set up language departments and committees in all districts in the country (Director of Culture, July 29, 2008, *personal communication*). The pace with which these departments work will, of course, depend on the conviction of the relevant officers as well as the articulation of the value attached to knowing indigenous languages well and the opportunities presented for learning them. Whatever the case, in most urban areas, Kiswahili can be foregrounded as the language of social and economic activity and contribute in inter-ethnic understanding. It is indeed already fulfilling this role but that function can be strengthened and focused. The language can be an engine of national development, the eradication of poverty and contribute in food security.

Currently, close to 50% of Kenyans live below the poverty line but by addressing issues of language we may change this pattern. In my view, Kenya's failure to address the language question in national development, consistently and deliberately, has contributed in the widening of the gap between the rich and the poor and this glaring difference played a role in the 2008 post-election violence. Increased school drop-out and transition rates, rising poverty and socio-economic inequities, and unemployment demand of us to think creatively about imparting relevant knowledge and skills in the languages available to the bulk of the people. Most school leavers operate within the nation-state, and not internationally, and greater proficiency in a national language would make them more productive than is currently the case. With Kiswahili as a regional lingua franca, citizens will easily cross borders and undertake economic activities without regard to levels of formal education.

Africa is endowed with abundant national resources. However, the continent's future economic growth will depend mainly on its labor skills and its ability to accelerate a demographic transition. Also, the continent will require to invest in people in order to promote their individual development. In order to achieve these, we need education, health, flexibility and a certain amount of economic security. But in the context of HIV and AIDS, war and conflict, drought, urbanization, unemployment, and massive poverty, the situation does look grim. Yet by focusing on protection against vulnerability, Africa can solve its crisis and language can play a major role towards this end. In view of the dismal levels of literacy, it is becoming quite important to explore if using African languages, such as Kiswahili, as engines of development can help solve the problem. They might open possibilities for the bulk of the people to be engaged in productive labour, and participate in politics and economic activities. Regional languages, such as Kiswahili, Zulu and Hausa, could be used to bolster cross-border trade, widen access to services especially for the rural people and increase community involvement in construction, maintenance and management of the infrastructure. Indeed, water systems in Kenya "built as part of self-help efforts proved far more reliable than those installed by the Water Ministry" (*World Bank Human Development Report*, 2000:152). The medium of the self-help efforts, made possible through the Harambee movement for social change, was indigenous languages. They were used for mobilization, mass participation, and the creation of a sense of identity and solidarity.

The link between languages and cultures on development cannot be ignored. This is because language is more than a means for the transmission of information. It is also a tool for creativity, innovation, affinity and solidarity. Kwesi Prah (2002: 35) considers the language of the masses the vehicle for undertaking development. By using a language such as Kiswahili, we increase public participation, facilitate affirmative action, broaden decision making processes, build on indigenous language systems and ensure Africans are enlisted for African development. Thus within the context of seeking a path to greater development for the Kenyan people by enlarging avenues for working directly with communities, African languages can be emphasized and modernized as engines of development. Development workers cannot effectively work through interpreters when in the rural areas. Instead, many of them are learning local languages in order to engage in meaningful communication.

There is no doubt that Africa is undergoing tremendous changes at the political level. A range of opportunities are now available for popular participation in politics, accountability of leaders, openness and transparency in the conduct of national affairs, and the pursuit of justice and fairness for all. These democracy markers are opening new possibilities for African languages. In pursuing national integration across ethnic lines and between socio-economic classes, indigenous languages are being sought and their functions expanded. Politicians would like to engage in intra-ethnic and inter-ethnic dialogue with the electorate without recourse to interpretation which can be quite alienating. Tanzania is a good example of how the challenge of national integration and unity could be resolved. By centralizing Kiswahili as the language of political action, the Tanzanian people have ensured broad public participation in national affairs. The country has one of the most politically informed citizenry in the region with a vibrant media and diverse outlets for news and information in Kiswahili.

The realignment of language practices are also influenced by economic factors which are equally important for the consolidation of democracy. Indigenous languages can be key to enhancing local and national markets, mobilizing workers and peasants, disseminating information on basic rights that have a bearing on production and providing economic solutions that challenge the phenomenon of dependence on the West. Thus, as African nations seek to delink themselves from the fetters of cultural and economic dependence they are likely to entrench certain African languages. For instance, the African Union passed a resolution making Kiswahili one of the organic official languages in July 2002 and it was implemented at the General Assembly in Addis Ababa in July 2004. The working languages of the

African Union are now Arabic, English, French, Kiswahili, Portuguese, Spanish and any other African language. Apparently, the continental body seeks to instill a sense of worth for African languages, here represented by Kiswahili, and to contribute in reshaping language related policies for Africa.

The Arena of technology

Information Communication Technology is an important context in our understanding of how indigenous languages operate in Kenya. Although internet growth has been fast in Kenya, access is mainly confined to urban centers due to lack of electricity, poor networks, costs of installation and maintenance. But there is a growing interest in kiosks, cyber cafés, hotels, and other sites for public internet access (schools, police stations, clinics). These spaces allow for information sharing, sometimes of linguistic significance. In reality, the greatest challenge for Africa's internet connectivity is not access but content generation. Africa, South of the Sahara, generates 0.4% of global content, and when one factors out South Africa, the rest of the Sub-continent gives only 0.02%. This is truly tragic and ought to be reversed. Kiswahili is one language that can be mobilized to change this state of affairs through deliberate engagement for the generation of content on the internet.

The internet is being used to exchange key information on health, agriculture, business, opportunities for self-advancement, and distance learning. Moreover, advances in information technology are creating opportunities for people to access their government through e-governance and civic engagement portals, increase public participation in politics and improve social services. But for Africa to participate effectively in global information economy, it will need to increase the generation and flow of local knowledge. Notwithstanding the slow pace of online engagement, the growth of communication technology – internet, mobile phones, and satellite networks – have truly compressed time and space. We are witnessing the emergence of online communities brought together on the internet by convergences of politics, ethnicity, gender, professional duty and shared social concerns. Communities are getting closer to the sources of information and are more informed than a decade ago. The entertainment and media industry are influencing culture and creativity in fundamental ways but we are also experiencing multilingual internet sites and radio programming in local languages. We can develop stronger internet communities of those who use African languages and a Kiswahili internet community is a good place to begin the conversation. Community radio stations have started gaining root and these have the effect of enhancing competence in the language of the broadcast.

In Kenya over 80% of households have access to a radio and in the rural areas and the informal settlements around the urban areas most audience members listen to Kiswahili or local language stations. With the push for greater democracy, free market economy and public participation in governance, many African countries have liberalized the airwaves and there is an increase in FM stations which encourage listener interaction through mobile phones and the internet. Whereas some of these stations promote English through programming that targets urban youth, a number especially community radio stations contribute in the development and promotion of community languages. Local language stations do also make economic sense, especially when they are well targeted. But they should be run professionally and with the consolidation of the nation-state in mind so that ethnic fixation is challenged and questioned. Local language stations should be spaces for the celebration of particularities and differences and not aimed at isolation and ethnic stereotyping. Let me elaborate this though further.

Even when they are not fully community based, local language radio stations add value to the development and promotion of African languages. They contribute in standardizing language use, expanding the lexicon and increasing mastery. The number of speakers of the language is also increased through on-air-teaching programs.

Local language radio and TV stations will undoubtedly have an impact on indigenous languages and democratization. Unfortunately, quite often some of the stations have used the space they occupy in the airwaves to balkanize and perpetuate ethnic mistrust, hate and intolerance. It has been claimed that the 2007-2008 post-election violence in Kenya can partly be blamed on the propaganda, misinformation and distortions perpetuated by vernacular radio stations. Instead of promoting democratic values, some of the stations retreated to narrow sectarian interests and violated the tenets of journalism through partisan reporting and patronage. They gave fodder to those interested in limiting freedom of expression and those opposed to the development of local knowledge. The radio journalist, Joshua Arap Sang of KASS FM, was indicted at the International Criminal Court on claims of statements made or facilitated through his programs and which may have led to crimes against humanity. He was acquitted of these charges but the potential misuse of airwaves had been flagged.

Kiswahili stations can provide a lead in the development of nationalistic content and the development of a culture of inter-ethnic tolerance, democracy and human rights. Equally, cultural workers and media practitioners can contribute in professionalizing local language stations so that they uphold ethical programming and the respect of human rights. It will be recalled that the Rwanda genocide was blamed to a significant degree on vernacular stations. It will be appreciated that the centralization of a national language is not a sufficient condition for justice, democracy, peace and human rights. Work must be done to improve the quality of local and national leaders.

The social Arena

In his essay *"Creating Space for a Hundred Flowers to Bloom: The Wealth of a Common Global Culture"* Ngugi wa Thiong'o (1993) identifies three traditions from Africa. First is orature such as is encapsulated in oral narratives, performances, *gicandi* poetry (poetic riddling in Gikuyu) and other poetic exchanges. Second is writing in European languages, which arose out of the colonial experience as a method of interrogating the Eurocentric worldview. But according to Ngugi, the writer writing in European languages,

> "... has colluded in prosperous uprooting of the African tongue... the African peasant and worker in this literature reappears on the stage of world history speaking not his gabble but perfect English, French or Portuguese, a remarkable case of literary surgery and transplant since in reality the masses of African people do continue speaking and using and creating in African languages." (1993: 20).

Thus when we are talking about promoting and developing African languages we cannot ignore the role played by writers. Through the skill of translation we can keep languages alive but this should be supported and undertaken deliberately. The third tradition according to Ngugi, is that of writing in African languages – a reconnection with the medium of orature. Yet this writing is not without difficulties. There are problems of readership, levels of literacy, orthography, diversity of languages, lack of a critical tradition and so on. Writing in African languages, nonetheless has immense implications for critical scholarship. For instance, critics of African literature will need to learn an African language in order to provide analysis. While borrowing from African orature and world literatures, this third tradition will play a key role in social and cultural renewal. For many years, many East African scholars have created imaginative and analytic works in Kiswahili as well as other indigenous languages. Consequently, non-Kiswahili speakers are finding it necessary to access literature as well as histories of the communities whose experiences are reenacted imaginatively. A new group of students of African languages is emerging and this might explain why a number of language institutions have sprung up around East Africa.

For example, the Nairobi Anglican Church of Kenya School of Language and Orientation trains preachers, researchers and students in Kenyan languages. At the school Gikuyu, Dholuo, Kimaasai, Kimeru, Kiembu, Kitaita, Kipsigis, Kamba and Luhya are taught alongside Kiswahili, French, Spanish, German, Japanese, Arabic and sign language. According to Rev. Samuel Njoroge, "the school was set up in the drive to evangelize as many indigenous people as possible in the languages they understand" (*The Standard* February 24, 2005). In 1965 the Church Missionary Society established a formal place to teach local languages. They knew the power of local languages in enhancing spirituality: "Missionaries would preach for six months and then take a six week break. It is during the break that they would learn local languages" (Rev. Njoroge 25 February 2005).

Institutions such as the School of Language and Orientation have tremendous potential for the promotion and development of African languages, although most are based in the capital cities. With more human traffic across nations, we are likely to see linguistic entrepreneurs cashing in on this goldmine and catapulting African languages to greater heights. They point to what needs to be done with Kiswahili as a national and regional language.

The educational Arena

A word on language in education. Although the Kenya Institute of Education provides guidelines on what should be taught in schools and contributes in vetting books that would be used in schools, teachers and students have a wide choice. In the case of Kiswahili, for example, general guidelines are given to curriculum implementers and publishers on which linguistic competences would be tested at the end of teaching cycles.

But children in Kenya are acquiring other languages, in addition to the home language, without prompting by parents or educational institutions. Peers in the street, cartoons, radio and television shows, interaction with tourists, neighborhood groups, house help involved in child rearing, stage performances and so on are important ways of informally learning new languages. Sheng, a youth slang derived from Kiswahili, other African languages, English and a host of tongues including Arabic and Hindi is picked in the streets as a marker of solidarity and inclusion. Young people are inducted into it swiftly by their peers and it is consolidating itself as a medium of cultural productions, such as music. There have been claims that it has a negative impact on the acquisition of English and standard Kiswahili (Mbaabu 1996: 215) and that it should be discouraged in schools. Whatever the case, it is a linguistic phenomenon, tied up with youth culture and the process of globalization. It might be worthwhile integrating it somehow into the school curriculum, instead of wishing it away.

The formal route to the acquisition of Kenyan languages is, of course, more vibrant and sustainable. Where a second language is not acquired naturally in the community, the school has been the most important institution for language learning. In the case of Kenya, most children learn Kiswahili in the streets and in school and the vernacular languages are acquired either within the family or in the community. Vernacular languages are supposed to be taught during the first three years of school but this hardly happens. Throughout the educational system, a system of code-switching seems to dominate.

The promotion and development of indigenous language can also be linked to the policy on adult education. In Kenya, statements related to literacy and adult education can be found in *Sessional Paper No. 10 on African Socialism and its Application to Planning in Kenya of 1965; the Education Commission Report (Ominde Commission) of 1964; The Board of Adult Education Act, 1996 (revised 1967); the Presidential Directive of 1978* that created the Department of Adult Education; *Sessional Paper No. 6 of* 1988 that renewed committee to eradication of illiteracy; and the *NARC Manifesto – 2002* (section 5:2:3) with its commitment to develop a comprehensive adult education programme. If literacy is the ability to acquire skills that will help an individual identify, understand, interpret, create, communicate and compute using printed and written texts, then it does provide one with a continuum of learning which facilitates an individual to realize his or her goals. Because adult education is related to the acquisition of reading and writing skills, as well as the development of other functions, it is only logical that it be conducted in indigenous languages and that foreign languages be taught as subjects.

The World Education Forum held in Dakar, Senegal in April 2000 renewed the world's commitments to Education for All by putting in place two goals to be achieved: (a) ensuring that the learning needs of young people and adults are met through equitable access to appropriate learning and life skills programmes, and (b) achieving a 50% improvement in levels of adult literacy by 2015, especially for women, and equitable access to basic and continuing education for all adults. The interest shown by the United Nations General Assembly (Resolution 56/116) in declaring the United Nations Literacy Decade (2003-2012) is indicative of some of the opportunities provided by world bodies for the growth of African languages. Literate adult populations are likely to contribute in writing and reading works in indigenous languages. They are also likely to encourage others to do so.

The Kenya literacy programme was launched in 1979 and it resulted in high enrolment rates in adult classes. However, due to a number of factors including the introduction of cost-sharing in all social services – recommended by the International Monetary Fund – and a shortage of personnel, the enthusiasm in the programme has waned. In 1999 for instance, the Population and Housing Census Reports showed that 4.2 million adult Kenyans (out of a population of about 14 million adults) were non-literate. In 1994, although 2.3 million women were non-literate, only 84,000 were enrolled in literacy classes. In 2003 when the National Rainbow Coalition (NARC) government introduced free primary education, there was renewed enthusiasm for learning and large numbers of adults and children were enrolled, many out of school youth went back to school as did the aged. In Eldoret, an 84 year former freedom fighter registered in class one so that he can read the Bible and count his compensation when it finally comes from the British government. He is motivated by a quest for spiritual and economic well-being.

At a national seminar organized for Faith-Based Organization on 6th-7th July 2004 by the Department of Adult Education and UNESCO, the role of literacy in realizing Education for All (EFA) goals, the UN Literacy Decade, and the Millennium Development Goals (MDGs) was reiterated. In my view, these goals will remain a mirage unless we link them with issues of language and culture. In Kenya, this will require reviewing the Education Act, the Board of Adult Education Act, National Adult Education policy (guidelines and the Non-formal Education Policy Guidelines. It will also require putting in place language specific organs that would ensure language planning work such as status and corpus planning. Matters of translation and lexical expansion will be crucial.

Revitalizing Kiswahili and African languages

According to Alamin Mazrui (1998: 42), Ali Mazrui has suggested that the Third World use the 'strategy of counter-penetration, on the political, economic, cultural planes, to counteract the growing Eurocentralization of the world.' Examples of Africa linguistic counter-penetration include the efforts of John Innis *Mtembezi,* the African American scholar who publishes Mfumbuzi and Ngugi wa Thiong'o, the editor of *Mutiiri*, a Gikuyu journal. Regarding Mutiiri, Ali Mazrui felt that an approach drawn from 'linguistic strength based on the unity of African languages' was more appropriate than one based on 'linguistic credibility' which Ngugi had chosen. Recalling this exchange, Alamin says:

> "Noting that at his institute [The Institute of Global Cultural studies at Binghamton university] could read an exclusively Gikuyu Mutiiri, Mazrui felt that the bilingualization of the journal would automatically quadruple its constituency and readership and, subsequently, multiply its own chances of survival in an otherwise unfavourable linguistic environment... Such cooperation between African languages...could strengthen Africa's capacity for the linguistic counter-penetration of the west. Ngugi, on the other hand expressed the concern that a bilingual Mutiiri would foster a kind of dependency relationship between Gikuyu and Kiswahili that might not be in the developmental interest of Gikuyu" (1998: 50)

Ngugi, also an advocate of Kiswahili, felt that linguistic counter-penetration would be enhanced if African language were separately developed in order to articulate intellectual discourse and to reach out to each other through translation.

But this counter-penetrative strategy is not limited to these two powerful Kenyan scholars. There is an emerging consciousness among Africans in the diaspora about the importance of learning African languages and contributing in their development. At the 2004 Distinguished Lecture held in Nairobi, Ngugi wa Thiong'o mentioned the impact of *Mutiiri,* the Gikuyu Literary Journal, started while he was at Yale and continued at New York University. Apparently, a contributor to the journal Gatua wa Mbugua, a graduate student in the Department of Crop and Soil Sciences at Cornell University wrote his dissertation in Gikuyu and provided an English translation for his examiners (Ngugi 2004: 11). It is possible that Gatua was partially inspired by *Mutiiri* to write in Gikuyu.

Also, in the course of the journal's existence, many writers have emerged. According to Ngugi most of these had never written in Gikuyu before or in any language for that matter. Others had written in English but never in Gikuyu. A few others had written a few pieces in the language but they had been discouraged by lack of publishing venues. The existence of a forum inspired them all. Among these, one Mwangi Mutahi "... went on to produce two novels in Gikuyu and numerous essays (Ngugi 2004: 13). If journals in African languages can be sustained, they are likely to inspire more writers to reflect on the histories of Africa and to create in the languages of the continent and to engage with their predecessors.

There is no doubt that, Ngugi and his followers are involved in understanding and re-inscribing the work of cultural and language scholars that wrote during the colonial days such as Bildad Kaggia, Arthur Barlow, Johanna Kunyiha, the 1909 Kambui readers and *Ituika* entrepreneurs (Peterson 2004: 222). By remembering and reconnecting the threads of linguistic history they hope to create a space for African languages to be heard locally and globally. Gikuyu will continue to benefit from work being undertaken in Kiswahili, as will other Kenyan languages. Some Kiswahili poems by Alamin Mazrui and Abdilatif Abdalla have been published in *Mutiiri* through translation. This has ensured that Gikuyu readers benefit from Kiswahili literature.

Equally significant is the recognition of Kiswahili as one of the working languages of the African Union and its use at the Pan African Parliament. This means that there is the possibility that in future Kiswahili might compete with English and French at continental meetings if Swahiliphone Africa is consolidated through a *lingua franca.* This action of elevating Kiswahili to the continental level is partly attributable to the lobbying and sensitization undertaken by linguists in Africa; linguists who see the irony of not having an African language at the continental forum.

There are also regional efforts to build language institutions for the development of Kiswahili. Article 137 of the East African Community recognizes English as the official language of the Community. In addition, Article 119 (d) of the treaty for the establishment of the East African Community provides for the development and promotion of indigenous languages, especially Kiswahili as the region's *lingua franca*. The treaty for the Establishment of the East Africa Community – Arusha, East Africa Community Secretariat: Article 137). Consequently the 3rd East African Tripartite Commission held in November 2001 directed the Secretariat to facilitate the formation of an East African Kiswahili Council which would serve such purposes as harmonization of vocabulary, promotion of Kiswahili literature, and advocacy of the language's use in the international fora.

To ensure that the three East African nations work together in developing and promoting Kiswahili, The East African Committee on Education, Culture and Sports set up a Task Force to expedite the process of establishing the East African Kiswahili Council. Earlier, the 8th Meeting of the Council of Ministers in the East African Community had urged individual countries of the Community to expedite the formation of the national Kiswahili councils at any rate not later than 30th June 2005 (Report of the Council EAC/CM8/2004 of September 9th 2004). The Task Force compiled the protocols leading to the establishment of the East Africa Kiswahili Commission located in Zanzibar. It started its operations in May 2015. In August 2016, the East African Legislative Assembly (EALA) passed a resolution urging the Summit of the East African Heads of State to amend the Treaty in order to provide for Kiswahili as one of the official languages of the Community. Member States have been urged to institutionalize Kiswahili as one of the official languages through the establishment of National Kiswahili Councils and National Kiswahili Associations. Earlier, Tanzania had established, through an Act of Parliament, the National Kiswahili Council – BAKITA in 1967 but Kenya and Uganda have not due to a number of challenges including bureaucratic bottlenecks and lack of clarity by sections of government over matters of language and culture. Encouragingly, the Constitution of Kenya which was promulgated on August 27th 2010 recognizes Kiswahili as a national and co-official language (Article 7). This has paved the way for the systematic development of Kiswahili nationally and within the region.

At the regional level there is the *Chama cha Kiswahili cha Afrika Mashariki* (CHAKAMA) – the East African Kiswahili Association formed by regional scholars and cascaded to the *Chama cha Wanafunzi wa Afrika Mashariki* (CHAWAKAMA) – the Kiswahili Students Association. Uganda has also set up the *Chama cha Kiswahili cha Uganda* (CHAKIU) and in addition to CHAKITA, Kenya has the *Taasisi ya Uchunguzi wa Waswahili ya Afrika Mashariki* (TUSIMA) – Research Institute of Swahili Studies of Eastern Africa (RISS-EA) –located in Mombasa. TUSIMA works primarily with local and international students and researchers as well as other groups such as diplomats, staff of the United Nations, and public servants. The Institute, formed under the auspices of the National Museums of Kenya, gives lectures on Swahili history, cultures and arts and offers lessons on Kiswahili language and literature. Similar courses are offered in a number of outlets in Zanzibar, Dar es Salaam and Nairobi. Other language bodies are underway in Uganda, Rwanda and Burundi and the East African Kiswahili Commission will have the task of linking them.

Conclusion

The development of a language for national integration is imperative and urgent. But even as we seek to develop Kiswahili in the East African region and on the continent, efforts should be made at the national levels to continue supporting community languages. This is especially because through globalization, Western languages and cultures are permeating spaces originally occupied by community languages and artistic modes of expression in a manner never seen before. We have an opportunity to extract the best from globalization and adapt it to our needs in order to come up with something both local and universal. The global does not fully erase the local; rather, it engages it to produce a sense of 'newness' and convergence that is both disintegrative and integrative. That newness can be encapsulated in community languages. At the national levels, language policies and implementation mechanisms in favor of national and community languages should be clear and enforceable and clear stipulations for their role in society, and their protection and development should be spelt out in national constitutions. Education, rural-urban migration, increased inter-ethnic interactions and inter-ethnic marriages, are some of the factors shaping language processes in the homes. If education can be used to entrench the English language in the national psyche it could also be used to reverse the trend in favor of local languages such as Kiswahili. This would not mean an erasure of English in the national curricula but a reassignment of its role through an endorsement of bi-lingual education. Multiethnic societies function best if they share sufficient common ground which allow for interaction and sharing of values. A deliberate crafting of nationhood and the development of national values in Kenya should be guided by Kiswahili. Kiswahili can be one thread and it can also be a transmission belt for national ideals. Local languages would undertake the task of consolidating these ideals in households and communities, instead of undermining them. Consequently, a multicultural nation defined by tolerance and the pursuit of humanist and democratic values would emerge and the Kenyan nation, recently challenged by the 2007-2008 post-election violence re-inscribed.

References

Abdulaziz, M.H. (1971). 'Tanzania's National Language Policy and the Rise of Swahili Political Culture'. In *Language Use and Social Change: Problems of Multilingualism with Special Reference to East Africa* (ed.) W.H. Whiteley, (pp. 160-78) London, Oxford University Press.

Chimerah, R. (2000). *Kiswahili: Past, Present and Future Horizons.* Nairobi University Press.

Fishman, J.F. (1996). 'Maintaining languages: What works? What doesn't?' In G. Canton (Ed.), *Stabilizing Indigenous Languages* (pp. 186-198). Flagstaff, AZ: Northern Arizona University.

Gorman, T.P. (1974). 'The Development of Language Policy in Kenya with Particular Reference to the Educational System'. W.H. Whiteley (ed.), *Language in Kenya* (pp. 397-454) Nairobi: Oxford University Press.

_____. (1970). *Language in Education in Eastern Africa*, Oxford University Press.

IDRC. (1997). *Language of Instruction: Policy Implications for Education in Africa*. Canada: IDRC.

Itebete, P.A.N. (1977). 'Some Thoughts on Reversion to an Indigenous Language as the Official Language of a Nation: The Swahili Case in Kenya'. *Lugha*: A Journal for Language Teachers in Kenya. Vol. 5 No. 2, pp. 44-51.

Kenya, Republic of. (1964). *Kenya Education Report* Part I (Ominde Report) Nairobi: Government Printer.

_____. (1976). *Report of the National Committee on Educational Objectives and Policies* (Gachathi Report) Nairobi: Government Printer.

Kwesi, P. (2002). 'African En Route, and Roots in Sustainable Development,' In *Governance, Globalization: African Perspective*, Nairobi: Heinrich Boll Foundation (p. 24-25).

Mazrui, Alamin. (1988). 'Language and Community Formation Among the Urban Poor: A Case Study of Nairobi's Kibera Slums'. Unpublished.

Mazrui, A. & Mazrui, Alamin. (1998). *The Power of Babel: Language Governance in the African Experience*. Chicago: University of Chicago Press.

_____. (1995). *Swahili, State and Society: The Political Economy of an African Language*. Nairobi: East African Educational Publishers, and London: James Currey.

Mazrui, A. & Tidy, Michael. (1984). *Nationalism and New States in Africa*. Nairobi: Heinemann Educational Books.

Musau, P. (2000). 'The spread of Kiswahili in Kenya in the New millennium: Prospects and Challenges'. *Kiswahili 2000 Conference Proceedings* (pp. 134-143), University of Dar-es Salaam.

Njogu, K. (2007). 'Reflections on Naivasha: Cultures, Leadership and Development'. In *Under the Tree of Talking: Leadership for Change in Africa*. London: Counterpoint (pp. 82-93).

_____. (2004). 'Utandawazi na Utambuzi wa Kiutamaduni.' In *Kiswahili na Utandawazi*. Dar es Salaam: BAKITA.

Okombo, O. (2001). "Language Policy: The Forgotten Parameter in African Development and Governance Strategies." Inaugural Lecture, University of Nairobi, October 4, 2001.

Peterson, D.R. (2004). Creative *Writing: Translation, Bookkeeping, and the Work of Imagination in Colonial Kenya*. Portsmouth: Heinemann.

Wa Thiong'o, N. (2004) 'Out of Africa: Language, knowledge and Empowerment'. The Second Ford Foundation Distinguished Lecture KICC, August 19, 2004.

_____. (1993). *Moving the Centre: The Struggles for Cultural Freedoms.* James Currey, Oxford.

_____. (1986). *Decolonizing the Mind: The Politics of Language in African Literature.* London: James Currey.

Transnational Africa(s): Ali Mazrui and Culture, Diaspora and Religion[1]

Timothy M. Shaw

> ...the rise of emerging societies is a major turn in globalization and holds significant emancipatory potential. North-South relations have been dominant for 200 years and now an East-South turn is taking shape. The 2008 conomic crisis is part of a global rebalancing process (Pieterse 2011: 22).

Ali Mazrui came from a transnational community, the Shirazis at the Kenyan Coast, and lived a very transnational life (1933-2014), especially in Uganda, the UK and the US. His continuing concerns about culture, diaspora, language, religion, among others, were generally considered avant-garde at least until the present era of 'religious' radicalization. His interest in multiple media was also in the vanguard, even if some such technologies were branded BBC. In short, Ali Mazrui was always discovering a variety of Africa as a rich tapestry to explore; his several legacies - from the intellectual and literary to policy and pedagogy - deserve to be continuously revived, revised and appreciated.

I am proud to have sat at the feet of Mwalimu Mazrui at Makerere in the late 1960s as he returned to East Africa with his new D.Phil from Oxford (www.binghamton.edu/igcs). But I did not appreciate then how prescient he was in his concern with 'transnational' communities, cultures, education, identities, languages, literatures and religions (Mazrui 1990 and 2008) as well as the orthodox foci of political science or international relations (Mazrui 1977); such as national security (right); national development, democracy (center or mainstream); class, or race, ethnic and gender dialectics (left). He moved across the perspectives effortlessly.

Similarly, I was too dismissive of the 'transnational' perspective advanced by Keohane and Nye (1970 and 1971) which, in the case of the latter, was informed by his pioneering analysis of the East African High Commission as Kenya secured independence (Nye 1965). But now in my twilight days, I have come to appreciate how Mazrui was ahead of his time, as the post-post-bipolar era brings us back to the realities of myriad possibly intractable 'differences' exacerbated by 'religious' radicalization, especially of young males.

After a generally disappointing half-century since attaining independence, Africa can now seize 'emerging' opportunities (Pieterse 2011) to move from fragile or failed towards 'developmental' political economies (Mbabazi and Taylor 2001; Mkandawire 2001; UNECA 2011). As suggested by Jan Nederveen Pieterse's opening citation, South-South in the 'Third World' may be in flux as 'emerging' countries, markets, powers, companies and classes evolve (Christensen and Xing 2016). Similarly Brazil, Russia, India, China and South Africa (BRICS), Emerging Markets (EMs) and now TICK (Turkey, India, China and Korea) may come to constitute a new, intermediary 'Second World' (Bergamaschi, Moore and Tickner 2016; Gray and Gills 2016).

Africa like Asia and Latin America is being rediscovered as a source of international relations in both theory and practice, as Mazrui would encourage. The recent collection by Bischoff, Aning and Acharya (2016) advances this idea, even in its title: *Africa in Global International Relations*. Its second chapter by Ahmed Ali Salem is based on Mazrui's work on culture, among others. Likewise, Bischoff, Aning and Acharya (2016: 7) recognize the salience of a parallel "international relations in Islam" project; suggesting that African scholarship or epistemologies contribute to "global international relations in general and to international relations theory more particularly". They conclude their introductory chapter:

> ...as Salem points out, citing the work of the late Ali Mazrui, Africa attests to the importance of cultural and civilizational forces in world politics and how these define worldviews, drive motivation and are a source of identity (Bischoff, Aning and Acharya 2016: 17)

Mazrui's lectures, writings and broadcasts were always topical as reflected in his 1990 discourses on "culture" which are "a celebration of the liberating power of culture" (Mazrui 1990: 10). Chapter titles in his *Cultural Forces in World Politics* are instructive and seductive, still resonating today: "The Culture of Power and the Power of Culture: the hidden agenda of world politics"; "The Moving Frontier of World Culture" and "The Third World and International Terrorism". His global status was enhanced by delivering the half-dozen BBC Reith Lectures in 1979 on "The African Condition" but he became a familiar global citizen/icon in 1986 with the nine-part BBC/PBS film series on *The Africans: a triple heritage*: Africa's attempted synthesis of the indigenous, Islam and the West. In the current digital world, Mazrui lives on via You Tube, Facebook, and others; a reflection of the endless 'disruption' of FANG, let alone China and other emerging economies.

Symptomatic of Mazrui's living legacy is positive mention of him in the introductions by Doreen Sibanda and Raphael Chikukwa to the Zimbabwe Pavilion at the 56th Biennale in Venice in 2015: a moving exhibition on "Pixels of Ubuntu/Unhu". Three Zimbabwean artists reflect on Zimbabwean histories and futures as their contribution to "All the World Futures". Their themes are "history, memory and urban conversations" (Zimbabwe Pavilion 2015: 22). They relate to "globalization, citizenship, diaspora, human rights, religion, identity and Ubuntu/Unhu" as "part of the world discourse" (Zimbabwe Pavilion: 17). The introductions conclude by asking:

> What is the meaning of Ubuntu/Unhu in the 21st Century? African Scholars like Professor Ali Mazrui and Chinua Achebe have different views about what Africa is and this is included in one of the artworks in this exhibition. (Zimbabwe Pavilion: 21)

Reflecting on and informed by insights generated by my "Mwalimu" Mazrui at Makerere in the late 1960s, this paper treats the continent's contributions to the development of comparative international relations (Bischoff, Aning and Acharya 2016) and International Political Economy (IPE) and International Development Studies (IDS) with a focus on the 'transnational' (Khagram and Levitt 2007; Held and Hale 2011). First, it examines diasporas, cultures and finances; second, 'new' or non- or semi-state regionalisms; third, transnational governance (Bevir 2011; Gray and Murphy 2013; Keohane and Nye 1970, 1971; Mukherjee-Reed, Reed and Utting 2012); and, fourth, novel directions in public policy or diplomacy for a range of state and non -state actors and the 'hybrid'. The paper also provides a thumb-nail sketch of aspects of the diverse range of the cultural, educational, infrastructural, medical and mediation work of the Aga Khan Foundation in East and Southern Africa, Pakistan, Afghanistan and Central Asia, Europe and

Canada: a very moderate variety of global Islam advocated through a nuanced form of public diplomacy.

As at independence and in the late 1960s and 1970s with structural adjustment conditionalities, the continent was again the focus of an intense debate about both data and direction (Jerven 2015) with relevance and resonance for other continents in the global South.

Seifudein Adem, who worked more closely with Mazrui than most of us, suggests that Mazrui was a pioneering 'postcolonial constructivist' because of his assumption or belief that culture, history and civilizations matter (Adem 2002), rather than the 'materialist' approaches or assertions of the Dar es Salaam School and other latter day 'Marxists'. Mazrui was never shy of disagreements or confrontations as is apparent in his heretical views of nuclear weapons or the state of Israel. And he certainly espoused values around civilizations, culture, race, religion, and others. But as always, his constructivism might be considered idiosyncratic.

The 'New' Africa: 'hopeless' then 'hopeful' even 'rising' 1965-2015

Africa is clearly part of the lowest caste in the international hierarchy (Mazrui 1977: 17).

In the middle of the second decade of the 21st Century, despite the recent precipitous decline in commodity prices as China's economic boom seems to be ending, as we anticipate a post-2015 world of development (*www.beyond2015.org; www.post2015.org*), Africa seems to still face an unanticipated 'second chance' (www.mckinsey.com). Concerns abound over how many 'developmental' (Mbabazi and Taylor 2001; Mkandawire 2001) versus 'fragile' states (*www.foreignpolicy.com/fragile* states) will be reported by 2020/2025 or the AU's anniversary of 2063? This optimistic scenario, shared by the World Economic Forum at its 25th regional forum (www.weforum.com) entails interrelated prospects as both BRICs (www2.goldmansachs.com/ideas/brics/index.html) – now BRICS with the inclusion of South Africa as the fifth member - and the continent are being transformed by the recent global financial crisis and as the South expands while the North contracts. What S-N, even E-S (Pieterse 2011) let alone S-S (Modi 2011; Taylor 2016), relations should we expect in future? The EU of 28 nations now includes the Eurozone's problematic PIIGS (Portugal, Ireland, Italy, Greece and Spain) plus Cyprus and Iceland: a disincentive to

African regions to sign EPAs, unlike the supposedly 'middle-income' Caribbean, which had little choice.

This paper relates somewhat to the artificially dialectical perspectives on (African) 'development' of, say, Bates, Collier, Easterley and Moyo on the one hand and Jerven (2015), Sachs or Taylor (2015) on the other. It inquires how to 'measure' African political economic/ development: orthodox economics/statistics or human development (UNDP)/capacity (ACBF 2011 and 2014) indicators, or the 'real' Africa including informal sectors, mobile communications/banking, social media, women, International Organized Crime (IOC) and others; such as 'African' versus other varieties of 'capitalisms'. So, for example, when the World Bank recalculated the size the economies of Kenya and Nigeria after 2010, did it include, say, M-Pesa and iHub on the one hand or Nollywood on the other? In short, Africa's relative growth along with continuing conflicts in the Horn, Great Lakes and the Sahel present challenges to analysis (Jerven 2015) let alone policy, and undermining some of the assumptions and explanations of orthodox disciplines/fields like economics, international relations, political science, psychology, sociology and even International Political Economy.

African political economies are now located in second, third and fourth worlds: will they identify with the G20 and/or the G192 (G193 with a formally independent Southern Sudan in the UN) and/ or BRICS, now including RSA? Half of the dozen fastest growing countries identified in the Economist's *World in 2011* were African (Economist 2010a): from Ghana to Liberia. Meanwhile, the CGD in DC now suggests that 17 African countries are 'leading the way' (Radelet 2010) and the BCG has identified 40 African corporations as global 'challengers' (*www.bcg.com*). At the beginning of the current decade, McKinsey (2010) Global Institute claimed to see 'lions on the move'; five years later, it has perceived a 'Brighter Africa' (McKinsey 2015). In the mid-1980s, I had over-optimistically suggested that the continent might enjoy a renaissance by the year 2000 (Shaw and Aluko 1985); but maybe in retrospect I was less than a decade premature in this prediction/desiderata.

African state and non-state actors are increasingly recognized to contribute insights into comparative international relations and International Political Economy (IPE), especially in terms of their transnational dimensions (Khagram and Levitt 2001; Held and Hale 2011; Mukherjee-Reed, Reed and Utting 2012). Since the turn of the century, African analyses have begun to inform international relations and international political economy as they seek to escape from an inheritance of US intellectual, disciplinary hegemony (Dunn and Shaw 2013; Cornelissen, Cheru and Shaw 2015). This paper reflects ongoing debates around the *fin de siecle* collections from Tickner and Waever (2009) on international relations and Phillips and Weaver (2010) on international political economy encouraged by reflections from both sides of the Atlantic by Lemke (2003 and 2011) and Brown (2006) on my initial foray into 'African' international relations with Kevin Dunn in 2001 and encouraged by Mazrui's endless interdisciplinary probing. Now over a decade ago, Douglas Lemke (2003: 116 and 138) lamented that:

> ...African international relations constitute the developing world activity most likely to be excluded from international relations research...

> ...standard international relations research describes the interactions of official states...In contrast, Africanist international relations scholars describe interactions between & among a variety of types of international actors...in the developing world, international relations *are more varied than standard international relations research recognizes.*

In revisiting the early history of Congo, which overlooks a range of non-state actors, what he characterizes as 'autonomous political entities', Lemke (2011: 69) has again contended that: "existing IR research on Africa offers a distorted image of African IR simply because existing data sets themselves distort African political reality." Lemke (2011: 64) does not abandon neo-realism just the orthodox exclusion of non-state actors: "...neo-realism is not "wrong" for Africa. Rather standard IR research practice is."

The extended rather affluent and influential Mazrui family/clan is itself transnational, juxtaposing elements of the changing African and Arab worlds over time in Mombasa. So it was natural that, as its mantle alighted on one of its new sons, Ali Mazrui would become an early advocate of incorporating non-Western 'cultures' or 'civilizations' into international relations, including issues of language and religion, as reflected in his mid-1980s BBC/PBS TV series on *The Africans: a triple heritage*. He was an early advocate of the global South, especially the more Arab, Islamic worlds of MENA. This facilitated his interest in the Commonwealth, particularly in terms of education and literature, film and music. Hence the timeliness of his 10th Commonwealth Lecture in mid-2007 (Mazrui 2008), reflecting my own interest in Commonwealth Plus or non-state/-governmental networks (Shaw 2008), including the possibility of discerning a distinctive Commonwealth perspective on IR encouraged by the evolution of the field towards a post-structural 'turn' (Shaw and Ashworth 2010), which would cut across inter-regional or cultural differences, such as an 'African' approach (Cornelissen, Cheru and Shaw 2015).

Ahmed Salem (2016: 32-33 and 34-36) celebrates the work of Ali Mazrui on culture in IR, that complements a larger project on IR in Islam, which is burgeoning yet has to develop its own perspective. He concludes, perhaps, idealistically that:

> Enriched by African epistemologies, and African critiquing of their own conceptual foundations, IR theories will not only become truly universal but also account for international politics in Africa and elsewhere more powerfully (Salim 2016: 36).

Yet to maximize its development and security, Africa would need to advance 'network' or 'public' rather than traditional 'club' diplomacy, involving civil society and private companies, as well as states and intergovernmental agencies (Heine 2006). But climate change may yet emerge as the spoiler, hence the importance of COP17 in Durban in 2011 and COP21 in Paris in 2015 where the BRICS-related BASIC group was ever more active than at COP15 and 16.

Mazrui, Africa and alternative development directions & debates post-2015

> ...there is the strategy of 'counter-penetration' into the developed world – the strategy of establishing a Third World presence in the Northern Hemisphere...(Mazrui 1977: 18)

This reflection, informed by Mazrui's own transnational career and concerns has four parts, which stake out paths towards a brighter future for the continent, including its myriad diasporas, like himself and his family of eminent children and grandchildren concentrated in the US (Adem 2015). First: post-Washington Consensus, Official Development Assistance (ODA) from the OECD is declining. Rather, a range of "innovative sources of finance" are appearing, encouraged by the "Leading Group": global solidarity fund, currency transaction tax, carbon taxes/trading, climate change funds, controls on money laundering and remittance taxes, and others. Others are the emerging donors like the Brazil, Russia, India and China (if not all five BRICS) and Gulf states along with Emerging Markets (EMs) like Korea and Turkey, some with Sovereign Wealth Funds (SWFs) or Faith-Based Organizations (FBOs). Added to this are new private foundation like Gates (www.gatesfoundation.org), Clinton (www.clintonfoundation.org) and Ibrahim (*www.moibrahimfoundation.org*) leading to AGRA (www.agra-alliance.org), GAVI (www.gavi.org) and others. So arguably, the Gates Foundation, for example, impacts health policy and outcomes in Africa more than the World Health Organization (WHO).

Second, Africa has generated an innovative range of 'new' transnational regionalisms involving non-state actors: from Maputo Corridor and Kgalagadi trans-frontier peace-park to 10 member-states in the increasingly contentious Nile Basin Initiative/Dialogue (www.nilebasin.org); and from the dozen states in the International Conference on the Great Lakes Region (*www.icglr.org*) to corporate supply chains. In the 1960s, Makerere was something of a regional factor or catalyst as it was the premier institution of higher education in East Africa; its illustrious alumni still help advance the new regionalism (Shaw, Grant and Cornelissen 2012).

Third, "transnational governance" or "new multilateralisms" with African dimensions, from International Campaign to Ban Landmines (ICBL) and Ottawa Process and Partnership Africa Canada/Global Witness (PAC/GW) and Kimberley Process and now Diamond Development Initiative (DDI) to Extractive Industries Transparency Initiative (EITI), Forestry Certification Scheme (FCS) and Marine Certification Scheme (MCS) (Cadman 2011, Gale and Haward 2011) to IANSA and ATT; yet coalitions over Small Arms and Light Weapons (SALW) and children/women's security are stalled due to US vetoes.

And finally, fourth, what implications of this trio of novel directions and players for our analyses and policies, state and non-state: who are the 'drivers', innovators and animators? How to transit from dependency and neoliberalism towards a Beijing Consensus? Where will African organizations like African Capacity Building Foundation (ACBF) and its partners be in 2030, 2040 or 2050 (ACBF 2011; Hanson, Kararach and Shaw 2012)?

Informed by the 2010 McKinsey report, the *Economist* (2011: 73) at the start of the new decade asserted that:

> Over the next five years…the African economy will outpace its Asian counterpart…

...Africa's economy will grow at an average annual rate of 7 per cent over the next 20 years, slightly faster than China's...Africa's changing fortunes have largely been driven by China's surging demand...but other factors have also counted...

...Without reforms, Africa will not be able to sustain faster growth. But its lion economies are earning a place alongside Asia's tigers (Economist 2011: 73).

Based on contemporary international relations (Cornelissen, Cheru and Shaw 2015; Dunn and Shaw 2013) development studies perspectives in particular, this paper examines emerging opportunities as well as challenges for Africa and its agencies like the ACBF, AU and UNECA (2011) at the start of the second decade of the 21st Century. It focuses on whether the emergence of the BRICS "second world" (Khanna 2009) presents unanticipated possibilities or threats to a heterogeneous continent, one which includes burgeoning 'developmental' as well as 'fragile' or 'failed' states; such as more formal and informal analyses?

Now arguably qualifying for the adjective/accolade 'miracle' (Dorr, Lund and Roxborough 2010), can Africa grow through the next decade given its quite stellar performance in the first decade (McKinsey 2010; UNECA 2011)? The *Economist* (2011) asserts that the continent contained more than half the top 10 economies from 2001 to 2010: Angola, Nigeria, Ethiopia, Chad, Mozambique and Rwanda – by contrast to the last two decades of the last century when only Uganda so ranked.

And now South Africa is one of the five BRICS, raising questions not only about whether they can become a bloc (Shaw 2010) but also whether they are better cast as 'emerging powers' rather than 'emerging economies' or 'emerging markets'. Certainly for Nel and Nolte (2010), South Africa is a regional power rather than emerging economy. But is its recognition and elevation in the BRICS with or without the support of its region, whether more narrowly (SACU/SADC) or broadly (SSA) defined? As Pieterse asks: emerging powers, emerging markets and/or emerging societies (Pieterse and Rehbin 2009: 1-3)?

As UNECA (2011: 2) report indicates: "...global developments have significant implications for African countries, though the direction and magnitude of impact naturally vary among countries. On the whole, African economies have recovered from the crisis better than expected." Such a welcome prospect poses challenges for public policy/ diplomacy: can Africa bring its non-state actors as well as resources to bear in focused and sustained/cumulative inclusive 'new' 'network' rather than traditional exclusive 'club' diplomacy (Heine 2006)? As suggested in the final section below, this is the welcome challenge or opportunity facing African institutions like the ACBF (*www.acbf-pact. org*): what has it learned and can it adapt in the past two decades given the significantly transformed global context at the turn of the decade (ACBF 2011; Hanson, Kararach and Shaw 2012)? How does it relate to the 'global' financial crisis since the global South is less negatively impacted than the trans-Atlantic core?

Varieties of innovative sources of finance

Even before the 'global' financial crisis, there was a looming gap in funding for African development. In fact, that undermined the Millennium Development Goals (MDGs) in 2015 and other global targets. This was despite some features of Peacekeeping Operations (PKOs) becoming Official Development Assistance (ODA)-eligible under revised Organisation for Economic Co-operation and Development (OECD) Development Assistance Committee (DAC) rules. In response to such deficiencies as well as the slowness of the 'Monterrey Consensus' to impact ODA effectiveness, France animated a 'Leading Group' of states (www.leadinggroup.org) to suggest other means to advance global public goods. In association with major international non-governmental organizations in a Forum on the Future of Aid (www.futureofaid.net), a Taskforce on International Financial Transactions and Development (www.innovativefinance-oslo.no) came to advance the notion of "taxation for the governing of globalization" at decade's end. The Addis Ababa conference of mid-2015 on the future of ODA recognized the diversities/choices of development partnerships plus the salience of the new Sustainable Development Goals (SDGs) over previous MDGs.

Other alternatives included ODA from new members of the EU of 28/27 and the BRICS as emerging donors, the latter reflected in the Forum on China-Africa Cooperation (FOCAC), for example. And new private foundations have emerged to parallel established ones like Carnegie, Ford and Rockefeller. These new ones are the Gates Foundation (*www. gatesfoundation.org*), the Blair (www.tonyblairfaithfoundation.org), Clinton (www.clintonfoundation.org) and Mo Ibrahim Foundations (*www.moibrahimfoundation.org*), among others. Similarly, faith-based organizations are increasing such as the Catholic Relief Services (*www.crs.org*), Islamic Relief (*www.islamic-relief,com*), Lutheran World Relief (*www.lwr.org*), World Vision (*www.worldvision.org*)) the Aga Khan Foundation (*www.akfc.ca*) and others. With new as well as established private foundations, they are increasingly partnering with international organizations such as the Global Alliance for Vaccines and Immunization (GAVI) (*www.gavialliance.org*) (Rushton and Williams 2011).

Among the dozen or so global levies, mainly on ubiquitous financial flows, proposed by the Taskforce to advance global public goods were the Currency Transaction Tax (CTT) along the lines of the original Tobin Tax which some E members are implementing; an airline ticket levy with revenues going to ATM, which is supported by UNITAID (www.unitaid.eu), already effected by Spain and Korea; COP-advocated carbon taxes being proposed by states or provinces like Alberta, California and Ontario; climate-change funds being offered by the World Bank's Global Environment Fund and UN's Reducing Emissions from Deforestation and Forest Degradation (www.un-redd.org).

These reinforce controls on money-laundering encouraged by the OECD and G8 including Financial Action Task Force/Caribbean Financial Action Task Force on Offshore Financial Centers over two decades (www.fatf-gafi.org) and leading to Publish What You Pay and Extract Industries Transparency Initiative. And there are parallel discussions about remittance taxes on North-South flows, which have blossomed to more than US$ 300 billion per annum annually.

But the largest flows to the continent come from a range of private sources such as Mutual Funds and Exchange Traded Funds, Sovereign Wealth Funds (SWFs), including those in Botswana and South Africa. Others are private and venture capital, pension funds like CALPERS and OMERS and others in collaboration with the proliferating stock exchanges on the continent and related financial services. Investments like Intel in South Africa in 2011 and IBM in the Nairobi high-tech sector in May 2014 are the vanguard, with Google planning to train a million Africans in information technology in Kenya, Nigeria and South Africa.

According to the *Financial Times* in May 2015, Africa was the fastest growing region for FDI, rising by 65 per cent in 2014 to US$87 billion. And a report from Ernst & Young in 2016 indicated that FDI to the continent reached a five-year high of US$128 billion in 2015, concentrated in technology, media and telecommunications, with agriculture expected to grow before the end of the decade.

However, getting from conceptualization to policies or politics is problematic; which is where African Capacity Building Foundation (ACBF) based in Harare and related agencies come in once its capacity is enhanced to engage in such public and open diplomacy as initiated through its series of novel indicator studies (ACBF 2011 and 2014). Hence, the imperative to animate a timely and extensive coalition to redefine and revive the continent's direction.

Varieties of 'New' transnational regionalisms

Africa has been the leading region in the South to advance regional innovations and institutions (ACBF 2014). In the initial one-party nationalist period, reflective of jealousy surrounding newly-realized independence, these were typically 'old' inter-governmental arrangements. But in the post-bipolar era, such regionalisms became less exclusively state and economic and more inclusive around emerging issues like ecology, energy, security, water, among others (Shaw, Grant and Cornelissen 2012).

First, the revived and redefined East African Community is emblematic: now six rather than initial trio of members, with innovative civil society, parliamentary and security dimensions, qualifying as an instance of 'new regionalisms' (Shaw, Grant and Cornelissen 2012). Given the scale and resilience of regional conflict on the continent, several attempts have been made at regional peace-building, from Darfur to Cote d'Ivoire, especially around Economic Community of West African States (ECOWAS), Great Lakes Region (GLR), Intergovernmental Authority on Drought & Development (IGADD), and others, such as the ongoing process around the International Conference on the GLR (*www.grandlacs.net*; *www.icglr.org*).

These increasingly involve a range of actors in heterogeneous coalitions, from international non-governmental organizations to multinational corporations. As such, conflicts are always about 'greed' as well as 'grief'; so resource extraction and accumulation proceeding in tandem with violence, all too often targeting women and children, as successive UN reports on the Congo have revealed. And as security is increasingly becoming privatized, so such coalitions become ever more problematic. This is particularly so around energy and mineral extraction and supply-chains as their products attract the attention of transnational as well as local criminal networks. Shorter-term peace-making is typically tied to longer-term norm-creation to advance sustainable development by regulating the flow of conflict minerals like coltan, diamonds (*www.ddiglobal.org*) and gold as indicated in the next section (such as Canadian-based but Afro-centric Intergovernmental Forum on Mining, Minerals, Metals and Sustainable Development (www.globaldialogue.info).

Second, regionalisms on the continent have come to cover a wide spectrum of levels – macro, meso and micro (Soderbaum and Taylor 2008) – and sectors such as civil society, corporate networks, ecology, energy, security, and others. While Export Processing Zones (EPZs) are associated with Asia and gas pipelines with Central Europe, development corridors and peace-parks are largely a function of Southern Africa's distinctive political economy. Similarly, Africa has its share of river valley organizations and other cross-border, more or less formal micro-regions. The Maputo Corridor has advanced growth in Southern Mozambique as well as the eastern Witwatersrand, reinforcing the cross-border dimensions of the Lesotho highlands water project for electricity and water (www.lhwp.org.ls); the latter was informed by the only global commission to be based outside the North – in Cape Town. This also included the multinationals as well as NGOs and states in its membership (Dingwerth 2008; Khagram 2004): the World Commission on Dams (*www.dams.org*). Southern Africa is the center of the trans-frontier peace-parks movement, which has led to the recognition of several such cross-border parks in the region (*www.peaceparks.org*).

Third, encouraged by growing recognition of climate change – the development of India, Brazil, South Africa (IBSA) into Brazil, South Africa, India and China on environment around Conference of the Parties (COP15) in Copenhagen at the end of 2009 - the continent's river basins are beginning to receive exponential attention as centers of biodiversity, energy, food and water as well as conflict: Congo (www. fauna-flora.org), Zambezi and others; and the Nile Basin Initiative (www. nilebasin.org) are arguably the most advanced to date. Symptomatic of emerging tensions is the discovery of oil around the Rift Valley lakes in northwest Uganda along the border with Congo; such oil production may propel Uganda into the ranks of the developmental states but it may endanger some of its environment and wildlife, let alone local communities. It is already generating allegations of corruption and political domination.

Fourth, the continent's pattern of inter-regional relationships is in flux, from classic, inherited North-South dependencies towards a novel South-East axis around China and India but also Japan and Korea. Symbolically, Africa's regions' reluctance to sign Economic Partnerships Agreements (EPAs) with the EU despite a mix of pressures and incentives may mark a turning point as global rebalancing continues: Europe of the eurozone crisis around the PIIGS and Asia of the BRICS transforms policy options and calculations for the continent as suggested in Cheru and Obi (2010). The tone of annual African-China FOCAC palavers (most recently RSA towards the end of 2015) can be contrasted with that at the third EU-Africa summit in Tunis in November 2010.

Fifth, given its numerous land-locked states, Africa has always experienced informal cross-border migration and trade, some in illegal goods like drugs and small arms. And as multinationals, now from China, India as well as South Africa, have increased their investments in energy and minerals, franchises and shopping malls, so their logistics and supply chains have come to define their own regional networks. Exponential infrastructural development will further new regionalisms, symbolized by the mobile-phone revolution and the roles of MTN and Celtel/Bharti, including the Mo Ibrahim Foundation (*www.moibrahimfoundation.org*).

Finally, sixth, Nollywood has begun to redefine the continent as its overwhelming production of DVDs reaches remote villages and myriad diasporas, just as soccer's African Cup now plays on mainstream TV in the global North. As the *Economist* (2010b: 88) indicated at the end of 2010:

> Film is now Africa's dominant medium, replacing music and dance. It links distant societies, fosters the exchange of ideas & drives fashion trends...

> Film also profoundly shapes how Africans see their own continent...

Mazrui was ahead of post-structural analyses in his interest in 'transnational' cultures, including religions, as seen in "The Africans" on BBC/PBS. Now, a quarter-century latter, we all recognize such transnationalisms given the ubiquity of Bollywood and Nollywood; whether we advocate such cultural turns or not.

Varieties of 'Transnational' governance

In a post-bipolar era, the mix of fragile and failed states, proliferating 'global' issues and pressures for democratization have generated some innovative forms of 'transnational' (Brown 2011) or 'private' (Dingwerth 2008) governance around the continent, symbolized by the early Ottawa and Kimberley Processes, now augmented by the Forestry Certification Scheme/Reducing Emissions from Deforestation and Forest Degradation and Extractive Industries Transparency Initiative (Oslo). These may not yet be authoritative and their scope still fails to reach continuing scourges like small arms and light weapons but they are changing the governance landscape (Bevir 2011). When combined with innovative sources of finance, they begin to transform the policy terrain for African agencies like the ACBF (ACBF 2011; Hanson, Kararach and Shaw 2012). They have served to encourage inter-state international law towards the recognition of myriad varieties of hybrid and changeable global governance, which may reflect varieties of sources of pressures (Hale and Held 2011; Mukherjee-Reed, Reed and Utting 2012).

Part of the unwelcome legacy of the Cold War is fields of landmines especially in parts of the continent. The comprehensive, heterogeneous International Campaign to Ban Landmines (*www.icbl.org*) led to the Ottawa Process, advanced by the 'celebrity diplomacy' of Princess Diana. By contrast, the subsequent Kimberley Process on conflict diamonds (*www.kimberleyprocess.com*) resulted from animation by a major and minor NGO: Global Witness (London) and Partnership Africa Canada (PAC) Ottawa, respectively. It has since spawned the Diamond Development Initiative to improve artisanal working conditions in the mines through formalization of labor (www.ddiglobal.org), a process which the World Bank has also encouraged through its network for Communities, Artisanal and Small-scale Mining Initiative (CACM) (*www.artisanalmining.org*). In turn, Partnership Africa Canada is advancing the International Conference on the Great Lakes Region (ICGLR) regarding the containment of negative, conflictual spill-over from artisanal mining through regional regulation.

More recent comprehensive innovations include the industry-supported Forestry Certification Scheme (FCS) (*www.fscus.org*) and G8-supported Extractive Industries Transparency Initiative (EITI) *(www.eiti.org)*; the latter being particularly timely given the dangers of 'resource curse' and windfall profits around BRIC demand for energy and minerals, including new African oil producers like Ghana and Uganda. Meanwhile, despite the US Constitution, an Arms Trade Treaty (ATT) is slowly being negotiated through the UN along with

ISO 26 000 on CSR (*www.iso.org*). And UN Programmes of Action (PoA) such as decade-old #1325 on women, peace and security and #1540 on SALW serve to keep sensitive issues on the agenda. Despite the scourges of small arms and of violence against women and children, progress on SALW and child soldiers and such like remains problematic notwithstanding advocacy through the International Action Network Against Gun Violence (*www.iansa.org*). Each of these governance processes include African regional programmes to which ACBF should relate with other African networks, including diasporas (Hanson, Kararach and Shaw 2012).

Finally, the continent might follow Central America in advancing beyond not only national security but also human security, towards 'citizen security'. This contemporary notion seeks to combine freedom from needs and want with issues around small arms and light weapons: how to keep citizens both safe and developing in sustainable ways? UNDP (2011) in the Caribbean and Central America at the turn of the decade began to explore such prospects in its regional human development research and reporting.

Insights from the Aga Khan Foundation

Founded in 1967, the Aga Khan Foundation has expanded into distinct transnational networks to advance development through culture, education, health, technology, urban and rural development concentrated in East Africa, Pakistan, Afghanistan and Central Asia (www.akdn.org). Its dozen overlapping networks now employ some 80,000 in 30 countries, especially Pakistan, Kenya, Afghanistan and Canada (*www.akfc.ca*). They bring together contemporary discourse and agencies for global development in a manner reminiscent of Mazrui's foci on civilizations, culture, language and the medias. The Foundation in Canada popularizes global development through an annual walk and run across, and in 2015-6 created a large articulated truck exhibit to cross the country, starting in the east in 2015 and heading to four Canadian Western Provinces: British Columbia, Alberta, Saskatchewan and Manitoba the summer or 2016: Together/Ensemble (*www.together.ca*).

And in terms of Mazrui's world view, it is moderately Islamic (see www.ismaili.net), advances both the Aga Khan University (AKU) (2500 students and more than 1,300 faculty and staff), especially its medical school in Pakistan, Afghanistan, East Africa and the University of

Central Asia (UCA) in a trio of ex-Soviet states: Kazakhstan, Tajikistan and the Kyrgz Republic (www.ucentralasia.org). AKDN has created Aga Khan Academies in Mombasa (Mazrui's hometown), Hyderabad and Maputo, which train for the International Baccalaureate (IB) exams. Earlier, the Aga Khan, who spent his earliest days in Nairobi before school in Geneva and university at Harvard, advanced the development of civil society and the media in East Africa by establishing in 1959, ahead of independence, the Nation Newspapers and later Nation Media Group comprising the *Daily Nation*, *Taifa Leo*, *Business Daily* and *The East African* and Nation Television in Kenya, *Citizen*, *Mwananchi* and *MwanaSpoti* in Tanzania; *The Monitor*, KFM and NTV-Uganda in Uganda (*www.nation.co.ke*). And the Aga Khan's investment in the upmarket Serena Hotel Group (*www.serenahotels.com*) reflects contemporary Ismaili regional interests: from Afghanistan, Tajikistan and Pakistan to East Africa, from Rwanda to Mozambique.

The AKF opened its impressive 'embassy' – the Delegation of the Ismaili Imamat - next to Global Affairs Canada (GAC) in December 2008 on Sussex Drive in Ottawa – a highly symbolic non-state mission in a very strategic location next to the Embassy of the Kingdom of Saudi Arabia. It is intended to connect the values of Islam with the increasingly diverse peoples of Canada. It hosts a series of development and education activities on its elegant premises in collaboration with GAC and NGO development community and think-tanks.

With others, the AKF has advanced notions of, and debates around, citizenship and pluralism. In Canada and elsewhere it is doing so by co-founding a Global Centre for Pluralism just opened in Ottawa (for our 150th), which will move into the restored historic buildings when renovated, between the National Art Gallery and the Mint on Sussex Drive overlooking the Ottawa River (*www.pluralism.ca*). And in Toronto, the AKDN animated the conception, design and construction of the $300 million Aga Khan Museum, opened in mid-2014: a center for education and discussion about the history of Islam globally, especially in Canada's multicultural cities (*www.agakhanmuseum.org*). It features the Aga Khan Park and is co-located with the Ismaili Centre. It indicates the long history of Islamic communities and empires in regions of Central Asia, the Middle East and the Mediterranean, including a special exhibit on Istanbul in spring 2016. The dozen agencies of the Aga Khan Network spans acadamies, hospitals and universities; art, cities and media. And Aga Khan Foundation (*www.*

akfc.ca) and Aga Khan Development Network (*www.akdn.org*) have several alliances with aid agencies like Global Affairs Canada (GAC), other INGOs, professional associations, universities in Canada, Europe and the US. For more on private philanthropy shading into FBOs (see Moran, 2013).

Onto varieties of innovative analyses/policies?

Burgeoning varieties of finance, governance and regionalisms pose challenges to public policy in and around the continent. They also present challenges to African and related analyses as they demand 'innovative' perspectives and policies, both state and non-state such as the civil society, private companies, and media. Hence the timeliness of ACBF's celebration in Harare mid-decade of its first quarter century with its support of a Pan-African network of think tanks and its several indicators studies (ACBF 2011) - most recently on capacity needs for regional integration (ACBF 2014; Hanson, Kararach and Shaw 2013) (www.acbf-pact.org).

Africa is currently at a crossroads in terms of growth, development, governance, regionalisms and sustainability. Can it seize its second chance and transcend its lacklustre past? In turn, can the African Union, African Capacity Building Foundation, United Nations Economic Commission for Africa and others advance into their own second comings by promoting inclusive public or network diplomacy of non-state as well as state actors for the most marginalized continent in the global South through its capacity-building perspective (Hanson, Kararach and Shaw 2013), especially given promising advocacy of developmental states, annual capacity (ACBF 2011 and 2014) and HDI indicators (www.hdr.undp.org)? Africa's place at the center of innovative sources of finance and styles of governance leads to optimism while the number of conflicts and fragile and failed states leads to skepticism even pessimism. What balance are we likely to see by 2020/2025/2030 or even the anniversary year already anticipated of 2063? And how should it compare or even relate to other futures – converging or diverging - such as Brazil, Russia, India, China and South Africa (BRICS) and other emerging markets?

Ali Mazrui pointed to possible futures in the late-1960s by participating in a World Order Models Project (WOMP) connected to the then-new *World Policy* journal (*www.worldpolicy.org*) (Mazrui and

Patel 1973). Perhaps in the rather promising context today, we can now all come to share his optimism. As Pieterse (2011: 31) suggests, reflecting some of Mazrui's extra-PS/IR or interdisciplinary perspectives, "global rebalancing is multidimensional. Although it is primarily discussed in economic and financial terms, it is as much a political, institutional, social and cultural process. Today, Africa increasingly reflects all such features of ongoing rebalancing, with intriguing possibilities of global restructuring (Shaw 2011): what prospects for sustainable African agency (Brown 2006 and Brown and Harman 2013).

Endnotes

[1] Research and writing in part funded through the Qatar National Research Fund (QNRF) National Priorities Research Program (NPRP) #6-1272-5-160, the research funding body of the Qatar Foundation (*www.qf.org.qa*); triennial project 2013-2016. An earlier, shorter version of this paper is to appear in Adem (ed) (2017, forthcoming).

References

Aall, P. and Chester, A Crocker. (eds.) (2016). *Minding the Gap: African conflict management in a time of change.* Waterloo: CIGI.

ACBF (2011). *Africa Capacity Building Indicators 2011: capacity development in fragile states,* Harare.

ACBF (2014). *Africa Capacity Report 2014: Capacity Imperatives for regional integration in Africa,* Harare.

Adem, S. (2002). *Paradigm Lost, Paradigm Regained: the worldview of Ali A Mazrui.* Provo, Utah: Global Humanities Press.

_____. (2015) Tribute: Ali A Mazrui: a great man, a great scholar.*Third World Quarterly,* 36(4) pp. 792-801.

Adem, S. and Njogu, K. (eds) (2017). *Global African & Universal Muslim: essays in honour of Ali A Mazrui.* Ayebia Clarke, Banbury, Oxon, UK and Newcastle: Cambridge Scholars Publishing, forthcoming.

Baert, F. and Shaw, Timothy M. (2014). Are you willing to be made nothing? Is Commonwealth reform possible? *International Affairs* 90(5), September, pp. 1143-1160.

Bassey, N. (2012). *To Cook a Continent: destructive extraction & the climate crisis in Africa.* Cape Town: Pambazuka Press.

Bergamaschi, I., Moore, P. and Tickner, Arlene, B. (eds.) (2017). *South-South Cooperation Beyond the Myths: a critical analysis of discourses, practices & effects.* London: Palgrave Macmillan, forthcoming.

Bevir, M. (ed.) (2011). *Sage Handbook of Governance.* London: Sage.

Bischoff, Paul H., Kwesi, A. and Amitav, A. (eds.) (2016). *Africa in Global International Relations: emerging approaches to theory & practice.* Abingdon: Routledge.

Boston Consulting Group (BCG) (2010). 'The African Challengers: global competitors emerge from the overlooked continent', Boston.

Brown, S. (ed.) (2011). *Transnational Transfers & Global Development.* London: Palgrave Macmillan.

Brown, W. (2006). Africa & International Relations: a comment on IR theory, anarchy & statehood. *Review of International Studies,* 32(1), January, pp. 119-143.

Brown, W. and Harman, S. (eds) (2013). *African Agency in International Politics.* Abingdon: Routledge.

Cadman, T. (2011). *Quality & Legitimacy of Global Governance: case lessons from forestry.* London: Palgrave Macmillan.

Cheru, F. and Obi, C. (eds) (2010). *The Rise of China & India in Africa.* London: Zed for NAI.

Cooper, A. F. and Daniel, F. (2013)Special Issue: foreign policy strategies of emerging powers in a multipolar world *Third World Quarterly,* 34(6), pp. 943-1144.

Cornelissen, S., Fantu, C. and Shaw, Timothy, M. (eds.) (2012). *Africa & International Relations in the Twenty-first Century: still challenging theory?* London: Palgrave Macmillan (revised pb edition 2015).

Christensen, S. F and Li Xing (eds.) (2016). *Emerging Powers, Emerging Markets, Emerging Societies: global responses.* London: Palgrave Macmillan.

Dingwerth, K. (2008). Private Transnational Governance & the Developing World. *International Studies Quarterly,* 52(3), pp. 607-634.

Dorr, N., Lund, S. and Roxborough, C. (2010) The African Miracle *Foreign Policy,* December: 80-81.

Dunn, Kevin C. and Shaw, Timothy M. (eds.) (2001). *Africa's Challenge to International Relations Theory.* London: Palgrave (revised pb edition 2014).

Economist (2010a). *The World in 2010: 25th anniversary edition,* London.

_____. (2010b). Lights, Camera, Africa 397 (8713), 18 December, pp. 85-87.

_____. (2011). The Lion Kings? 398 (8715), 8 January, pp. 72-73.

_____. (2015). *The World in 2015,* London.

Fanta, E., Shaw, Timothy M. and Tang, Vanessa T. (eds.) (2013). *Comparative Regionalisms for Development in the 21st Century: insights from the global South.* Farnham: Ashgate for UNU.

Gale, F. and Haward, M. (2011). *Global Commodity Governance: state responses to sustainable forest & fisheries certification.* London: Palgrave Macmillan.

Grant, J Andrew and Soderbaum, F. (eds.) (2003). *The New Regionalism in Africa.* Aldershot: Ashgate.

Grant, Andrew J., Nadege, Compaore W.R. and Matthew, Mitchell I. (2014). *New Approaches to the Governance of Natural Resources: insights from Africa.* (London: Palgrave Macmillan)

Gray, K. and Murphy, Craig N. (eds.) (2013). Special Issue: rising powers & the future of global governance. *Third World Quarterly.* 34(2).

Gray, K. and Gills, Barry K. (eds.) (2016). Special Issue: rising powers & South-South cooperation. *Third World Quarterly,* 37(4), pp. 557-748.

Hanson, Kobena T. (ed.) (2015). *Contemporary Regional Development in Africa.* Farnham: Ashgate.

Hanson, Kobena T., Kararach, G. and Shaw, Timothy M. (eds.) (2013). *Rethinking Development Challenges for Public Policy: insights from contemporary Africa.* London: Palgrave Macmillan for ACBF.

Heine, J. (2006). 'On the Manner of Practising the New Diplomacy'. Waterloo: CIGI. Working Paper #11.

Held, D. and Hale, T. (eds.) (2011). *Handbook of Transnational Governance.* Cambridge: Polity.

Hertzenberg, T. *et al* (eds.) (2012). *The Trilateral Free Trade Area: towards a new African integration paradigm?* Stellenbosch: TRALAC.

Hicks, C. (2015). *Africa's New Oil: power, pipelines & future fortunes.* London: Zed.

Jerven, M. (2015.) *Africa: why economists get it wrong.* London: Zed.

Kararach, G., Besada, H.and Shaw, M. Timothy (eds.) (2015). *Development in Africa: refocusing the lens after the MDGs.* Bristol: Policy Press.

Keohane, Robert O. and Nye, Joseph S. (eds.) (1970). *Transnational Relations & World Politics.* Cambridge: Harvard University Press.

Keohane, Robert O. and Nye, Joseph S. (eds.) (1971). Transnational Relations & World Politics. *International Organization* 25(3), Summer: 329-349.

Khagram, S. (2004). *Dams & Development: transnational strategies for water & power.* Ithaca: Cornell University Press.

Khagram, S. and Levitt, P. (eds.) (2007). *The Transnational Studies Reader.* New York: Routledge.

Khanna, P. (2009). *The Second World: how emerging powers are redefining global competition in the twenty-first century.* New York: Random House.

Kokole, O. (ed.) (1998). *The Global African.* New Jersey: Africa World Press.

Lemke, D. (2003). African Lessons for International Relations Research. *World Politics,* 56(1), October, pp. 114-138.

Lemke, D. (2011). Intra-national International Relations in Africa. *Review of International Studies,* 37(1), pp. 49-70.

Mazrui, Ali A. (1967). *Towards a Pax Africana.* London: Eeidenfeld & Nicolson.

_____. (1977). *Africa's International Relations: the diplomacy of dependency & change.* Boulder: Westview.

_____. (1990). *Cultural Forces in World Politics.* Oxford: James Currey.

_____. (2008) 'The Power of Language & the Politics of Religion' *Round Table,* 97(394), pp. 79-97.

Mazrui, Ali A. and Hasu, H Patel (eds) (1973). *Africa in World Affairs: the next thirty years.* New York: Okpaku Communications.

Mbabazi, P. and Taylor, I. (eds) (2005). *The Potentiality of 'Developmental States' in Africa: Botswana & Uganda compared.* Dakar: CODESRIA.

McKinsey (2010). *McKinsey on Africa: a continent on the move.* New York, June.

McKinsey (2015). 'Brighter Africa: the growth potential of the Sub-Saharan electricity sector', Johannesburg, February.

Mkandawire, T. (2001). Thinking about Developmental States in Africa. *Cambridge Journal of Economics,* 25(3), pp. 289-313.

Modi, R. (2011). *South-South Cooperation: Africa on the centre stage.* London; Palgrave Macmillan.

Moran, M. (2013). *Private Foundations & Development Planning: American philanthropy & global development agencies.* Abingdon: Routledge.

Mukherjee-Reed, A., Reed, D. and Utting, P. (eds) (2012). *Business Regulation & Non-State Actors: whose standards? Whose development?* Abingdon: Routledge.

Nel, P. and Nolte, D. (eds) (2010). Regional Powers in a Changing Global Order. *Review of International Studies,* 36(4), October, pp. 877-974.

Nye, Joseph S. (1965). *Pan-Africanism & East African Integration.* Cambridge: Harvard University Press.

Nye, Joseph S. and Keohane, Robert O. (1971). Transnational Relations & World Politics: an introduction. *International Organization,* 25(3), Summer, pp. 329-349.

Patel, H. and Mazrui, Ali A. (eds) (1973). *Africa in World Affairs: the next thirty years.* New York: Third Press.

Phillips, N. and Weaver, C. (eds) (2010). *International Political Economy: debating the past, present & future.* Abingdon: Routledge.

Pieterse, Jan N. (2011). Global Rebalancing: crisis & the East-South turn. *Development & Change,* 42(1), pp. 22-48.

Pieterse, Jan N. and Rehbein, B. (eds) (2009). *Globalization & Emerging Societies: development & inequality.* London: Palgrave Macmillan.

Radelet, S. (2010). 'Emerging Africa: how 17 countries are leading the way'. Washington. DC: Center for Global Dialogue.

Ritchey, L. and Ponte, S. (2014). New Actors & Alliances in Development. *Third World Quarterly,* 35(1), pp. 1-195.

Ritchey, L. and Ritchie, S. (2012-4). 'How Celebrities Shape North-South Relations'. Project: http://celebnorthsouth.wordpress.com.

Rushton, S. and Owain, David W. (eds.) (2011). *Partnerships & Foundations in Global Health Governance.* London: Palgrave Macmillan.

Salim, Ahmed A. (2016). A Critique of Failing IR Theories in African Tests, with Emphasis on North African Responses in Bischoff, Aning & Acharya (eds.) *African in Global IR,* pp. 22-42.

Scholvin, S. (ed) (2015). *A New Scramble for Africa: The rush for energy resources in Sub-Sahara Africa.* Farnham: Ashgate.

Shaw, Timothy M. (2008). *Commonwealth: inter- & non-state contributions to global governance.* Abingdon: Routledge.

_____. (2010). 'Can the BRICs become a bloc?' in The Emerging Politics of the Emerging Powers: the BRICs & the global South. *China Monitor,* 52, June, pp. 4-6.

_____. (2011). "New" Regionalisms in the Global South after the Global Crisis: from rebalancing to reordering? Addis Ababa for NETRIS, November.

_____. (2012). Africa's Quest for Developmental States: 'renaissance' for whom? *Third World Quarterly,* 33(5), pp. 837-851.

_____. (2015). African Agency: Africa, South Africa & the BRICS. *International Politics,* 52(2), January, pp. 255-268.

_____. (2016). 'African Agency Post-2015: the roles of regional powers & developmental states in regional integration' in Daniel H Levine & Dawn Nagar (eds.) *Region-Building in Africa: political & economic challenges.* London: Palgrave Macmillan for CCR.

Shaw, Timothy M. and Olajide, A. (eds.) (1985). *Africa Projected: from recession to renaissance by the year 2000?* London: Macmillan.

Shaw, Timothy M. and Ashworth, Luke M. (2010). Commonwealth Perspectives on International Relations. *International Affairs,* 86(5), September, pp. 1149-1165.

Shaw, Timothy M., Grant, Andrew J. and Cornelissen, S. (eds.) (2012). *Ashgate Research Companion to Regionalism.* Farnham: Ashgate.

Shaw, Timothy M. with coeditors (2014). 'Prospects & Trends in the Governance of Africa's Natural Resources: reflections on the role of external & internal actors' in J Andrew Grant, W R Nadege Compaore & Matthew I. Mitchell (eds.) *New Approaches to the Governance of Natural Resources: insights from Africa.* London: Palgrave Macmillan, pp. 267-284.

Smith, Matthew L. and Reilly, Katherine M.A. (eds.) (2013). *Open Development: networked innovations in international development.* Cambridge, MA for IDRC.

Soderbaum, F. and Taylor, I. (eds.) (2008). *Afro-Regions: the dynamics of cross-border macro-regionalism in Africa.* Uppsala: NAI.

Struenkel, O. (2015). *India-Brazil-South Africa Dialogue Forum (IBSA).* Abingdon: Routledge.

Taylor, I. (2015). *Africa Rising? BRICS – diversifying dependency?* Martelsham: James Currey.

This is Africa: special report. Building inclusive economies: can Africa bridge the development divide?(2015). *Financial Times* for Rockefeller Foundation, pp. 1-20.

Tickner, Arlene B. and Waever, O. (eds.) (2009). *International Relations Scholarship around the World.* Abingdon: Routledge.

UNDP. (2012). *Caribbean Human Development Report 2012: Human development & the shift to better citizen security,* Port of Spain.

UNECA. (2011). *Economic Report on Africa 2011: governing development in Africa – the role of the state in economic transformation,* Addis Ababa.

Van, der Merwe J., Arkhangelskaya, A. and Taylor, Ian C. (eds) (2016). *Emerging Powers in Africa: a new wave in the relationship?* London: Palgrave Macmillan.

West African Commission on Drugs (WACD) (2015). 'Not Just in Transit: drugs, the state & society in West Africa', Accra, June.

Zimbabwe Pavilion (2015). 'Pixels of Ubuntu/Unhu: exploring the social & cultural identities of the 21st century', Harare: Patchy Light.

www.acbf-pact.org

www.afdb.org

www.africaprogresspanel.org

www.agakhanmuseum.org

www.akdn.org

www.akfc.ca

www.au.int

www.agra-alliance.org

www.bcg.com

www.beyond2015.org

www.celebnorthsouth.wordpress.com

www.cgdev.org

www.cop21.gouv.fr

www.clintonfoundation.org

www.cnbcafrica.com

www.ddiglobal.org

www.eiti.org

www.foreignpolicy.com/fragilestates

www.gatesfoundation.org

www.greenalliance.org.uk

www.hdr.undp.org

www.iansa.org

www.icbl.org

www.icglr.org

www.gavi.org

www.globaldialogue.info

www.globalwitness.org

www.grandlacs.net

www.kimberleyprocess.com

www.leadinggroup.org

www.mckinsey.com

www.moibrahimfoundation.org

www.nilebasin.org

www.nyererefoundation.org

www.post2015.org

www.smallarmssurvey.org

www.thisisafrica.

www.uneca.org

www.wacommissionondrugs

www.weforum.org

www2.goldmansachs.com/ideas/brics/index.html

Ali Mazrui: Transformative Education and Reparative Justice

Horace G. Campbell

Introduction

The Reparations Movement inside the Global Pan African Movement has grown in the past 25 years and in the process registered new milestones. One of the most important of these interventions has been the reassertion that *Black Lives Matter* and charting new directions for the repair of the planet earth; the retreat from the ideas that justified enslavement and the understanding that humanity must embark on a new direction in the era of the Third Technological Revolution. This revolution is unfolding at an exponential pace and is characterized by the fusion of technology that is blurring the lines between the physical and biological spheres. The technological changes in the fields of solar power, information technology, cognitive technologies, genetic engineering, nanotechnology, and robotics are at the same time heralding the transformation of entire systems of production, consumption and the relations between human beings. In fact, this revolution also brought to the fore who or what will be humans in the 21st century. John Markoff in a new book entitled, *Machines of Loving Grace: The Quest for Common Ground between Humans and Robots* has raised fundamental questions about the role of designers in deciding what human beings will be and what will be robots. Will technological innovation expand human activities or create transhumant?[1]

Human relations are being rapidly transformed yet the educational systems in Africa reflect the ideas of the era of candles, the era of the so-called 'enlightenment.' The Pan African Reparations is a movement that has always organized against hierarchies of human beings and the justification for these hierarchies that had been articulated by

Enlightenment thinkers such as Voltaire, Immanuel Kant, David Hume, Thomas Jefferson, and F. Hegel. The memory of freedom and dreams of seizing it had sustained generations who had understood how their labor had contributed to the wealth and power of hegemonic global forces. One central component of the freedom dream was that of the spirit of reparative justice that had been conceived out of solidarity and the need to restore dignity to the global African family and, particularly, the descendants of the enslaved.

This new thoroughness of reproducing the call for reparative justice had raised fundamental questions of the ideation systems and models of accumulation that dehumanized the African. The most recent books by Edward Baptist, *The Half Has Never Been Told: Slavery and the Making of American Capitalism* and Hillary Beckles, *Britain's Black Debt: Slavery and Native Genocide* drew clear linkages between the First and Second Indust rial Revolution and African labor power internationally. Would this model of accumulation and accompanying forms of education and culture survive the crusade of reparative justice? These questions are now front and center in a world of ferment and boundless uncertainties. Pan African institutions of higher learning from Cape to Cairo, Lisbon to Berlin and from Halifax to Bahia are faced with energetic youth who are seeking outlets for self-expression and an affirmation of their humanity.

Forty years after the African youth stirred the world in Soweto by challenging the language policies of apartheid and five years after the youth of Tunisia and Egypt demanded freedom and justice, the African Union continues to follow a path that declines to embrace the agenda of reparative justice. From North America and the Caribbean, the establishment of robust Reparations Commissions has engaged scholars, cultural leaders and thinkers with books, articles and films seeking to popularize the basic tenets of the contemporary reparations movement. These are the elements of rehabilitation, compensation, rehabilitation and guarantee of non-repetition.[2] In particular, the CARICOM Reparations Commission (CRC) was established in 2013. This is a bold initiative by the peoples and governments of the Caribbean region with a mandate to prepare the case for reparatory justice for the region's indigenous and African descendant communities who are the victims of Crimes against Humanity (CAH) in the forms of genocide, slavery, slave trading, and racial apartheid. In the formulation of the Caricom

Reparations Justice Program (CRJP), the Caribbean Commission asserted "that victims and descendants of these crimes against humanity have a legal right to reparatory justice, and that those who committed these crimes, and who have been enriched by the proceeds of these crimes, have a reparatory case to answer."[3] Hilary Beckles the current Vice Chancellor of the University of the West Indies was elected as the first chairperson of the Commission.

The scholarship of Hillary Beckles had been maturing in the context of the Durban reparative process that initially found concrete diplomatic expression in the *Third World Conference Against Racism* and is continuing within the context of the *International Decade for People of African Descent of the United Nations*, 2015-2024. The Durban Declaration of 2001 and the Durban Declaration Programme of Action (DDPA) had underscored the centrality of transformative education to unleash a comprehensive programme to both combat racism globally and prepare the next generation to meet the challenges of the 21st century.

Education to redress the crimes against humanity was viewed as a strategic tool encompassing formal education, adult education, awareness campaigns, and information dissemination along with the democratization of media resources accessing the latest tools of the information and communications revolution.[4] Since Durban 2001, it became increasingly clear that the transformation of the entire educational system will be central to the project of reparative justice. In this regard, this chapter lines up with the observations of Joyce King who made a distinction between *transformative education* and *education for submission*. She had written:

> "Transformative education...is the production of knowledge and understanding people need to rehumanize the world by dismantling hegemonic structures that impede such knowledge. Alternately, education for submission, recapitulates knowledge which has been used as a tool of white imperialist hegemonic rule. It is a deliberate and aggressive means of perpetuating the disenfranchisement of the masses."

Ali Mazrui was unique among the African intellectuals who were at the forefront of the Global Reparations Movement. Ali A. Mazrui had been reared in the context of a colonial Kenya where the activities of the Phelps Stokes Commission had been operationalized to lay down a system of Education for Submission.[5] Mazrui grew up in this colonial context but was humanized by the struggles around him to the point where he had emerged as one of the Eminent Persons of the Organization of African Unity Commission for Reparations. Despite starting out his life as an 'Afro Saxon' who had internalized the linear ideas of Social Darwinism and progress, after his relocation to North America, Ali Mazrui embraced the anti-racist struggles and emerged as a foremost champion for the dignity of all human beings. Even while he was celebrated as a distinguished user of the English language, Ali Mazrui had recognized the tensions between dignity and linguistic rationality among those who celebrated the use of European languages in Africa. Mazrui had recognized the complexes among those who he had identified as Afro-Saxons.[6] In clearly identifying with this strata of Africans in the period of his rise as an intellectual, Mazrui was to later appreciate the pitfalls of the brand of liberalism and alienation that grew out of a certain model of education.

As a teacher Ali A. Mazrui demonstrated that there was always room for growth. In the process of seeking clarification about the heritages of humanity, Mazrui embraced education which re-humanizes and challenging Western imperial narrative of the transformation of humans. From his base in Binghamton University in New York, Mazrui had grasped the importance of African languages in the process of reconstructing African educational systems. As a teacher in the United States, Ali Mazrui was brought face to face with militant Zionism when he relocated to Binghamton to occupy the Albert Schweitzer Chair. His defense of the rights of the Palestinian peoples had earned him the label of being an anti–Semite and many of the journals that sought him out in an earlier period poured scorn on his advocacy for reparative justice. Though his maturation within the 'crusade for reparations' came swiftly, the reverberations of the Northern Liberal Traditions still echoed in some of his writings and Mazrui himself became embroiled in many of the debates about the future of education, culture and reparations. Some of these debates about the place of Ali A. Mazrui in higher education have been captured in an earlier text edited by Willy Mutunga and Alamin Mazrui.[7] In the book, *Race, Gender and Culture Conflict: Ali Mazrui and His Critics,* the reader is exposed to the reality that the intellectual flexibility of Mazrui was manifest in the ways in which he made connections between different ideas and different axioms within his writings. The books and articles on Ali Mazrui trace his life from his birth in Kenya and much of the biographical details can be found in books such as *Africanity Redefined: Collected Essays* of Ali A. Mazrui, edited by Ricardo René Laremont, Tracia Leacock Seghatolislami and

Michael Toler. The other major source of the biographical details can also be found in the annual Newsletters that were published by the Institute of Global Cultural Studies at Binghamton and the Annual Mazrui Newsletter published by Ali for more than 40 years. Professor Sulayman S. Nyang and Seifudein Adem have also contributed to a branch of scholarship that is now termed "Mazruiana".[8]

The voluminous writings of Mazrui have been analyzed from differing ideological positions. However, in this analysis the author wants to associate with those aspects of the scholarship of Ali Mazrui that are linked to his stewardship in the project for reparative justice. The celebration of the life and work of Mazrui is faced with the challenge of focusing on his biography and his contribution as an individual or the task of locating him in the present global struggles for human dignity. His tenure as one of the 12 Eminent Persons of the Organization of African Unity (OAU) is one of the highlights of this paper; and one of the lesser known aspects of his life was his advocacy for the Pan African Project of the union of the peoples of Africa at home and abroad. Mazrui was one of the intellectuals whose formulation of the Global African facing global apartheid that emerged with the African Union adoption of the position that Africans outside of Africa constituted a sixth region of Africa. In his newsletter, he defined the Global African as follows:

> "We define Global Africa as the continent of Africa plus, firstly, the diaspora of enslavement (descendants of survivors of the Middle passage) and secondly, the diaspora of colonialism the dispersal of Africans which continues to occur as a result of disruptions of colonization and its aftermath."

Along with the concept of Global Africa, Mazrui had long argued that Africans needed to unite in order to assume responsibility for the maintenance of peace and security on the continent.

The intersection between education, linguistic diversity, transformation and reparations is crucial for the leap necessary to make a break with the limits of Eurocentric educational ideas and structures. The life and struggles of Ali A. Mazrui offers one opportunity to grasp the need to escape complacency and submission promised by those who want the current mode of economic organization to deepen the dehumanization that emanated from enslavement.

Growing up in the shadows of colonial education

Ali Mazrui was born in Mombasa, Kenya, on February 24th, 1933 at the height of last great capitalist depression. Two years after his birth, the Italian fascists invaded Abyssinia and his formative years had been one where the question of the African dignity and the recovery of national independence were burning questions. Despite the clear viciousness of the colonial project, the planners and intellectuals of the colonial states were intent on establishing eugenic societies where the ideas of inferiority and superiority were championed. Members of the Eugenic societies in North America and Europe were dedicated to "furthering the discussion, advancement, and dissemination of knowledge about biological and sociocultural forces which affect the structure and composition of human populations." German capitalists had taken eugenic ideas about sociocultural forces that affect the composition of human populations to the highest point of capitalism in the fomenting of wars and industrial genocide.[9]

The formal educational structures to which Mazrui was introduced as a youth was one where the colonial state worked overtime to regulate the processes of class and racial hierarchy in Kenya (with Europeans on top, Africans at the bottom and Asians as the buffer in the middle). Colonial education was for domestication. The missionaries disparaged African education and frowned on the Islamic schools that sought to maintain some autonomy from the Eurocentric conceptions of the foundation of knowledge. It was Mazrui's Islamic background and knowledge of Kiswahili that provided a buffer against an educational system whose goal was primarily for the propagation of the gospel to "win souls for Christ." Colonial education was elitist; it was biased for males and the base for the creation of ethnic identities. It was the breeding ground for the ideology of 'tribalism' in Africa. The principal route was through the development of African orthographies. Though Mazrui had come from a prominent family of Islamic scholars, the education that was prized in Kenya was that which had been inspired and influenced by the Phelps Stokes Commission to train Africans as low level technical workers. Mazrui had been trained at a technical college in Mombasa in the traditions of education for submission that had been reserved for Africans. But Ali Mazrui would not be satisfied with being a clerk in the colonial state and his energetic rendering of the English language earned him a scholarship to Huddersfield Technical College in the United Kingdom after the outbreak of the liberation war by the Land and Freedom Army.[10]

In 1909, twenty-four years before Mazrui was born, the President of the United States Theodore Roosevelt had visited Kenya and after the tour of hunting big game, facilitated the travel to the USA for Mohamed Juma Yohari, one of the servants who had been employed to look after the touring party. Six years later, Yohari was one of the first East Africans to be enrolled at the Tuskegee Institute in Alabama. Mohamed Juma Yohari became one of the first Africans to experience the philanthropic push at the start of the 20th century to promote education for adaptation. The Phelps Stokes Fund had been founded in 1911 with the intended mission of "managing the education of Negroes both in Africa and the United States."[11] Thomas Jesse Jones, the Educational Director of the Phelps Stokes Commission, had been at the forefront of the eugenic ideas about the possibilities of education for blacks and had recommended a system of 'vocational' education because of their perceived low levels of intelligence.[12]

After the establishment of the Tuskegee Model of Education, Thomas J. Jones had taken two trips to Africa to make recommendations about the education of Africans. The Tuskegee educational philosophy had been one where the corporate funding of black education greatly influenced the ways in which blacks during the 19th and 20th centuries were being educated. Capitalists and wealthy American elites like Rockefeller, Carnegie, and Peabody all began investing in "negro" education, as an essential means of control. Through such funding they were able to control and dictate what the curriculum consisted of and what knowledge was being spread and propagated among the black masses. This corporate influence in education often sought to maintain the social hierarchy of blacks being subordinate as a means to insure white supremacy and power. The corporate funders insisted that agriculture, general history, Bible study, and civics be main composites of the curriculum. Such fields essentially worked to maintain blacks in their share-cropping and manual labor positions, as well as a variant of the European interpretation of Christianity.

Britain specifically requested the Phelps Stokes Education Commission to tour their colonies and see how their educational model could translate for the African 'natives.' The Phelps Stokes Commissioners travelled throughout Sierra Leone, Liberia, the Gold Coast, Nigeria, Cameroon, Belgian Congo, Angola, and South Africa during 1920 and 1921. Within his findings, Jones found that the education of the natives should focus on health, appreciation for and use of environment, effective development of the home, and recreation. In the Gold Coast, specifically, Jones proposed that four male natives travel to the United States to learn the Hampton-Tuskegee model and then implement back in their home country.

The second Education Commission tour of Eastern and Southern Africa had greatly influenced the British colonial education policy in Africa. Numerous scholars have written on how the educational policy guideline issued by the British Colonial Office in 1923 echoed many of the recommendations of the Phelps Stokes Reports.[13] The Phelps-Stokes Commission illustrated the immense sway that Western opinions on education had at this time. The influence was mainly due to the notion that their educational models and findings were empirically sound and rooted in the social sciences. Consequently, the Commission espoused throughout the United States and African colonies the idea that only a certain kind of education is suitable for black people. Ingrained in this educational philosophy are assumptions about the racial organization of society, the intellectual inferiority of black people, and the "naturalness" of black's sociopolitical and economic conditions. Jones and the Commission further supported the idea that a few "exceptional Negro men" could be entrusted with literary knowledge that would enable them to lead the Negro masses. One of the prized images of the book on Pan-African education was a picture of a young Johnstone Kenyatta, 'working with his hands.' From the outset of the contact between the colonial state and the African peoples there was a distortion of what constituted education and whether Africans could attain the highest levels of education. When one speaks of education in the African context, quite often this refers to what was introduced by the colonialists. It is often forgotten that education was taking place in Africa long before the arrival of the colonialists. This acknowledgment is very important whenever reflecting on transformative education in Africa.

What is Education?

Education is the way in which a society transmits values and information from one generation to the next. In this sense, there is always formal and informal education in a society. Education is a central component of social reproduction; the combined mechanism to ensure the recreation of the physical, social, political and ideological conditions for the functioning of a given society. The reproduction usually brings to mind the regeneration of the productive forces. The productive forces involve not merely the static recreation of the conditions of production, but also the dynamic expansion of the productive apparatus. In this sense, education is always central to the expansion of the productive apparatus. Education is never neutral. The dominant social forces in society organize education to strengthen their position.

The decolonization process in Africa did not include the decolonization of education. In fact, the reverse occurred in Africa where once the speed of the decolonization exercise had caught the Atlantic planners by surprise, after being destabilized for a moment, they doubled down to train a cadre of Africans who could maintain the system. Many Africans such as Ali Mazrui, Ngugi wa Thiongo and Micere Mugo have written at length of the special training that had been reserved for those who had been identified as being willing to adjust to the existing social order. Mazrui has written at length on the tensions that had emanated for his exposure to this colonial education.[14]

Ngugi has written forcefully about the decolonization of the mind and the necessity to use African languages in the curriculum of African schools to unearth the richness of the history of Africa and African knowledge systems.[15] Writing about contemporary globalization and the challenges for African youth, Ngugi has argued that "the linguistic incorporation of the African elite into the European memory has dire consequences for Africa, the most obvious being the almost universal acceptance by educated Africans that English, French, and Portuguese are the proper languages for producing and storing knowledge and information. This has meant that the masses, the social agency of change, are being denied access to the knowledge and information they most need to change the world. Trickle-down economics, so beloved by capitalist fundamentalists, becomes reflected in trickle-down education and information."[16] Ngugi continues with the observation that "the more I look into the situation, the more I feel that the linguistic incorporation of the African educated elite into the European bourgeois memory is an active contributor to Africa's backwardness."

For progressive African thinkers and activists, the necessity for educational transformation was to get Africa out of this backwardness and exploitation. Ngugi wa Thiongo, Frantz Fanon, Cheikh Anta Diop, Joseph Ki-Zerbo, Julius Nyerere and Thomas Sankara were among the progressive pan-African males who understood that education could not be understood outside of the history of a society. Education that seeks to enlighten the African must be attuned to the history of Africa and the entire history of humanity. This history recognized that Africa had a complex and varied education. There was nothing traditional about this education. It changed with the balance of class forces. Because of the matricentric base of production there was knowledge that women possessed and owned for the community. This was especially so for those who were the guardians of the ancestral spirits. Joseph Ki-Zerbo in writing on *Thoughts on the Prospects of Education for All* had warned that it was imperative to end the form of education that alienated the African youth from their environment. This education and alienation created social misfits in societies where the forms of economic organisation produced surpluses that were siphoned outside of Africa. According to historian Joseph Ki-Zerbo, Africa needs an "educational system properly rooted in both society and environment and therefore apt to generate the self-confidence from which imagination springs."[17]

Transformative Education

In East Africa, it was only in Tanzania where the founding President Julius Nyerere had sought to make a break with colonial education by seeking to implement a policy of Education for Self-Reliance (ESR). One of the underlying objectives of ESR was to realize the goals of *Ujamaa* (African Socialism) and transform society through education. The objective of ESR was to ensure that children leaving primary school were able to engage in meaningful economic activities to transform their society. This was to be done through a curriculum that emphasized practical training. Another area was language. Kiswahili, an indigenous language, was made the medium of instruction in primary schools, with plans to replicate the same in secondary education. Another area was Universal Primary Education (UPE); with the target that by 1975, all eligible children would be in school.

Tanzania made some significant gains towards UPE. At one point, 85 per cent of school-age children were in school, and Kiswahili was the language of instruction throughout primary school education in all government schools. Similarly, international school for children of foreigners, private primary schools were not allowed in Tanzania. However, none of these changes addressed the essential knowledge base of the curriculum. There were efforts to Africanize the curriculum, but this primarily meant focusing on Africa in geography, history and literature. However, the colonial mentality was so strong that many of the changes were resisted by both those who were charged with implementing them and the students and their parents. Hence the education system in Tanzania was never transformed.

This experience and the deterioration in the standards of education in the era of neo-liberal policies sharpened the understanding of the need for a new kind of educational system. This kind of education ought to incorporate ways to sharpen critical cognitive and creative aspects of African knowledge system to ensure responsible use, renewal and conservation of Africa's biological resources. Ki-Zerbo underscored the reality that economic transformation cannot be separated from educational transformation, just as agricultural transformation and the transformation of energy cannot be separated from health, housing and the building of a new infrastructure. It is in the context of a 21st century pan-Africanism where the question of transformative education and transformative research comes to the fore. According to Joyce King (2005): "Transformative education...is the production of knowledge and understanding people need to rehumanize the world by dismantling hegemonic structures that impede such knowledge."[18]

This analysis of Joyce King was a rejection of the Tuskegee Model of Education for submission which had been used as a tool for reinforcing alienation among the educated African. In the logical conclusion from this position, education which rehumanizes, challenging historical spaces of colonialism, capitalism, and imperialism would naturally promote liberation in the Pan-African world. First, this knowledge must endorse a connection which bridges the chasms constructed by white racist hegemony. Second, it must repeal subscriptions to ownership of knowledge which castigate Black heritage as devoid of substance and sustenance. Third, it must propose a new paradigm, or the tools by which to engage and articulate the new knowledge – the foundation of which must be based on, and routed in authentic African experiences, scholarship, and redemption.

Joyce King outlines some key important points that are significant in establishing a transformative education for liberation in the Pan African world. First, the perspective must be centred in the African reality. Second, priority ought to be on family over individual. Third, adopting what is useful; improvising what is sensitive to our culture; resisting what is destructive. Fourth, revive arts and humanities to demonstrate life and experiences of black people. Fifth, the search of meaning and understanding beside research and statistics. Sixth, inculcating African traditions; hegemony within systems effected by Western thought; equity, beneficial practice from childhood to adulthood. Seventh, undertaking cultural, political, and professional research of African peoples. Eigth, taking back the destiny of black people: health, mental state, and entire well being. Ninth, creating positive learning environments for students and teachers; and tenth, removing the idea of dependency. These factors would contribute to the development of transformative education in the African content and the diaspora.

Building on the foundations of the African knowledge systems

Like Cheikh Anta Diop, Joseph Ki-Zerbo and Ngugi wa Thiong'o, Joyce King understood that education could not be fully empowering outside of the history of a society. This history recognized that Africa had a complex and varied education. There was nothing traditional about this education. It changed with the balance of class forces. But because of the matricentric base of production there was knowledge that women possessed and owned for the community. This was especially so for those who were the guardians of the ancestral spirits. To simplify, Ki-Zerbo broke down the needs of African education as inclusive of many domains of knowledge.

African education ought to be based on:

- Moral education that inspires a heritage of sharing and generosity and seeks to restore social collectivism;
- Democratic approach to education and democratic approach to bringing up children, respect for youth and the aged;
- Religious education, respect African gods and goddesses. That there are many gods and goddesses, respect and tolerance for other beliefs. This brings back the secular and spiritual nature of Africa which was interwoven for tolerance and respect for differences;
- Economic education, community based systems and to break crude consumerism;
- Physical education, dance, running, games and work;
- Language education, dialectics, myths, riddles, proverbs and other stories – called orature;
- Gender education on the breakdown of sharp construction of masculinities and femininities;

- Environmental education that deals with building clean societies for human beings where there is democratic access to land, air and sea.

Ki-Zerbo reflected on the themes of education as language and language forms; religion and belief systems; aesthetics, beauty in construction and in life; technology; family and family forms; economy; government; health; recreation.

Importance of language and transformative education

What is significant about many of the observations on educational transformation was clarity that there could be no separation between moral, scientific religious, physical and environmental education. African education today favors foreign consumption without generating a culture that is compatible with the history of African achievements. The expedient for the transmission of the foreign culture is the foreign language which is the language of higher education in most parts of Africa. The present educational system and language education breeds socially unadapted persons.

Pan African education encourages initiative, curiosity, cultural awareness, responsibility, and respect for collective rules and a taste for menial work. There is a need for education that inspires the self-confidence of Africans. In his outline of the major steps towards the unification of Africa, the rehabilitation of African languages was at the top. In his book on *Black Africa: The Economic and Cultural Basis for a Federated State,* Diop called Africans for the restoration of the historic unity of Africa. Step Two was "To work for linguistic unification on a territorial and continental scale, with a single African cultural and governmental language superseding all others; the European languages…would remain relegated to the status of foreign languages taught in secondary schools." And Step Three was "To raise our national tongues to the rank of governmental languages used in Parliament and in the writing of the laws."

The major theme of the writings of Diop is that precolonial Africa had a cultural, economic, political, psychological, and linguistic unity. His call for work for linguistic unification on a territorial and continental scale, with a single African cultural and governmental language was a central aspect of regaining the independence of Africa. According to Diop, if this unity does not now exist, because of the colonial interlude, it could be recreated. All that may be lacking is the political will to do so. Ngugi and Diop spent a lot of writing on the importance of education as one form of interpreting reality. "If a kindergarten child does not see himself or herself reflected in what he or she is reading, the education process will reproduce self-hatred." This self-hatred was evident in the Africans who assimilated European education. These were the foreign agents, the evolues, the assimilated persons or the Black English persons. Ngugi outlines the story of the person in "The Nervous Condition" by Tsitsi Dangaremba who goes to a missionary school. When this person returns to the village, he pretends not to know the language. For the villagers, this person was brain dead. The rehabilitation of African languages would be the foundation of a program of education for emancipation.

Cognition and the new educational terrain in Africa

Today the importance of the work on African languages for transformation is being driven by an awareness of the importance of cognitive technologies. The content of education in Africa is for the most part a Eurocentric education which does not begin with African languages. The large numbers of foreign experts and 'donors' is a clear manifestation of this dependency and dominance of enlightenment thinking. Such dependency is also conveyed through the rituals of schooling that denigrate African traditions, especially traditions of respect for elders. New rituals encouraged the disparagement of African knowledges and African languages with the celebration of the mastering of European languages as the major medium of instruction in schools. There are so many Africans from the current elite who are proud that they do not know African languages. Franz Fanon and Carter G. Woodson have written on the miseducation that was involved in the education models planted in Africa and in the USA. Woodson in his now famous book The *Miseducation of the Negro* alerted us to those Negroes who were proud of their classical education, of their knowledge of Greek, Latin and Hebrew, but knew nothing of the contribution of Africa to the world of knowledge. This is also the case of those Africans who are proud of their knowledge of euclidean geometry and know very little of fractal geometry.

Pan African organs such as the African Mathematical Union have been striving to bring to the curriculum the richness of mathematics in Africa as it is expressed in everyday life. Ron Eglash (1999) in his study, *African Fractals: Modern Computing and Indigenous Design,* brought to the world the contribution of African mathematical thinking to modern science and technology. Fractal geometry opened new areas of understanding of the world and liberated humans from the linear and hierarchical ideas of enlightenment thinking. Reawakened in the western world through the work of Benoit Mandelbrot, fractals along with insights from the field of chaos theory, have helped humans to make tremendous breakthrough in understanding the universe. Fractal geometry and fractal thinking have inspired scientists in many disciplines - including architecture, cosmology, medicine, engineering and genetics.

Some of the same international scientists who studied African geometry, especially fractal geometry, are now studying the cognitive skills of Africans. We are informed by the futurists who are grappling with the *Physics of the Future* that we are in the midst of the merging of information technology, robotics, biotechnology, nanotechnology and cognitive sciences. It is in the matter of the cognitive skills of Africans where the peoples of Africa have a storehouse of knowledge to share with the world as the articulators of the Human Cognome project seek to map the DNA of the linguistic structures and the mental basis for African languages. The strength of African ways of knowing, grounded in African culture, history and languages, is affirmed by the integration of mind and body. It is in East Africa where this study of language is most intense. African societies such as the Hadza, the Iraqw, the Maasai, the Samburu, Sandawe, Shilook, Nuer, Turkana and the Dinka from Kenya, Sudan and Tanzania share the distinction of having peoples with a large repository of the history of humanity. Biocolonolialists and bioprospectors have been studying their languages and cognitive skills. These people were part of the 100,000 indigenous groups that were being studied under the Genographic Project, a project financed by National Geographic Society and IBM. As a group, many of these people constituted the populations selected to track the migratory pathways through which humans have populated the globe.[19] Brain mapping like mapping the genome is part of a new thrust in the development of information computing. Hence, the Human Cognome Project is one more expedient to tap into the brains and cognitive skills of Africa as part of the new scramble for resources for the Third Technological Revolution.

Africa and Africans have become more important in an era where life-sciences research and the development of increasingly powerful tools for obtaining and using biological data are rapidly transforming economic planning. The demands of the life sciences research are also accelerating this interest in the cognitive skills of Africans. Western scientists are studying the cognitive skills of Africans in their rush to reverse engineer the brain. From the White House in the United States there are clear plans for a massive Brain Initiative that will advance brain research through advancing innovative neurotechnologies.[20]

Within the planning for the revolutionary breakthroughs in neurosciences, the scientists are going back to the cognition skills of early humans. These scientific breakthroughs in the fields of biology and genetic engineering require expertise in the languages and cultures of the societies where the new economic transformations are taking place. In the transition from chemical based products to biologics, we are entering a period when preparations, such as drugs, vaccines, or antitoxins that are synthesized from living organisms or their products can then be used as diagnostic, preventive, or therapeutic agents. This aspect of the scientific transformation enmeshes Africans in multiple ways and there are not clear research priorities in Africa that recognize the pace of technological transformations in this regard.

In an attempt to grasp the possibilities of educational transformations within the Pan African ideals, it is important to restate the basic position that African independence and freedom was at all times about the restoration of the dignity of human beings. The concept of dignity and humanity has gone through many iterations, from the period of demand for independence to the present period when the peoples are asserting that they cannot have dignity when they live in slum conditions bedevilled by exploitation and pandemics such as HIV and AIDS and Ebola. In the era of clones, cyborgs, robotics, artificial intelligence and genetic engineering the question of what or who is a human and the dignity of the human person has been reopened. African peoples are demanding that the science and technology plans of the African Union and the Specialised Technical Committees focus on their demands to live in peace and live as healthy human beings.

The bio-political questions that are arising in this century of revolutionary technologies challenges all of humanity, but more so the African and indigenous peoples who have been threatened with genocidal violence in past periods of "scientific" advancements in capitalist societies. In this century, the conceptual skills along with the creative spirit and cultures of African peoples remain one of the frontline weapons against the attempts of capitalism to dehumanise and to turn certain humans into mere body parts providing needed tissues and organs for the rich. The possibilities of harnessing the cognitive skills and knowledge of Africa to chart a new direction offer exciting possibilities for African renewal in the 21st century, and education systems across the continent much be retooled to meet this challenge. Such a retooling will be more urgent in the long battles for intelligence augmentation, the scientific work that seeks to expand human abilities. Such an approach to the cognitive technologies and artificial intelligence is very different from the futurists believe that in future humans will be an endangered species. Stephen Hawking warned that "the development of full artificial intelligence could spell the end of the human race... It would take off on its own, and re-design itself at an ever increasing rate." Hawking noted that "humans, who are limited by slow biological evolution couldn't compete and would be superseded."

It is in the context of the struggles to maintain the full human potential that we now turn to the career of Ali Mazrui as a crusader for reparative justice. In his writings he had compared the long struggles for reparative justice as a crusade,

> "The crusade for reparations, inevitably, has to be multifaceted. Western direct support for African democracy and Western direct support for institutionalized African leverage in the world system have to be included in the agenda for reparations. If love is a many-splendored thing, so is reparations."[21]

The humanization of Mazrui in the Reparations Movement

Mazrui's autobiographical writings have left enough information on the different periods in his life and in this section we are primarily concerned with his ability to grow and to learn. Mention has already been made of the fact that Sir Phillip Mitchell had in mind a technical education for Mazrui but Mazrui wanted to develop as a scholar. The first 21 years of his life was thus the effort to transcend the Phelps Stokes Model.

As a youth Mazrui yearned to be part of Makerere University in Kampala. He was recruited from Oxford University by Colin Leys after he completed his doctorate to teach at Makerere. Ali Mazrui had studied western political science at the height of the Cold War when Lockean principles of private property and the Walt Rostow ideas of modernization were in vogue. Ali Mazrui wanted his name to be associated with US realist scholars such as David Apter, Hans Morgenthau, Aristide Zolberg, David Easton, James Coleman and the other leading lights of the US political science establishment. In the face of the popularity of the African liberation movements western foundations such as the Ford and Rockefeller invested heavily into the training of new responsible African intellectuals in the traditions of education for modernizing an African elite to manage the decolonization process.

A component of this training was the efforts to dictate the terms of social science debate through conferences, graduate training, journals and magazines. One such platform was the *Transition* magazine which had been funded by an organization called Congress for Cultural Freedom. Professor Michael West in outlining the role of *Transition* magazine in African politics noted that, "based in Kampala, Uganda, *Transition* was a magazine of the arts, culture, and politics. Necessarily, the faculty at nearby Makerere University College (later Makerere University), where Mazrui taught, played an outsize role in the magazine."[22] Rajat Neogy, the Ugandan-born founder of the Magazine worked very hard along with Ali Mazrui to make this journal the flagship for western thinking on African political processes. *Transform* became influential in Africa, and was read quite widely beyond the university. It was in this period that Mazrui could be termed a 'liberal' in his outlook in so far as he gravitated to the principles of the market, private property, individualism and the other shibboleths of western democracy.

It was in this intellectual milieu that Ali Mazrui wrote on "Kwame Nkrumah as the Leninist Czar" and wrote about 'Tanzaphalia,' in reference to the experimentation with another form of economy in Tanzania under Julius Nyerere. Kwame Nkrumah who was then still alive and had read the essay on Nkrumah the Leninist Czar said the 'essay was penned by one with a colonial mind.' Later in his life Mazrui became one of the most steadfast proponents of the Nkrumahist vision of African unity and liberation. Twenty years later after Mazrui had relocated to the USA, he demonstrated his ability to learn from Nkrumah by building on Nkrumah's formulation of the *Triple Heritage of Africa*, consisting of indigenous, Afro-Asian-Islamic, and European-Christian civilizations. This concept of the Triple Heritage was a new direction away from the eugenic idea that Europe was the foundation of human civilization. The ideas of the Tripe Heritage of Africans were first presented in 1986 as a BBC/PBS television documentary and then as a book. Mazrui's Triple-Heritage idea reached a mass audience worldwide and became controversial for the establishment in Europe and North America. It was disavowed by Lynne V. Cheney, chairman of the National Endowment on the Humanities, who branded it an ''anti-Western diatribe.''

Cornell West attributes Mazrui's Triple Heritage to Nkrumah and points out that Mazrui admitted this in his correspondence with Gamal Nkrumah:

> "In response to Gamal Nkrumah's question, Mazrui replied that his triple-heritage trope came from "three great teachers." The first was Edward Wilmot Blyden, perhaps the outstanding black intellectual of the 19th century and author, in 1887, of Christianity, Islam and the Negro Race, which indubitably anticipates Mazrui's triple heritage. His "second great teacher," Mazrui told Gamal, was Kwame Nkrumah, the lessons coming largely from *Consciencism*. "My third great teacher was my own life," Mazrui finished off. Growing up in the Indian Ocean port city of Mombasa, Kenya, he "crossed those three civilizations several times every 24 hours. I was getting Westernized at school, Islamized at home and at the mosque, and Africanised at home and in the streets. I was myself a triple heritage in the making."[23]

For ten (10) years when at Makerere University, Kampala, Uganda, the social questions of the paths towards independence and transformation could not be kept out of the University. Ali Mazrui was supposed to be a master of the English language and was hailed as the best debater in East Africa. His public debate with Dr Akena Adoko (of the General Service Unit) in the Town Hall of Kampala in early 1969 was his own effort to establish the independence of intellectuals in Uganda. In the face of the intellectual and political choices that were then placed before the society by the liberation struggles in Africa, there was a grand debate between Walter Rodney and Mazrui. In *Race, Gender and Culture Conflict: Ali Mazrui and His Critics*, Al Amin Mazrui and Willy Mutunga, say that, "the debate between Walter Rodney and Ali Mazrui pitted two giants of the intellectual divide." The debate was televised live in Uganda, and caused a stir among both academics and politicians on and off campus in Uganda and beyond.

For many, this would have placed Rodney and Mazrui as ideological opponents but, as we will see, as Mazrui matured on his journey to the vision of openness, he became one of the most unflinching supporters of Rodney and spoke out against the government of Guyana when they refused him employment in Guyana. As many are aware, Rodney was assassinated in Guyana on June 13, 1980. When Mazrui later travelled to Guyana in 1988 as a guest of President Desmond Hoyte, Mazrui made a public appeal for the restoration of Rodney's name to "national legitimacy." The appeal was made in the president's presence and was broadcast live. Mazrui was always at the forefront of the call for an inquiry into the assassination of Walter Rodney. In 2016 when the Commission of Inquiry into the assassination of Rodney delivered its report that the state of Guyana killed Rodney, progressives in the Justice for Rodney Committee acknowledged the role of Mazrui in raising the question of the legitimacy of Rodney.

Face to face with racism in the USA

Of the 50 years of Mazrui as a public intellectual, more than 40 of those years were spent in the terrain of the North America academy and it was in the face of the day to day racism and chauvinism that Mazrui became clearer politically and became most outspoken against all forms of oppression. Mazrui left Uganda after Idi Amin acceded to power in 1971 and initially taught at Stanford University, at the University of Michigan and in 1989, he was appointed to the faculty of Binghamton University, State University of New York as the Albert Schweitzer Professor in the Humanities and the Director of the Institute of Global Cultural Studies (IGCS). Prior to taking up the appointment at Binghamton there were demonstrations by those supporters of the state of Israel who believed that Mazrui was unworthy of being chosen as a distinguished Professor. Mazrui was not afraid to speak out about the degrading conditions of the occupation of Palestine and wrote and spoke out against the conditions of the Palestinian Peoples. In 1992 he had delivered a lecture at the University of Michigan entitled, "Apartheid is dying, but Zionism Persists." In his newsletter, he described the lecture thus:

> The thesis was that both Zionism and apartheid had been ideologies of macro-segregation - creating a Jewish state separate from Arabs, and a white state separate from Blacks. The separatist ambition of white South Africans is in the process of collapsing. The separatist ambition of Jews to maintain a distinct "homeland" from Palestinians is still powerful. Both forms of "macro-segregation" have inevitably entailed a degree of what is now called "ethnic cleansing" - sometimes taking the form of outright collective deportation of groups or population transfers.

Such a thesis on the treatment of the Palestinians by the Israeli state was unwelcome then in 1992 as it is unwelcome now in 2016. Not only was Mazrui opposed by the militant Zionist but in his rendition he recounted that:

> In 1991 there were demands that I should be dismissed from my job as a professor at the State University of New York at Binghamton. In 1992 there were renewed demands that my appendix on "Comparative Holocaust" should be expunged from the official report of the Syllabus Review Committee. The Weisenthal Centre urged the Board of Regents of the State of New York to "reject" the appendix on the grounds that any denial of Jewish uniqueness was a denial of the very diversity and multiculturalism which our Syllabus Report sought to promote.[24]

If Ali Mazrui was prone to controversy his battles with the extreme Zionist brought his ideas to the pages on the mainstream newspapers when in his own words, "there have been Zionist extremists in 1992 who wanted to incite people against me." His newsletter noted that in their organizing these Zionist extremists fully expects President DeFleur [of Binghamton University] to assist them in having Mazrui removed from his position.

Mazrui's presence in North America at this time coincided with the raging debates about whether Zionism was a form of racism akin to apartheid. The campaigns in the United States against apartheid had drawn attention to the support of the Israeli state for the apartheid regime and in the eighties global anti-racist campaigns had linked the civil rights struggles in the USA, to the anti-colonial struggles in Africa, the anti-apartheid struggles in South Africa and the struggles for basic human rights. These global campaigners had placed the question of racism before the international community and especially the United Nations. In November 1972, the United Nations General Assembly had designated 1973-1982 as the First Decade to Combat Racism and Racial Discrimination. Ten years later, in December 1982, the General Assembly designated 1983-1992 as the Second Decade of Action to Combat Racism and Racial Discrimination. One important aspect of this Second Decade was the attention of the international community on the question of apartheid. It was in this second decade that the UN had declared that apartheid was a "crime against humanity."

This formulation assisted the moral challenges of those involved in the political, cultural, diplomatic and military struggles against apartheid. One important component of the Programme of Action of the Second Decade was based on the declaration of the United Nations General Assembly that condemned apartheid "as the most extreme form of racism."[25] When this discussion deepened in the United States there was a popular Free South Africa campaign across the campuses while the mainstream sought to find ways to cover up the odious aspects of apartheid and zionism. Mainstream academia did not support this anti-racist campaign and Mazrui was no longer held up as a great intellectual. He was no longer gracing the pages of the mainstream political science journals. In fact, in the academic world, his status as a political scientist was being questioned by the mainstream departments of political science and at Binghamton the mainstream political scientists shunned him. This questioning of his scholarship intensified after Mazrui became a clear advocate of reparations for the Trans-Atlantic slave trade.

Mazrui as a reparations activist

The release of Nelson Mandela from incarceration in 1990 had been a major milestone in the global anti-racist struggles and it was in this international context where the issue of reparations was placed before the OAU for the first time. Resolution 1339 of the OAU was approved by the Council of Ministers of May 27 - June 1, 1991. By this resolution, the OAU under the Chairperson, Salim Ahmed Salim, had decided to establish a group of Eminent African and Africans to the Diaspora in the relevant fields to set out clearly the extent of Africa's exploitation, the liability of the perpetrators and the strategies for achieving reparation.

Resolution 1373 adopted by the Council of Ministers of February 24 - 28, 1992, mandated the Secretary-General to form the support structures to the Committee of Eminent Personalities, thanking Chief M.K.O. Abiola of Nigeria for his commitment to reparations agenda while Resolution 1391 adopted by the Council of Ministers of June 22 - 28 1992, called on the Committee of Eminent Persons and the Member States to give their full support to the measures undertaken by the OAU in reparations for the wrongs done to Africa with the exploitation and the slave trade. This was the genesis of the Eminent Persons Group of 12 appointed by the OAU to mobilize and organize about educating Africans at home and abroad on reparations and reparative justice. The original Chair of the Group was the Nigerian politician-cum-businessman, Chief Bashorun M. K. O. Abiola, who was later elected President of Nigeria. Other members were the Nigerian historian, J.

F. Ade Ajayi; Professor Samir Amin of Egypt; US Congressman R. Dellums; Professor Josef Ki-Zerbo of Burkina Faso; Mme Graca Machel, formerly First Lady of Mozambique and later wife of Nelson Mandela. Others were Miriam Makeba; Professor M. M'Bow, former Director-General of UNESCO; former President A. Pereira of Cape Verde; Ambassador Alex Quaison-Sackey, former foreign minister of Ghana; and the Jamaican lawyer /diplomat Dudley S. Thompson. Of these 12 eminent persons, the three who were the most active and attended international meetings and conferences such as the World Conference against Racism were, J. F. Ade Ajayi, Ali A. Mazrui, and Dudley Thompson.

The momentum for reparative justice had taken the form of a major Pan African Conference on Reparations in Abuja from April 27 to 29, 1993 sponsored by the Committee of Eminent Personalities and by the Reparations Commission of the Organization of African Unity. After deliberating the Abuja Proclamation,

> upon the international community to recognize that there is a unique and unprecedented moral debt owed to the African peoples which has yet to be paid - the debt of compensation to Africans as the most humiliated and exploited people of the last four centuries of modern history... Further urges the Organization of African Unity to call for full monetary payment of repayments through capital transfer and debt cancellation [...] Convinced that the claim for reparations is well grounded in International Law, it urges on the Organization of African Unity to establish a legal Committee on the issue of Reparations [...] Serves notice on all states in Europe and the Americas which had participated in the enslavement and colonization of the African peoples, and which may still be engaged in racism and neo-colonialism, to desist from any further damage and start building bridges of conciliation, co-operation, and through reparation [...]

These demands for capital transfer, debt cancellation, skills transfer and direct power transfer formed an important component of the scholarly activism of Mazrui in the nineties.[26] This reparations campaign was so feared by the international powers to the extent that when the chairperson of this group, M. K. O. Abiola was elected President of Nigeria in 1993, he was prevented from taking office. He was to die in custody in Nigeria five years later in 1998. Mazrui had this to say of his involvement in the case for reparative justice,

> In 1993, I embraced the reparations cause seriously not only as an assignment of the OAU entrusted to us but also as an intellectual

challenge. After all, issues like colonial damage analysis or comparative slavery were of academic value independently of any activism.

One of the limitations of the work of this period was the paucity of real scholarly work on reparative justice. Two main publications by Mazrui on the reparations did not reflect deep and committed research.[27] However, these texts served to inspire the wider research and scholarship that was later exposed in books by Hilary Beckles, *Britain's Black Debt: Reparations for Slavery and Native Genocide* and Edward E Baptist, *The Half Has Never Been Told: Slavery and the Making of American Capitalism*. What has emerged from these new studies is the major work that still has to be done to roll back the ideas about 'modernity' and the civilizing role of western capitalism.

The World Conference against racism in Durban 2001

When the African National Congress (ANC) took over the South African government in 1994, the new government recognized its debt to the international community over the role that the anti-racist forces had played in the isolation of the apartheid regime. While the global NGO movement for reparative justice was gaining momentum, Mazrui spoke out in Accra and Addis Ababa for African intellectuals and activists to support the reparations movement. Mazrui was active in the debates among the activists in North America who were building a broad coalition ranging from the Black Radical Congress (BRC) to the N'COBRA organization. The BRC elected to promote a campaign against "war, racism and repression" and to struggle for "peace, reparations, justice". Though Mazrui was not formally a member of the grassroots organs of the Reparations Movement his activism (working with Dudley Thompson and Ajayi) jelled with the activists who had convened the African Descendants caucus of the WCAR process.[28] By 1997 the activism lobbying of several African, Asian, Latin American, and Caribbean groups cooperated with the Eminent Persons Group to pressure the UN to call the Third World Conference on Racism.

The ANC-led government offered to host the Third World Conference against Racism in Durban in 2001 but the permanent members of the Security Council were, in the main, lukewarm, (if not hostile, as in the case of Britain and the USA) to the meeting. Hence, there was very little funding for the meeting. The United Nations Commission on Human Rights in Geneva supported the role of the South African government in hosting this meeting. From the time of her appointment as High Commissioner in 1997, Mary Robinson, a former President of Ireland dedicated herself to supporting the goals of the Third Decade of bringing the issues of racism and racial intolerance to the center of the international agenda. However, under intense pressures from the USA, the UN Secretariat in Geneva sought to use bureaucratic measures to undermine the NGO Forum and the WCAR meeting itself.

The format of the UN World Conferences (Environment –1992; Population and Development -1994; Social Development – 1995; Women -1995) had been standard over the previous 10 years. There had been a special effort to have the input of civil society inform the deliberations of the UN conference that were attended by representatives of governments and invited organizations. Hence, at all of these international meetings, there are two sessions, the NGO meeting followed by the UN conference. These UN meetings were usually preceded by regional meetings in Africa, America, Asia and Europe. There are also regional NGO meetings. It is in these regional meetings where the draft documents are prepared. The UN World Conference on Racism (WCAR) of 2001 was the first meeting where there was no agreement on the draft document. However, despite the absence of a draft, the African descendant's caucus representing Africans from Africa, the Caribbean, Europe, Latin America, and North America (the USA and Canada) had agreed on language reflecting the mass support for the recognition of the Transatlantic Slave Trade as a crime against humanity.

By July 2001 the caucus of Africans and African descendants had agreed on language relating to the following points:

- The Trans-Atlantic Slave Trade, Slavery and Colonialism are crimes against humanity;
- Reparations due for Africans and African Descendants;
- Recognition of the economic basis of racism;
- Adoption of corrective national (domestic) public policies with emphasis on environmental racism and health care;
- Adoption of culture specific development policies;
- The adoption of mechanisms to combat the interconnections of race and poverty, and the role that globalization (caused by governments and the private sector) has in this interconnection;
- Adoption of mechanisms to combat racism in the criminal punishment (penal) system;

- Reform of the legal system including national constitutional reforms and development of international and regional mechanism for dismantling racism;
- Adoption of policies specific to African and African Descendant women that recognize and redress the intersection of race and gender;
- Support for the adoption of policies that recognize and address the intersection of race and sexual orientation.

The first three points were studied and circulated widely throughout the African world before the meeting and in the final declaration of the conference the language of the declaration reflected these positions. These points remain the core organizing ideas within the Pan African movement for reparations.

It was in light of the preparations of the peoples of African descent that the US and Britain started to organize internationally before the meeting to take the issue of reparations out of the official discussion of the WCAR. The issues of Palestine, the Dalit and the Roma Peoples question surfaced as major dividing points before the meeting and caused a sharp division between the countries that were formerly colonized and the countries of the EU and the USA. Time and space does not allow for the depth of the issues of Palestine, but it is important to note that the Palestinian question brought out more information on the real strength of the Israeli lobby in the United States.[29] The issue of the nature of the Israeli lobby in the United States again came to the fore again in 2009 over the matter of US participation in the Durban Review Conference in Geneva. By the start of the 21st century the question of reparative justice was mobilizing progressives in all parts of the World. China and India argued for Europe to return cultural artifacts. China successfully demanded the return of cultural artifacts that had been looted by France and Britain and India demanded the return of the glasses of Gandhi that had been on auction in the USA. Ngugi was among the many scholars who called on Africans to intensify the struggles for reparations by quoting Frederick Douglass who argued that power concedes nothing without a struggle:

> No, Africa must not let the West off the "moral hook." The continent must heighten its demands for global social justice and the rectification of glaring historical injustices like the slave trade and colonialism.[30]

Fault lines in the Reparations debate

The masters of the universe were not sitting quiet while this campaign for reparative justice was gaining momentum. First, prior to the Durban Conference there were promises of more aid to Africa under the Millennium Development Goals (MPGs). After the Durban Conference in 2001, the West suggested to the AU that it should no longer support the Eminent Persons Group and pushed to promote the New Africa Partnership for Development (NEPAD) instead of a programme for reparations.

Then, there was the debate that had begun in Abuja in 1993, whether there should be reparations for the Arab Slave Trade and for colonialism. These questions were linked to an intensified debate within the Pan African Movement as to "who is an African." This question along with the challenges of a proper historical account of the trade in human cargoes across the Sahara and across the Red Sea constituted one of the underdeveloped areas of research and a contentious one in framing the questions of reparative justice. Some commentators argued that Mazrui as a member of the GEP had not paid sufficient attention to the distortions and destruction of the Arab slave trade. For this author, one of the outstanding tasks of the Pan African movement will be to develop an intellectual infrastructure to unleash research on the nature and consequences of the Arab slave trade in the search for the healing of the relations between the peoples of the South.

After Alpha Oumar Konaré of Mali became Chairperson of the Commission of the AU, there was renewed activism by that AU with the call for the debate on slavery in all African parliaments, with the aim of declaring it a crime against humanity and discuss on the nature of reparations in 2005. Faced with these stirrings from the African descendants and from the AU, Tony Blair, the British Prime Minister, sought to head off the reparations discussions by expressing regret at the consequences of the slave trade and calling the G8 Summit at Gleneagles, Scotland, to 'Make Poverty History.' Despite this maneuver, there were meetings and conferences held all over the world to intensify pressures on the West at the time of the 200th anniversary of the abolition of the Slave Trade in 2007. On September 23, 2009, in New York, during the 64th Session of the United Nations General Assembly, the then president of the African Union Muammar al-Gaddafi stated that Africa deserved reparations, which amounts to 77.7 trillion dollars for the resources and wealth stolen in the past. He also declared that colonization should be criminalized and people compensated for the suffering endured during the reign of colonial powers. This same Gaddafi, as chairperson of the African Union, made reparative claims against Italy. The government of Italy made a payment of US$5 billion dollars. However, Gaddafi refused to take a clear stand on racism against fellow Africans by the Libyan state. He also met in secret with the conservative Italian leadership to deny the free international movement of African workers. The West was not asleep in this bold claim by Gaddafi and in 2011 there was the conspiracy to overthrow him on the grounds that he was about to kill his people. Mazrui, even in failing health, joined in the condemnation of the NATO intervention in Libya and the assassination of Gaddafi.

Mazrui enriched by feminism

Mazrui was brought up in a patriarchal atmosphere of colonial Kenya and when he came to the USA, he came face to face with the progressive feminist movement. Black women had taken the questions of Pan Africanism to a new level. Mazrui had been present at the 7th Pan African Congress in Kampala in 1994 when the Pan African Women's Liberation Organization (PAWLO) had been formed. From the period of the Congress one could see the engagement of Mazrui with Pan African feminists. Scholars such as Micere Mugo had made clear and concise contributions to the centrality of grassroots women and the need to pay attention to the lived experiences of African peoples.

Micere Mugo in her essay on *Re-Envisioning Pan Africanism: What is the role of gender, youth and the masses*, noted that:

> "...though not cited in intellectual discourses that have so far come to be the literary cannon on Pan-Africanism, in their activism, as well as participation, women were and have always been the heart of the Pan-Africanism's essence, or if you like, substance. My point is that Pan-Africanism may be seen as manifesting itself in two major ways, which are equally important: through the movement itself and through its lived aspects. As a movement, Pan-Africanism has been characterized by fluctuation, registering bouts of life and dormant lulls. On the other hand, its lived aspects, actual substance, or essence, have always remained alive and persistent over historical time. Ordinary people, or the masses, including the majority of Africana women, have been the key keepers or carriers of this essence.

Mazrui drew from these struggles and became an outspoken opponent of what he termed 'malignant sexism.' Malignant sexism is defined as the "most pervasive and most insidious; [because] in most cases [it subjects] women to economic manipulation, sexual exploitation and political marginalization.'[31] The Nigerian feminist Molara Ogundipe Leslie challenged the dichotomies between benign, benevolent and malignant sexism and after these debates Mazrui acknowledged his own growth from the exchange.

The scholar Etin Anwar from Malaysia made an invaluable contribution to the understating of Mazrui's grasp of the oppression of women. In her chapter, "Mazrui and Gender: On the Question of Methodology", drew out some of the real challenges that Mazrui faced in grasping the feminist standpoint. She argued that:

> Indeed, Mazrui's greatest contribution to the question of gender is a consistent portrayal of the confluence of Islam, the West and Indigenous Africa. Growing up in a traditional African Muslim household and reaching maturity in a western household have shaped the way Mazrui theorizes about women's issues.[32]

Ali Mazrui was brought up as a follower of the Islamic faith and he was a spiritual person. Yet, he was a secular person who as a believer wanted all people to have their rights and dignity. Mazrui was not a proselytizer. Mazrui like most followers of Islam felt the deep persecution and harassment of the USA after the Islamophobia craze was fueled by the neo-conservative forces. Mazrui himself was stopped and held at the airport in Miami and questioned about his connections to international terrorism. It was at this point where Mazrui was carving out a space for decent humans everywhere. Mazrui was an outspoken critic of extremism and fundamentalism of all sorts and he was critical of both the US imperial war on terror and those extremists such as Boko Haram and other Jihadists. Because of his challenge to the conservatives, his writings were not liked in Saudi Arabia and the Gulf where the Wahabists were using their billions of dollars to foment hatred and divisions.

From his struggles to affirm the voices of women in Islam such as Ingrid Mattson and Amina Wadud, Ali Mazrui supported the view that: "The issue of gender equality is a very important one in Islam, and Muslims have unfortunately used highly restrictive interpretations of history to move backward." When she was seeking to make history in New York Amina Wadud stated: "The voices of women have been silenced by centuries of man-made traditions, and we're saying, 'No more.' ... We're going to move from the back of the mosque to the front of the mosque."[33]

Mazrui's gift to Kenya and Africa

Mazrui's mortal remains were interred in Mombasa, Kenya, and Kenyan youth will have an opportunity reflect on the ideas of Mazrui as they seek to work to overcome education for submission. The long history of Pan African cooperation and solidarity in Kenyan society has been blurred by the Frank Kitson plans for ethnic and religious differences. Kenyan freedom fighters such as Dedan Kimathi, Wangari Maathai, Pio Gama Pinto, Ngugi wa Thiong'o, Micere Mugo and countless others have reflected the reality of the depth of dreams of freedom in the society. Wangari Maathai has made her contribution to the repair of the planet by her focus on the healing attributes replenishing the earth.[34] This brand of reparations linking the future of Africa to the future of the planet earth has now been taken further by the struggles for climate justice. Increasingly, it is becoming clearer the responses to global warming and pandemics such as Ebola cannot be done in the context of the Berlinist states.

The African Union has responded to the calls for the regeneration of Africa in the 21st century and adopted *Agenda 2063* to accelerate the processes of social and economic transformation. One component of this Agenda has been the establishment of Specialized Technical Committees (STC) to jumpstart the transformation of Africa.[35] However, this initiative from the African Union is being undertaken when the top political leaders are seeking to retreat from the international call for Black reparations. One concrete contribution that can be made by those celebrating the life and work of Mazrui will be to call for the establishment of the African Union Reparations Commission as one of the Specialized Technical Committees to pursue the multifaceted tasks of reparative justice for Africans at home and abroad. The Science, Technology and Innovation Strategy is seeking technical understandings of how to 'spearhead the revitalization of education systems' without a comprehensive understanding of the harms done to Africa by colonial education and colonial languages.

Such a call for reparative justice and reparative history will seek to heal the divisions within Kenya that have been sown and nurtured by the colonial state and the commissions for education that seeks to hide from the Kenyan people the real linguistic diversity of the region that is now being tapped for cognitive technologies by bioprospectors. The Kenyan society is undergoing massive challenges especially in the areas of unleashing the potential of the youth who are not yet fully aware of the extent of the history of the mass internment and murder of thousands of Kenyans. This society is faced with its own legacies of the crimes of colonialism and the need to incorporate a solid understanding of the nature of colonial barbarity.[36] The prolonged struggles of many Kenyans for the truth of the imperial crimes shattered the cover up of colonial atrocities and demanded a new cadre of researchers to explore the secret Hanslope files that had been the subject of a clumsy effort at archival erasure.

It is this lack of understanding of history of colonialism that impels the bureaucracy in Kenya to turn their back on the *Agenda 2063* of the African Union and launch their own *Vision 2030*. Central to this Vision 2030 is the creation of Africa's Silicon Savannah at the proposed Konza city which will be a "sustainable, world-class technology hub and a major economic driver for the nation, with a vibrant mix of businesses, workers, residents, and urban amenities." In the past decade the ingenuity of young Kenyans in establishing Kenya *M-Pesa* (cell phone banking service) and *Ushahidi* (a platform for crowdsourcing information during disasters), has brought Kenya to the attention of technology experts in all parts of the world. Information and telecommunications technologies are serving as essential components of the new push by the Kenyan leaders to generate economic diversification. The plan is for this Konza Technology City to be the information technology hub of the African Union creating more than 200,000 IT jobs by 2030.[37]

As one of the key bases for the African Union, Specialized Technical Committee on Education, Science and Technology, Kenya is at a crossroad in the approach to education and the real innovative breakthrough's that are being fashioned by the youth. With each passing day there are new revelations on the technological revolution that is underway. Whether it is the potential of the Tesla solar storage batteries or the perovskite solar cells,[38] the breakthroughs promise is that in the next five years solar power will do for the energy sector what cell phone communications had done for the telecommunications sector. Just as the mobile phones enabled Africans to leap frog one hundred years of fixed telephone lines, the emerging solar technologies will speed up new forms of diversified economic activities. The connection between mobile telephones and the deployment of solar power is already evident with the forms of electricity that power cell phone towers in the most remote parts of Africa.

In his discussion of emerging technological opportunities Juma Calestous writes:

> Information and telecommunications technologies serve as essential motherboards for other industrial activities. Unfortunately, most African countries view these technologies as products and services, not as platforms for industrial development. There are many other emerging platform technologies of relevance to Africa. For example, the rise of 3D printing could do for Africa what semiconductors did for Taiwan in the 1960s. The expiring of critical 3D printing patents has resulted in explosive growth in the sector, estimated at 23 percent per year. Another emerging platform technology of relevance to Africa is genetic engineering. So far the role of this technology has been discussed in the narrow context of genetically modified (GM) foods. The intensity of the controversies surrounding the issue, however, has blinded African countries to the benefits of acquiring and applying the same techniques in fields such as the development of vaccines and drugs against emerging infectious diseases.[39]

Juma has argued that with the right policies African institutions of higher learning can be hubs of innovation. Writing on the necessity to tune higher education into an engine for innovation Juma laments the low levels of investment in research in Africa and argues for more robust research and entrepreneurship. Noting that,

> For African higher education institutions to be centers of excellence and prime movers for community development, there has to be a systematic educational design that is relevant to African societies, particularly in the field of agriculture, through which the majority of African families support their livelihoods. African higher education needs to be reinvented in ways that equip graduates with the right skills to trigger innovation, societal development, economic growth and competitiveness… Without reshaping the discourse and creating transformative higher education enriched by innovative thinking, the African continent will be less likely to leverage its economic growth path into a prosperous future.[40]

This author will add that though some leaders are arguing that Kenya is well placed to push the changes necessary for the STC – ETC. This paper contends that such changes in education cannot take place outside of a framework of a transformed educational system.

Ali Mazrui: Transformative Education and Reparations

When Mazrui was born in 1933 the dominant philosophy of education in Africa had been that of education for submission and he began his schooling with a slate. Though his Islamic background and his life was buffered by three heritages the dominant colonial ideology was most appealing and Mazrui was a spokesperson of liberalism until he came face to face with militant Zionism and racism in the USA. By the time Mazrui joined the ancestors in 2014 the dominant ideology for humanization was Ubuntu and most children in good schools used the ipad instead of a slate. Mazrui confessed in one of his newsletters that he was not completely literate in information computer technologies. "With regard to the computer revolution, I have been more fascinated by its cultural consequences than by a personal desire to use computers."

Basic literacy and access to the resources for transformed knowledge environment are some of the requirements of a transformed educational system in the era of the ipad. One Caribbean scholar who wrote on starting school in the era of the slate noted that in the current era,

> "A modern competitive economy needs people who can communicate clearly and efficiently, who can work independently but within a team, who can adapt to changing technology, and who are self-motivated and self-disciplined. This translates into strong language skills in English and at least one of the other principal regional languages - Spanish, French and Portuguese - and/or Mandarin (Chinese).

It means that our students must develop strong analytical skills from mathematics that equip them to have a basic understanding of the sciences. It is analytical thinking that students must learn from mathematics because calculators, computers and iPads now do the calculations which I had to do as a child in my head or on my slate. Kids today are certain to live through rapid technological changes that have to be harnessed for the production of wealth and the generation of incomes, and not just entertainment that distracts their minds from reality."

The writer continues:

> "The iPad generation cannot be taught like the slate generation. New and more relevant techniques utilizing information technology have to become basic tools that are expertly used by the modern teachers, instructors and lecturers. Perhaps the emphasis should be shifted to learning, and away from teaching, with the leaders of the instructional processes focusing more on stimulating the students to discover information on their own."[41]

This writer concurs with the view that youths today are far away from the instructional processes that alienate them and need new innovative techniques that can accelerate the transformation of Africa and the Global South. Mazrui could communicate effectively and his spirit of love and openness placed him as an ancestor to whom we can call for guidance and inspiration. He demonstrated that he can grow and learn. The tribute to him by Wole Soyinka demonstrated the graciousness of Mazrui to show that while he may have an intellectual disagreement with someone, he did not hold grudges.[42] If one were to summarize the key elements of Mazrui these were: his ability to grow and learn; his attitude and practice of inclusiveness; thinking global, being a secular person who respected persons of different faiths; carrying forward African optimism; transcending gender boundaries; and working for the rights of women and mixed gender persons.

Mazrui attracted controversy and was noted because he stood up to be counted for social justice and peace. In his 81 years Mazrui spoke, wrote and dramatized enough in film to place an unmistakable stamp on the intellectual culture of the 20th century. In his well-publicized texts there will be contradictions, some inconsistencies and positions that alarmed those in power. These positions were forthright enough for the New York Times to state in its obituary that "Ali Mazrui was a scholar who divided US audiences." There was no vagueness on where Mazrui stood on human dignity. In his life, he stood for many things, but in this paper, I chose the question of his service for Africa in the OAU Reparations Commission. Mazrui was not parochial; his call for reparative justice included oppressed peoples such as the Palestinian people. Convening this memorial two weeks after the visit of the most conservative Israeli Prime Minister to Kenya, in August 2016, it is fitting that we use this commemoration of Mazrui to highlight his support for Palestine and the ways in which the apartheid condition s of Israel discriminates against Africans and Palestinians.

Endnotes

[1]   John Markoff, *Machines of Loving Grace: The Quest for Common Ground Between Humans and Robots,* Harper Collins Publishers. New York 2016.

[2]   United Nations, Office of Human Rights, "Basic Principles and Guidelines on the Right to a Remedy and Reparation for Victims of Gross Violations of International Human Rights Law and Serious Violations of International Humanitarian Law," Adopted and proclaimed by *General Assembly* Resolution 60/147 of 16 December 2005.

[3]   A Ten Point Action Plan for Reparatory Justice was endorsed by Heads of Government, in March 2014, see Caricom Reparations Commission, "REPARATIONS FOR NATIVE GENOCIDE AND SLAVERY," http://www.caricom.org/reparations-for-native-genocide-and-slavery.

[4]   Report of the World Conference Against Racism, Racial Discrimination and Related Intolerance, *http://www.un.org/WCAR/durban.pdf*

[5]   Kenneth King, *Pan-Africanism and Education: A Study of Race Philanthropy and Education in the Southern States of America and East Africa, Clarendon Press, London 1971.*

[6]   Ali A. Mazrui & Alamin M. Mazrui, *The Power of Babel: Language and Governance in the African Experience*, University of Chicago Press, 1998, page 24. This section also outlines the definition of an AfroSaxon. See also Ali A. Mazrui, *The Political Sociology of the English Language*, Mouton, London 1975, p. 76.

[7]   Mazrui, Alamin and Mutunga, Willy M., *Race, Gender and Culture Conflict: Ali Mazrui and His Critics*) (Trenton, NJ: Africa World Press, 2003. For an updated bibliography see *https://en.wikipedia.org/wiki/Ali_Mazrui*

[8]   For an early collection of the writings on Mazruiana see *The Global African: A Portrait of Ali A. Mazrui*, edited by Omari H. Kokole, Africa World Press, 1998. See also *The Mazruiana Collection Revisited: Ali A. Mazrui Debating the African Condition,* Compiled by Abdul Samed Bemath, Africa Institute of South Africa and New Dawn Press, India 1998.

[9]   Zygmunt. Bauman, *Modernity and the Holocaust*, Cornell University Press, New York 2001.

[10] Mazrui recounted how in his interview with the British Governor Sir Phillip Mitchell he intimated that he wanted to study law and literature but instead the British encouraged him to go to a technical college to pursue technical education. See Ali A. Mazrui, *The Political Sociology of the English Language*, Mouton, London 1975, pp. 25-28.

[11] Franklin Giddings, first chair of sociology at Columbia University had promoted the view that citizenship should be at heart of any educational program. Citizenship was defined by him as an individual adjusting him/herself to the existing social order. He believed that black people could be educated so long as they adhered to Euro American developmental paradigms. Thomas Jesse Jones had been one of the prominent students who believed that blacks should adjust to the existing social order and he was employed by the Phelps Stokes Commission to put these ideas into practice. James D. Anderson, *The Education of Blacks in the South, 1860-1935*, University of North Carolina Press, Chapel Hill, 1988.

[12] James D. Anderson, *The Education of Blacks in the South, 1860-1935*, University of North Carolina Press, Chapel Hill, 1988.

[13] John K. Marah "Educational adaptation and pan-Africanism: developmental trends in Africa.' Journal of Black Studies 17, no. 4: 460-48 AND Kenneth King op cit, Chapter 4, The Phelps Stokes Commission in Kenya, pp. 94-127.

[14] Ali Mazrui, "Growing Up in a Shrinking World: A Private Vantage Point" and "The Making of an African Political Scientist" (International Social Science Journal No 25, 1973).

[15] See Ngũgĩ Wa Thiong'o, *Decolonising the Mind: The Politics of Language in African Literature,* James Currey, and London 1986. See also Micere Githae Mugo, *Writing and Speaking from the Heart of My Mind*, Africa World Press, New Jersey, 2012.

[16] Ngũgĩ Wa Thiong'o, "African Identities: Pan-Africanism in the Era of Globalisation and Capitalist Fundamentalism" *Macalester International*, Vol. 14 article 9 2004.

[17] Ki-Zerbo, J., 1990, *Educate or Perish: Africa's Impass and Prospects*, Dakar/Abidjan: UNESCO-UNICEF.

[18] King, J., 2005, *Black Education: A Transformative Research and Action Agenda for the New Century*, Mahwah, New Jersey: Lawrence Erlbaum Associates, p. 5.

[19] For a discussion of the Genographic Project see MacIntosh, Constance, 'Indigenous Self-Determination and Research on Human Genetic Material: A Consideration of the Relevance of Debates on Patents and Informed Consent, and the Political Demands on Researchers', *Health Law Journal*, No. 13, 2005.

[20] See 'White House Brain Initiative', Washington, D.C, April 2, 2013. *http://www.whitehouse. gov/sites/default/files/whitehouse_files/infographic/wh_brain_mapping_2013_0.pdf*

[21] Ali A. Mazrui, Global Africa: From Abolitionists to Reparationists, *African Studies Review*, Vol. 37, No. 3 (Dec., 1994), pp. 1-18.

[22] Michael O. West, "Kwame Nkrumah and Ali Mazrui: An Analysis of the 1967 Transition Debate," *Journal of Pan African Studies*, vol.8, no.6, September 2015.

[23] *Ibid* p. 134.

[24] *http://binghamton.edu/igcs/docs/Newsletter17.pdf*

[25] For the details of the resolutions from the 1978 United Nations Conference, World Conference to Combat Racism and Racial Discrimination, Geneva, August 14-25, 1978 see *http://www. racism.gov.za/substance/confdoc/declfirst.htm*

[26] Ali A. Mazrui, Global Africa: From Abolitionists to Reparationists, African Studies Review, Vol. 37, No. 3 (December 1994), pp. 1-18.

[27] Mazrui, A.A. 1999 "From Slave Ship to Space Ship: Africa between Marginalization and Globalization", *African Studies Quarterly: the Online Journal for African Studies,* 2 (4), *http://www.africa.ufl.edu/asq/v2/v2i4a2.htm.* Also *Black Reparations in the Era of Globalization* (Binghamton, N.Y.: Institute of Global Cultural Studies), 2002.

[28] African Descendants Caucus brought together reparations activists from across the diaspora, including representatives from many U.S. groups: The December 12th Movement, N'COBRA, All for Reparations and Emancipation—a group associated with the Lost/Found Nation of Islam—the Black Radical Congress, and the National Black United Front (NBUF). They formulated an agenda for Durban that stressed three goals: to characterize the institution of slavery and the transatlantic slave trade as crimes against humanity, (crimes against humanity have no statute of limitations in international law); to assert the economic motive of white supremacy; and to call for reparations. See Martha Biondi, "The Rise of the Reparations Movement," *Radical History Review*, Issue 87 (fall 2003): 5–18.

[29] John J. Mearsheimer and Stephen M. Walt, *The Israeli Lobby and US. Foreign Policy*, Farrar, Straus and Giroux, New York 2007.

[30] Ngugi Wa Thiongo, "African Identities: Pan-Africanism in the Era of Globalization and Capitalist Fundamentalism" *Macalester International*, Vol. 14 article 9, 2004.

[31] Ali A. Mazrui, "The Black Woman and the Problem of Gender," in Global African, pp. 225-247.

[32] Etin Anwar, Mazrui and Gender: on the questioning of methodology, in *The Mazruiana Collection Revisited: Ali A. Mazrui Debating the African Condition: an Annotated and Select Thematic Bibliography, 1962-2003*, Sterling Publishers Pvt. Ltd, 2005.

33   quoted in article by ANDREA ELLIOTT, "Woman Leads Muslim Prayer Service in New York," New York Times, March 19, 2005, *http://www.nytimes.com/2005/03/19/nyregion/ woman-leads-muslim-prayer-service-in-new-york.html.*

34   Wangari Maathai, *Replenishing the Earth: Spiritual Values for Healing Ourselves and the World*, Doubleday Books, New York, 2010.

35   There are 14 STC's: 1. Agriculture, rural development, water and environment; 2. Finance, monetary affairs, economic planning and integration; 3. Trade, industry and minerals; 4.Transport, infrastructure, energy and tourism; 5. Gender and women empowerment; 6. Justice and legal affairs; 7. Social development, labour and employment; 8. Public service, local government, urban development and decentralization; 9. Health, population and drug control; 10. Migration, refugees and internally displaced persons (IDPs); 11. Youth, culture and sports; 12. Education, science and technology; 13. Communication and information communications technology (ICT); and 14. Defence, safety and security. *http://www.au.int/ en/organs/stc*

36   Caroline Elkins, *Imperial Reckoning: The Untold Story of Britain's Gulag, Holt, New York 2005.* For an account of the efforts to gain access to the hidden files of the British see Marc Perry, "A Reckoning: Colonial atrocities and academic reputations on trial in a British courtroom," *Chronicle of Higher Education*, June 1, 2016, *http://chronicle.com/article/A-Historians-Day-in-Court/236656*

37   In January 2013 the President of Kenya launched that Konza Technopolis Development Authority (KTDA) to oversee the building of the IT hub.

38   Perovskite is a light-sensitive crystal that has the potential to be more efficient, inexpensive, and versatile than all other existing solar solutions to date. Over the past five years, perovskite's conversion efficiency has increased dramatically — from four percent to nearly 20 percent, making it the fastest developing technology in the history of photovoltaics.

39   Calestous Juma," It Will Take More Than Natural Resources for Africa to Rise," Op-Ed, Aljazeera, October 22, 2014.

40   Calestous Juma, "Universities as Engines of Innovation" in *New African*, July 2015, p. 78.

41   Michael Witter, "From slate to iPad" Sunday Gleaner, August 5, 2012, *http://jamaica-gleaner. com/gleaner/20120805/cleisure/cleisure2.html*

42   Wole Soyinka, "Remembering Ali Mazrui," *Transition*, Issue 117, 2015.

Ali Mazrui and *The Trial of Christopher Okigbo*

Chris L. Wanjala

Introduction

An intellectual should not only be seen as an acrobat: "a person who has the capacity to be fascinated by ideas and has acquired the skill to handle some of those ideas effectively," as Ali A. Mazrui once claimed,[1] but he or she must represent values which go beyond the orthodoxy of his or her society and relate them to the holy Scripture.[2] Mazrui saw the anguish of the writer, specifically, as continental. In June 1971 he gave a vote of thanks for Professor Wole Soyinka at a writers' festival in Nairobi. Wole Soyinka had been arrested by the Federal Government of Nigeria. Writers around the world showed concern about this arrest. They wrote "telegrams of concern" to the Federal Republic of Nigeria and operated on the notion that society should protect the creative writer with more diligence than any other type of intellectual because the writer belongs to a special breed of gifted people higher than the common person.[3] When there was a crackdown on writers in Nigeria, Ali Mazrui reminisced on all the Nigerians from various ethnic backgrounds he had known from his undergraduate days and the way they had been part of his growth, and how then they were picking up guns and killing each other.[4]

African writers arrogate to themselves a very special role in their communities. Wole Soyinka, for instance, emerges in *The Man Died* as a greatly maligned prodigy vis-a-vis the "brawny, hairy monsters" that the thick-headed soldiers are. We are back to role of the African writer as a prophet. Wole Soyinka summarized it for them when he said that: "The artist has always functioned in African society as the record of the *mores* and the experience of his society *and* as the voice of vision in his own time."[5]

The influence of Swahili Poetry is more pervasive in Ali's literary undertakings, than the influence of Swahili Prose. Mazrui grew up in a culture of pamphleteering and non-fiction authorship. He was a student of English Literature in England and although he was different from his British classmates who had been prepared by their upbringing of learning English through nursery rhymes and play songs which had formed an integral process of their growing up, he had to be "resocialized" into an English literary culture.[6] His clarity of mind and his literary ability were evinced by his power to express himself effectively. He was exposed to the English language and English classics by such authors as Milton, Dryden, Pope, Wordsworth and T.S Eliot when he was an "O" Level student in Great Britain.[7]

Mazrui's literary criticism and creative writing

The Trial of Chistopher Okigbo is a memoir on the multitude of persons who, like Mazrui himself, lived in the turbulent times of the 1960s. In writing this work from his memory of Nigeria of his time, Mazrui is what one would call a "self-biographer." Mazrui fictionalizes the debate about the role of the literary artist in his society in this novel. We are told, the main character, Christopher Okigbo, is charged "with the offence of putting society before art in the scale of values" (Mazrui 1971:41).[8] Hamisi defends the role of the artist in society and, as the story unfolds, he is less glamorous than Christopher Okigbo. The author has less sympathy for him in this novel. During the defence, the audience in the courtroom spares only few moments of pity for him, Salisha and her background (Mazrui 1971). Apolo-Gyamfi, who is painted more glamorously by the author, is a debater and a prodigy of sorts, and in many ways, he is the author's voice, representing the author's view regarding the issue of the role of the writer (read 'intellectual') in society. He also represents the author's view of the intellectual's stand in the face of the masses. The life of the intellectual seems to be more important than the life of the farmer, for instance.

In the novel, we witness the triumph of the Western-derived idea that the individual should be treated differently from his brothers and sisters who are members of the common people in the society. But, in contrast, African intellectuals like Ngugi wa Thiong'o, Ousmane Sembene, and Alex La Guma, who are committed to their communities, blame the individualistic views of the alienated members of the intelligentsia on their Western upbringing.

From what we see of Mazrui's *The Trial of Christopher Okigbo,* and his works of non-fiction, Ali Mazrui compares very well with Ngugi wa Thiong'o in so far as wide reading and wide experience of many literary traditions, are concerned. The difference between Ali Mazrui and Ngugi wa Thiong'o is that for many years Mazrui stuck to his own definition of an African intellectual and espoused wide learning almost for the sake of wide learning.[9] On the issue of commitment in African literature, Mazrui has no resolute decision. Judging him by the verdict in Okigbo's case in his novel, we find him saying: "The verdict on Counsel for Biafra was *Guilty;* the verdict on Counsel against Biafra was *Not Guilty;* and the verdict on Biafra herself was *Not Proven (Mazrui 1971: 144)."*

For the liberal Anglo-Saxon Black man, the choice falls on Apolo-Gyamfi, who triumphs over traditional Africa whose cause is only feebly defended by Hamisi. Here we see how Mazrui prejudges the issues of commitment by saying that Okigbo had no right to consider himself a patriot first, and an African artist only second.[10] That was to subordinate the interests of generations of Africans to the needs of the Ibos at an isolated moment in historical time.

Relying on his erstwhile English high school education very well and using his journalistic approach from his family's tradition as pamphleteers, Mazrui etches a large canvas in his writings; this is no exception to the space he dedicated to the issue of the role of the intellectual in society as portrayed in *The Trial of Christopher Okigbo.* Mazrui remains very topical in his approach to issues in the novel and he discusses the Nigerian crisis in the context of other crises on the continent like the Congo crisis which he studied in the early part of his career. Mazrui can compare with Peter Abrahams who blends the Ghanaian reality with the Kenyan reality in his novel, *A Wreath for Udomo (1956).* African writers of the earlier generation like Peter Abrahams and Ali Mazrui are able to contrast the role of the artist in Africa with the role of the artist in Europe and America because of their wide experience. Unlike Ngugi wa Thong'o and the Nigerian literary critic, Obiajunwa Wali, Mazrui is ambivalent about the choices which an African intellectual makes when discussing the African dilemma. Obi Wali, unlike Mazrui describes a viable option that the African novelist has to take when he says:

This very challenge may well be one of his (the African novelist's) opportunities to develop the much talked about new form in his adventure to create a written tradition.[11]

According to Ngugi wa Thiong'o, on the other hand, traditions of African narratives have evolved over the years, just as the role of the African artist has changed. In his essays collected in a volume entitled *Homecoming,* Ngugi shows that there have been two kinds of societies in Africa: the feudal societies with their wealth and privileges restricted to a section of the society and the stateless societies. In the feudal society, the role of the artist is to entertain the feudal overlords in the court. In contrast, in the stateless society there is no division of labor and people identify with each other according to the skills they own. The whole stateless society, however, participates in its creative activities as a community. They tend their farms, play their music, participate in ceremonial recreation and entertainment like dancing, reciting stories at the fireside, and young adults become warriors and participate in war as it occurs.[12]

Ngugi reaches these conclusions by outlining elements of African performance traditions like song, dance, and occasional mime rooted in the ritual and ceremonial practices of the country. He notes the centrality of song and dance in the celebration of the coming of rain, the first birth, the second birth, circumcision, marriage, funerals, and all ordinary ceremonies. In his analysis of the role of the artist, Ngugi reaches a conclusion which he shares with other critics of African literature.

From their pronouncements, African writers of the 1970s seemed to be unanimous about the role the African writer should play in the African revolution. The African writer must face the stark realities of the continent and actually name them in his or her writing. Most of them repudiated the metaphysical terms about human suffering which seemed to dominate the criticism of African literature in the mid-1960s. The criticism which tallied with the more progressive writers picked culture conflict as a predominant theme, especially in West African literature. Apartheid and its racial laws were the major themes in the literature of South Africa.[13] The writer and the politician joined hands to fight against colonialism in Africa. The writer faced the challenges of the African writer and the politician who was alienated. While the politician talked about decolonization, the educational model that he put across to his people was based on Western and capitalist values.

The politician failed to implement the programme of decolonization. He maintained the power structure which he inherited from the colonizer. The two - the intellectual elite and the political elite - were thus alienated from the masses.

They betrayed the masses. Their struggle against the white people remained at the level of racial equality, but now that they had access to what the white people had denied them, they had settled down to vigorous consumption of Western values. They hold their glasses of whisky in toasts and yodel a few songs in their native tongues and they consider themselves to be close to their people. These are the same people who fought for the land which was forcefully occupied by the white people; they fought for a European lifestyle – clothes, shoes, salary, western-style mansions – and they had to acquire an education to help them feel properly integrated into the new values. They were locked up in close imitation of the white man and his values.

The African writer who had fought alongside the politician did not find himself or herself in an exceptional situation. Through his or her own filter of alienation, owing to the education he or she had picked from the West, and the shock of disillusionment of being left out by the politician and the masses, the African writer created lonely, perceptive and sometimes self-righteous bystanders of the 1960s typified by Gabriel Okara's novel, *The Voice,* Achebe's Chief Nanga, in *A Man of the People,* Ayi Kweyi Armah's main character "the man" in *The Beautyful Ones Are Not Yet Born,* Gerald Timundu in Kibera's *Voices in the Dark* and Joe Musizi in Robert Serumaga's *Return to the Shadows.* Ali Mazrui's fictional Christopher Okigbo is no exception.

The individual in the literature of the nationalist period is the prophet of doom, tantalized as he is by the paradox of collaboration between the national political elite and the agents of multinational monopoly in the Western metropolis.

Ali A Mazrui and *The Trial of Christopher Okigbo*

In a letter to Ali Mazrui, I told him that it had occurred to me when I was teaching his novel *The Trial of Christopher Okigbo* to an undergraduate class; that the novel could be read in the same way as *The Republic* by Plato and *Messingkauf Dialogues* by Bertolt Brecht. From this standpoint the novel could be seen as the first vivid comment in the theory of African literature, highlighting the issue of commitment that has engaged the African writer in the nationalist period. I wanted to know what result this approach of mine would yield towards theories of African literature.

Mazrui's novel and the works of the Sudanese writer, Taban Lo Liyong, should be read in the same way as the works of theory of literature, and African political thought respectively. The two writers have been able to excite a lot of dialogue which is often lacking when literary critics are dealing with other East African writers. Mazrui and Lo Liyong are provocative writers. They are the only two East African writers who are given a special place in Ezekiel Mphahlele's critical work, *The African Image* (1974). Mazrui delved into African political thought, Islam and Christianity. He discussed religion and politics as inseparable domains of knowledge. From a brilliant and perceptive exposition apparent in his work, *On Heroes and Uhuru Worship*, he gave us insights into the psychology of African Nationalism. He specifically draws his theoretical perspectives from Edmund Burke. As Es'kia Mphahlele ably demonstrates in his chapter in *The African Image* entitled "Dialogue of Two Selves"[14] Mazrui makes a distinction between the indigenous consciousness and the one derived from western civilization (Mphahlele 1974: 280).This divided self is noted mainly among African poets.

Christopher Okigbo, for example, is a prodigal who prostrates himself before Mother Idoto (Mphahlele 1974: 282-283). Taban Lo Liyong, on the other hand, dramatizes himself before Susan Sontang, an English woman. In Mphhlele's words: "His intellect commutes easily (maybe too easily?) between Africa and figures of English literature" (Mphahlele 1974: 284-285), Taban Lo Liyong is described as being a writer who possesses "sparkling wit" (Mphahhlele 1974: 285). This essay demonstrates how Ali Mazrui, like Eskia Mphahlele above, celebrates Okigbo's talent on the one hand, while regretting that the great Nigerian poet put his talent to a poor cause, on the other hand.

I followed *The Guardian* in its accounts of Mazrui's Reith Lectures on the BBC. I learnt that *The Listener* published them in full. I wanted a full copy of the lectures and asked Mazrui to spare one for me. Professor Mazrui became very important in the subsequent days as an Anglophone scholar from East Africa. For his novel, *The Trial of Christopher,* he was criticised by younger colleagues, despite his influence on East African intellectual life. Besides the Reith Lectures and the novel, he came up with *The Africans,* a nine-part series exposing his thoughts, as an intellectual, about Africa as his continent. For these series Mazrui was seen by his critics in the United States of America as "anti-West" (Howard, 1987: 77).

In Kenya there were echoes of his novel in a play that was performed at the Kenya National Theatre. The play was called *Hereafter*. In it we had characters that remind us of those in *The Trial of Christopher Okigbo;* namely, the Counsel for Damnation and the Counsel for Salvation. In the play we recognized that existentialist tone which was only familiar to us in our study of Western literature and which came across as resignation to fate and unmitigated disillusionment. Individualism and loneliness were creeping into our lives. We had "the maverick, the dissenter, the man who steals the fire... each man, in awful and brutal isolation, is for himself, to flower or to perish."

In the *Hereafter* play there were no real mentions of God. We saw man refusing to love his God. He became arrogant: "You talk of Nyakalaga, who is he? I have not seen him face to face. Therefore, I cannot worship him. I worship three Ws: war, wine and women." This cynicism (or was it nihilism?) had echoes of existentialism in the West. And yet we could not gloss over it and dismiss it as sheer irresponsibility. The play used drumming at the back of the stage. There was "a soft humming of a tune portraying resurrection."

In Mazrui's *The Trial of Christopher Okigbo*, the trial is conducted by Hamisi Salim and Apolo-Gyamfi. Values are introduced in the *Hereafter,* which become very important in the contrast between individualism and universalism. Tudi in the script of the *Hereafter* play, says: "Individualism is the deeper loyalties to one's inner being, a capacity to retain a private area of distinctiveness in one's personality. The black sheep of the family is the greatest individual dualistic member."

The issue of commitment in the writing of Mazrui and his contemporaries revolves around collective consciousness which is equated to African socialism. But Mazrui's novel was not given a fitting attention in the criticism of African literature in East Africa when it was published in the early 1970s. We had a couple of reviews of *The Trial of Christopher Okigbo* by Timothy Wangusa,[15] Peter Nazareth in *Standpoints on African Literature* edited by the present literary critic,[16] and Dr Okello Oculi in *Ghala*.[17] An expanded version of Okello Oculi's review appeared in the *Presence Africaine*.[18]

The reviewers of the novel accused Mazrui of having written prose that was pedantic and full of flawed logistic and of having a cluster of abstract, stilted words which failed to communicate what he set out to say. He allegedly used clichés in an attempt to portray characters.

Mazrui's critics also picked on his treatment of sex. Nazareth picked on the situation in which Mazrui describes the activities of the people in the Hereinafter:

> It took a minute or two for Hamisi's vision to adjust itself to the dimmer lighting of the Refresher Room. But visual adjustment was to constitute a psychological stumbling-block for, as the contents of the refresher room became clear to his vision, the shapes were reduced to a bizarre spectacle. There seemed to be about two dozen naked men, with a similar number of women. Some of the men still wore the beads which had differentiated them on the football ground a few hours ago. The red or white beads, according to whether they were eleventh or sixteenth century, continued to adorn a number of masculine bodies in the room. But in some cases the beads had been removed, and the nakedness of the soccer player had been made complete. There was an air of agitated activity in the group, but on the closer observation it became clear that each couple was engaged in one of the two possible activities. Either the woman was massaging the man nearest to her, or the man was making love to the woman. These two alternating activities formed an interspersing pattern on the carpeted floor of the Refresher Room (Mazrui 1971: 50-51).

The lack of vitality in Mazrui's lines comes from an intellectual detachment in his analysis. That sensuality in the prose of fellow writers like Ngugi wa Thiong'o, and indeed, the poignancy and anguish which we find in Ezekiel Mphahlele *Down Second Avenue* (1962, an autobiography) is absolutely lacking in Mazrui's writing. Mazrui himself seems to be unaware of this because he later says his task in this novel is one of "unearthing the depths of meaning of otherwise simple events and the hidden links in otherwise disparate phenomena." As you read through his prose you may think this is easier said than done. The feeling in his writing is like that of a man who says, "I'm very angry with you. I'll beat you just now," but he instead laughs and taps you on the shoulder.

We may argue that Mazrui's critics were flippant and sometimes naïve. In many instances, Nazareth, for one, picked an isolated sentence from Mazrui's novel, and howled over it. The rape scene in the novel is certainly an elaborate one. The line: "Lolia stiffly received the soldier into her body," in the rape scene (Mazrui 1971: 105) is an anti-climax to a beautiful recreation and sex scene which has taken place between Lolia and Pete Kawesa before they are rudely interrupted by the soldiers. Pete Kawesa is a suave Ugandan taxi driver with a soft tongue which seems to go very well with women of moral turpitude. He is described by his creator as having "some compensating qualities including a great capacity for hard work, and some genius in elementary strategy" (Mazrui 1971: 102).

The rape scene starts as a case of unfaithful conduct between Pete Kawesa and Lolia, his friend Ali Mayanja's mistress. From the start we are told that Kawesa is the sort of man who will woo his friend's mistress and in fact sleep with her. He does this with Lolia by first taking her to a night club, sponging her with intoxicating liquor and then taking her to bed in Ali Mayanja's absence. Ali Mazrui gives a banal description of the sexual intercourse between Kawesa and Lolia precisely because it is cheap sex:

> Then, arms round each other's shoulders, giggling away, they stumbled back into the bedroom. Kawesa put her on the bed and stood and undressed himself in the dim light of Lolia's room. After that he removed the remaining items of clothing on Lolia's body – the bra came off first, next the sweaty pants. He left the cheap gaudy necklace hanging round her neck, forming a pattern of some kind between her two breasts. Kawesa proceeded to make love to Lolia twice, each a prolonged session. Then exhausted, they both lay naked and fell asleep (Mazrui 1971: 104).

But Mazrui must be commended in this scene for creating credible confusion which follows the Kawesa – Lolia love scene. When the soldiers come in, it is Ali Mayanja that Kawesa has in mind. Mazrui graphically captures the drama:

> "It must be Ali Mayanja back already!" exclaimed Kawesa. They were not quite sure what to do. He had time only to put his shirt on, unbuttoned, when Lolia pushed him under the bed. She was afraid the door would be knocked down, and that she might have to pay from her own savings for its repair (Mazrui 1971: 105).

This scene portrays the brutality of the army men in Uganda during Amin's foul regime. But Kawesa emerges in the scene as a sympathetic character. His pathos is apparent in his penitence directed at the soldiers who do not understand in the least what he is sorry for. The narrative ends on a sour note, and rather than isolating the sentence which talks about the soldiers sliding into Lolia's womanhood, as Nazareth does, the passage has to be read in whole. Mazrui writes:

> He was protesting in agitated Luganda, while one of the soldiers dragged him by the scruff of his neck shouting in Swahili "*Nyamaza! Wacha*

Kelele!" The first soldier lets his comrade deal with Kawesa while he returns to the bedroom. Lolia's sheet falls off her, and she tries to cover herself again. The soldier crossed the threshold and closed the door behind him. A minute later, as Lolia stiffly received the soldier into her body, they heard two shots outside (Mazrui 1971: 105).

The sour note relieves the tragedy of the taxi driver. It also explains why Pete Kawesa is in After – Africa as we speak.

In their eagerness to find fault with Mazrui, the reviewers of his novel said that Mazrui was not being sufficiently erotic. Peter Nazareth, for one, said that the tragic scene above was: "A pretty inadequate sexual description in the post Lawrence, Harris, Miller and Mangua era!" (Nazareth 1973: 149).

I do not want to speak about other sex scenes in *The Trial of Christopher Okigbo*, but the one I have discussed at length was not meant by the author to be scintillating. Nazareth said Mazrui used what Christopher Booker calls "nyktomorphic" words and quickly adds: "This is the excessive use of vague words in the hope that the reader will fill in the blanks out of his own imagination or experience since these words carry little meaning in themselves." (Nazareth 1973: 149).

This is also my belief. But the examples that Nazareth gave actually showed that Mazrui failed to capture the excitement, which came with events like sex and football because he was communicating something else about the tense post-colonial times that these characters were living in.

This point in the reviews, in hindsight, brings us to another fact in Mazrui's style. What is really the significance of football in Mazrui's novel? Was Nazareth being illuminating when he said: "One wonders, then, why Mazrui decided to introduce a football match into an alleged novel of ideas, and one cannot help concluding that he was getting bogged down in his story and decided to introduce something where the reader would do all the work that the novelist should have done"? (in Wanjala 1973: 150). Nazareth misses the real nature of the novel that Mazrui was writing. The novel is an allegory and if you will, anti-utopian. It speaks about the commitment of African writers and represents the thoughts and the experiences of the majority of them through Christopher Okigbo who in this work is fictitious and, therefore, an image. The idea of commitment in art comes to us in the simplified literary way. Mazrui is a scholar and a debater, and Nazareth himself says so. At the time of reviewing the novel, Nazareth sounded to me as decidedly immune to ideas, because, to my mind, he failed to evaluate the novel in its own terms.

I am now convinced that *The Trial of Christopher Okigbo* must be read as a discourse in the theory of literature, in the same way as *Plato's Republic*, and Bertolt Brecht's *Dialogues*. It is an exercise in dialectics where commitment in the criticism of African literature is the subject. Probably if I had not become the Assistant Editor of *Nairobi Stadium* and heard Professor Henry Odera Oruka, my editor, explain the meaning of *Stadium* I would have thought about the Gymnasium in which the *Trial of Christopher Okigbo* takes place in the literal sense. In *The Trial of Christopher Okigbo*, Mazrui sees the Gymnasium as an intellectual arena in the classical terms where scholarship was seen as a rigorous devotion. Mazrui uses the football stadium deliberately to imply that *stadium* which Odera Oruka explains as a "place of intensive academic and intellectual exchange." The main drama of the grand play in *The Trial of Christopher Okigbo* takes place as intellectual football. The stadium in this case in a traditional African *Baraza* and/ or an Anglo-Saxon courtroom. As Okello Oculi noted, the game takes place with poetry forming the background. Oculi observed:

> The novel and the play have to reckon with and in fact give way to the invocation of poetry as a terrestrial voice that rides high and powerful in the winds. The poetry of Okigbo and of Byron intervenes on several occasions like supernatural forces reminiscent of spirits in traditional farina thought and life. This structural trinity at the centre of the book, and the setting of the stage of action in the realm of life after death on earth, will certainly be seen as a worthy addition to literary experimentation in east Africa (Okello Oculi 1972: 39).

Mazrui's characters are autobiographical in many places. Hamisi's only qualification in participating in the trial of Christopher Okigbo is his "participation in panel discussion for the BBC in London..." We are told: "He recalled especially the panel discussion he had arranged to discuss the implications of the assassination of Sylvanus Olympio in January 1963." No wonder on being assigned the task of defending Christopher Okigbo in the After-Africa, Hamisi is asked "to think out his case, try to grasp the judicial system of After-Africa, assess modes of potential impact *in the debating arena*" (my emphasis).

The Trial of Christopher Okigbo is about an obscurantist Nigerian poet who suffered from misplaced allegiances. Rather than engaging in the intellectual mudslinging that East African literary intellectuals dabbled in in the 1970s when the novel was published, we should ask about Mazrui's stand in the perennial debate on commitment in African intellectual life. We must ask of him the reason why he picks on Christopher Okigbo. *The Trial of Christopher Okigbo* was not meant to be read by people who have never heard of the word commitment (or indeed engagement), and one should know from the start that it was not meant for people who were unfamiliar with the problems of choice facing African writers in that era . It is ironical that Peter Nazareth should glibly say: "To sum up: in terms of the use of words, *The Trial of Christopher Okigbo* is an awful novel."

I have a sneaking suspicion that Nazareth is operating like all the products of the Makerere School of English who, especially in the 1960s and 1970s, saw form as the be-all in the evaluation of works of literature. I am surprised that a man who wrote an essay in defence of commitment in Ngugi's first novel was not amenable to a discussion of this pet subject in Mazrui's novel. Nazareth failed to see that Mazrui took up the debate Nazareth himself broached in his book of essays, *Literature and Society in Modern Africa* (1972*)*. I am surprised that a man who had tried to liberate himself from the Makerere literary thinking was himself bogged down by formalism in his criticism of African literature. When Nazareth tried to discuss values in *The Trial of Christopher Okigbo*, he unwittingly settled into discussing the plot.[19] Peter Nazareth engaged a stereotype approach to *The Trial of Christopher Okigbo* where the critic dismisses an author because of the setting he has chosen.

Mazrui's writing was tolerable to Nazareth to the extent that it reminded him of Swift's *Gulliver's Travels*, Butler's *Erewhon* and Orwell's *Animal Firm*. Generally speaking, Nazareth spoke of Mazrui as if to say the questions which were raised by the professor were important, only that they are raised in a flawed style.

But in the classical use of *dialogue,* Mazrui used living personalities from past and contemporary history to make his novel sound realistic. He invoked the names of dead African statesmen - Chaka, Lumumba, Tom Mboya, who were long dead at the time the novel was published. Mazrui says: "The Nigerian Civil war had shaken Africa at least as profoundly, as ever the Congo troubles had done a few years previously" (Mazrui 1971: 28).

The journalist in Mazrui came out here where the writer remained contemporary and topical:

Abiranja then referred to the Congo situation soon after independence. The death of Lumumba had indeed caused a diplomatic convulsion in the Herebefore. But there were few ripples in After-Africa. The really important trial in After-Africa connected with the Congo was that of an unknown mutineer in the Force Publique who had helped in sparking off the military insurrection soon after Belgian withdrawal, and set loose the torrents of anarchy in that country. The elders in After-Africa decided to have this particular mutineer arrested immediately on arrival beyond the grave, and the mutineer was judged both for himself, and as an embodiment of the guilt or possible innocence of the Congo as a whole (Mazrrui 1971: 28).

The realism of the novel is etched by references to actual historical names representing the oppressive world of colonialism. We know that nothing like After-Africa ever existed. But the novelist tries to convince us by a self-confident description of what After-Africa might look like. What is important about Mazrui's novel is that he is looking introspectively into his own career as a political scientist and writing about it. We often talk about "Science Fiction"; when we read *The Trial of Christopher Okigbo,* it is time we talked about "Political Science Fiction." In a much fairer analysis of the novel, Dr Okello Oculi argues that Mazrui has transported political science to heaven. He hails the Pan-Africanist stand which Mazrui takes in this novel: It is an Africa that is united across all generations and centuries. We meet Lumumba playing football against Tafawa Balewa and Tom Mboya, in their Africa of After-Death. This is Mazrui coming to terms with African reality.

Okello Oculi is critical of Mazrui's exclusivity in his portrait of Africa.

> It is a Mazruian pan-Africanism for it excludes Berber and Arab Africa. The Egyptian, Algerian, Northern Sudanese, Moroccan, and even Ethiopian and Somali dimensions of after-Africa are significantly silent. Mazrui's after-Africa is; disturbingly, an Africa without the Sahara and the pyramids (Okello Oculi 1972: 40).

The novel is said to be a study of Mazrui's own guilt: "The burden of Mazrui's effort," writes Okello Oculi, "is to put on record his agony and problem as an African Anglo-liberal who is being harassed by the voices of African socialism and the ethic of collective social familyhood" (Okello Oculi 1972: 40).

The author of *The Trial of Christopher Okigbo* was born in the 24th of February in 1933, in Mombasa, Kenya. He went to a Sunni mosque in Mombasa; his primary and secondary schools were not more than a mile from his home. His father was a Chief Kadhi of Kenya until his death in 1947 – a very learned man in the Islamic law. As a Muslim boy he did not pay much attention to the impact of Christianity on Kenyan societies. But he was later exposed to a literature that evokes a Christian world-view.

Ali Mazrui's mother on the other hand was moderately educated in Islam. He has a brother and four sisters, none of whom is a writer like himself. His brother was a Liwali of Mombasa until he retired from the civil service and went into private business. Young Mazrui went to school at the age of six. His father was a pamphleteer. He aroused young Mazrui's interest in writing. His interest in Nigerian writers is shown by the fact that not only has he written a novel on the late Christopher Okigbo, but he was also the man who gave a vote of thanks, in honour of Wole Soyinka, following Soyinka's Plenary Address on "The Writer and Society in Africa" at the colloquium held at the University of Nairobi in June 1971. But from my interviews with him, the writers who interested him included Wole Soyinka, William Shakespeare, William Wordsworth, Edmund Burke, Chinua Achebe, Frantz Fanon, Charles Dickens, Agatha Christie and Okot p'Bitek.[20]

Ali Mazrui went to school at the Arab Boys Government School before leaving for Huddersfield College in England. He attended the University of Manchester in England, Columbia University, New York, USA, and Oxford University, England. Nothing seemed to delight Mazrui more than dispelling ignorance and creating an intellectual sensation in an audience. He attended conferences and gave lectures in Africa, Asia and Europe, North America and Australia. His novel, *The Trial of Christopher Okigbo* created an intellectual sensation which was apparent in the lecturer – audience relationships. Mazrui's audiences always stirred and exchanged admiring comments whenever they were intellectually titillated by him. As we have seen above, the lecture hall for Mazrui was like a football field. It is referred to by his character Apolo-Gyamfi as "an open forum," and "that assembly of returning listeners."

The lecture hall for Ali Mazrui was a forum indeed which was borne out by the enlightened and witty exchanges between people of such intelligence as Apolo-Gyamfi and the Lord George Byron. The author says: "The audience nearly burst out in applause. It had been a memorable exchange." In the whole discourse of *The Trial of*

Christopher Okigbo, Mazrui is decidedly morefond of Apolo-Gyamfi than Hamisi. There is something autobiographical about Apolo-Gyamfi. His brilliance and his ability to handle ideas effectively are aptly summed up by the author as "probing thoroughness" and they remind us of Mazrui. Apolo-Gyamfi is adroit in debate and in his turn of mind. Like his creator, Ali A Mazrui, Apolo-Gyamfi is shown to have received the best education that Britain could offer. The author says:

> Byron agreed. And, with a brilliantly timed triviality, Apolo-Gyamfi capped the informality with the words, 'I was at that other place, Lord Byron – I read Greats at Christ Church. You are a Cambridge man, Byron, aren't you?" Apolo-Gyamfi in a man who is straight away respectable for his "probing thoroughness" (Mazrui 1971: 120).

As a student, Ali Mazrui lived in Europe and America for twelve years. His stay and study outside East Africa had a considerable emotional and intellectual impact on him since most of his university education took place abroad. In this novel he prepares us very well for the trial. Tin Abiranja's says to Hamisi:

> I told you yesterday that Christopher Okigbo, the poet, had arrived in After-Africa. He was killed in the Nigerian Civil war and is now awaiting trial (Mazrui 1971: 40).

The case against Christopher Okigbo is that he has the commitment to Pan-Africanism and communalism to art and universalism: "He is to be charged with the offence of putting society before art in his scale of values" (Mazrui 1971: 41).

All said, Mazrui was an erudite scholar on African nationalism. His flair for comparative politics was apparent in the liberal switch from Nigerian ill-fated nationalism to Scottish nationalism. The debate even compares the unequal participation in Britain's leadership and intellectual activities by the Scottish elite with the unequal participation in Nigeria's leadership and intellectual activities by the Ibo elite.

Mazrui belonged to a generation of scholars in Africa who witnessed African nationalism at its peak point. He watched, from close proximity, African nationalist leaders erect nation-states from a quagmire of tribal conglomerations. These nationalists saw tribalism and any form of cultural schism as a negation of nationalism. The debate in *The Trial of Christopher Okigbo* reveals the stand taken by Ali Mazrui vis-à-vis the analysis of traditionalism and anti-traditionalism. In this debate, Mazrui stands for "a partial retreat from westernism in our education and way of life and a partial revival of African cultural ways."[21] For him Africa is "The meeting point of three continental cultures – African, Asian and European." His character Apolo–Gyamfi condemns tribal chauvinism of any kind when he gives an account of the break-up of the British Empire, the disintegration in the former colonies like Nigeria, Kenya and the strife between the Ibo and the Nigerians who stood for a federal republic. The character addresses the rifts between the Luo and the Kikuyu in Kenya.

Christopher Okigbo had the marks of a national poet, if not an international poet. This is apparent in what Salisha Bemedi, a defense witness says about him. Mazrui's literary and intellectual endeavours were continental. He saw the spirit of nationalism as a common factor among African countries, especially after independence. Okigbo's commitment to the narrow nationalism of the Ibo cause was a betrayal of Nigerian nationalism. The question which Mazrui puts in his stadium are theoretical and not sufficiently prone to investigation by his characterization.

The author makes a declaration which he does not develop on the psychological or philosophical planes. The declaration remains a question that awaits further exploration. The theme of crisis pervades the novel. But the crisis which is supposed to face Christopher Okigbo" is not felt nor is it articulated by the character himself as a personal experience. He does not go beyond what he said about "The Anguish of the Writer" in 1973. The statement that Mazrui makes in *The Trial of Christopher Okigbo* and in his 1971 Vote of Thanks for Wole Soyinka is not improved on in his fiction.

Perhaps the other question that Ali Mazrui would have asked when he heard that Soyinka had been detained would have been: "What did it matter if one writer was detained?" Mazrui himself tried to ask this question in discussing Okigbo's tragic death in the Nigerian civil war. Should we react differently where a gifted person is victimized? Should humanity be extra-protective of its specially gifted individuals? Should we do a little extra to preserve the great inventor in our midst? The great biologist? The inspired surgeon? The brilliant poet?

In his novel, Mazrui avoids the resolution of the debate on the place of the artist in his society. He leaves it open-ended for further debate:

> The verdict on Counsel for Biafra was *Guilty*; the verdict on Counsel against Biafra was Not *Guilty*; and the verdict on Biafra herself was *Not Proven*.

In the whole novel, however, the author is for the autonomy of art and indeed the autonomy of the artist. The man who defends integration of the artist into his society is weak, and less glamorous. Hamisi and what he stands for in the novel are treated less seriously than Apolo-Gyamfi and what he defends. The reader feels that Mazrui is all the time wagging his tail to please his imperial master. In the portrayal of the two counsels, Hamisi and Apolo-Gyamfi the scale tilts against Hamisi. Although he derives his strength from the community and its past he does not win the case. He ends up as a poor defender of the role of the artist in traditional societies.

Hamisi's past affects the way he is to perform as the Counsel for salvation. He becomes one of the tormented recipients of the evils of the Nigerian holocaust. Although he is a Mombasa-born Moslem, Hamisi commits an atrocity by sleeping with Pomedi, a Moslem Hausa girl from Northern Nigeria. By being brought up in eastern Nigeria, Bemedi has experienced some form of cultural alienation. She is exposed to the religious ideas of an aunt who is not a fervent believer in orthodox Islam. She has been brought up as 'a woman of real consequence," in a non-Muslim world. She is a university graduate from Ibadan. She was among the very first girls to be admitted into Ibadan." She later proceeds to Leeds University in the United Kingdom, to work on Alexander Pope. Her final catastrophe (and the reason why she is in After-Africa) is her rejection by her compatriots: She cannot stay in London much longer because she cannot face a number of friends. She is finally raped to death by an anti-Hausa gang, and loses the baby she had conceived from the Mombasa-born broadcaster at the BBC. No wonder Hamisi Salim and Salisha are "doomed to walk the night" in some nook in West Africa.

The story of Hamisi is told as if to say the evils of the Nigerian Civil war have to dawn on him so that he blames it all on people like Christopher Okigbo who started it. The author later says: "Many in the audience spared a moment of pity for Hamisi, as well as for Salisha and her background. The old-timers in the grand stadium knew, of course, why it was that the woman bore a different name in After-Africa from that which she had borne in the Herebefore. It was the way in which she died. The grand ambiguity between birth and death – a mother dying because a child was struggling to be born. This by itself would have meant a change of name for the mother. The assembly of the Ages had decreed a long time ago that demise by ambiguity negated the previous name. After all, such a capitulation was a blurring of the essence of things – a struggle to give life culminating in exhausted death.

The theme of alienation in *The Trial of Christopher Okigbo* has been described by Okello Oculi as "the psychological disease that affects all Black European" (Oculi 1972:39). We are talking about the pathological alienation described by Frantz Fanon's *Black Skins, White Masks*. 'Black Europeans' are the carriers of European aspirations. This alienation is reflected in the judgement by the Ghanaian lawyer, who, so to speak, is the mouthpiece of the author. This is apparent in the way the author scales favour for Apolo-Gyamfi.

Here we argue with Peter Nazareth: "Having started to ask such vital questions – Mazrui then draws a red herring across our path!" (Nazareth 1971: 153) He raises the important question of commitment, but he suddenly prejudges the issue, saying: "The prosecution is going to suggest that Okigbo had no right to consider himself an Ibo patriot first, and an African artist only second. That was to subordinate the interest of generations of Africans to the needs of a collection of Ibos at an isolated moment in historical time."(Nazareth 1973:153) Like Achebe and Ngugi, Mazrui contrasts the role of the artist in Africa with the role of the artist in Europe. To do this he brings in Lord Byron who also died fighting for a collective cause.

But Ali Mazrui does not solve the questions that he raises. The development of the novel indicates the switch of the words of judgement from one mouth to another. In the issue of commitment the individual is tied to the society. He is a worshipper of what his kith and kin stand for. But Ali Mazrui's novel is decidedly out to disprove this.

Conclusion

Ali Mazrui decided to fictionalize ideas about the artist in Africa. He ended up projecting a Western view of the artist, as opposed to his contemporaries like Wole Soyinka, Chinua Achebe, Ngugi wa Thiong'o and Alex La Guma. *The Trial of Christopher Okigbo* is a novel of ideas demonstrating the dilemma of the artist in Africa. The dialectical poise of the novel does not, however, give us a synthesis. What we have is a paradox, nay a dilemma, which is not solved. The type of intellectual Mazrui wants is different from what the history of Africa has defined for herself. There are many examples of commitment which people express as a collective and even as a government. Making literature available in translation, taking theatre to the people, and writing autobiographies that describe the elements of the way of life in the writer's region. Mazrui not only wrote his novel, but also placed it in the context in which he debated with colleagues and government officials of his day.

Endnotes

1   Peter Nazareth, "The Trial of a Juggler" In *Standpoints On African Literature,* 1973, pp.147-157.

2   *Ibid.,* p.157.

3   Ali A. Mazrui,"The Anguish of the Writer ," Remarks in honour of Wole Soyinka following the latter's plenary address on "The Writer and Society," in Gurr and Calder, (Editors) *Writers in East Africa,* Nairobi, Nairobi, East African Literature Bureau, 1974, p.34.

4   Gurr and Calder (Editors), *Writers in East Africa,* Nairobi, East African Literature Bureau, 1974, p.97.

5   Wole Soyinka in *The Writer in Modern Africa*, Ed. Per Wastberg, Scandinavian Institute, Uppsala, Stockhom, 1968, p21.

6   Ali Mazrui, "Aesthetic Dualism and Creative Literature in East Africa," in *Black Aesthetics*, Papers from a Colloquium held at the University of Nairobi, June 1971, edited by Andrew Gurr and Pio Zirimu, Nairobi, East African Literature Bureau, 1973, pp.32-57, p.34.

7   Ali Mazrui, *Ibid.,* pp.34-35.

8   Ali Mazrui, *The Trial of Christopher Okigbo.* Heinemann Educational Publishers. African Writers Series.All page references in this chapter are from this edition, 1971.

9   See his definition above.

10   Peter Nazareth, "The Trial of a *Juggler*," in Chris L Wanjala (Ed.)*Standpoints On African Literature,* Nairobi, East African Literature Bureau, 1973, pp.152-53.

11   From personal communication, 1986.

12   Ngugi wa Thiong'o, *Homecoming*, London, Heinemann Education Books, 1972, p.6.

13   *Ibid.* 1986

14   Mphahlele, Es'kia, *The African Image.* London, Faber and Faber, 1974, pp.60-61; 281-285.

15   In *Mawazo III,* No 3, 1992, pp.46-48.

16   Peter Nazareth, "The Trial of a Juggler," in *Standpoints On African Literature,* Nairobi, East African Literature, 1973, pp.147-157.

17   *Ghala IX*, No. 1, 1972, pp. 39-40;

18   *Presence Africaine,* No. 81, 1972, pp.183-184.

19   For more discussion of Peter Nazareth's approach. see reviews of his critical work, *Literature and Society in Modern Africa* ,by Angus Calder in *Afras 1,*1973, No. 81, pp.183-184 and G. A. Heron, Joiliso No. 1,1973, pp.67-73.

20 From personal communication, 1986.

21 French, Howard, January-February 1987." Mazrui's Continent" In *Africa Report*, pp.17-18.

References

Brecht, B. (2014). Bloomsbury Methuen Drama. An imprint of Bloomsbury London New Publishing Plc. Delhi New York Sydney.

Kermode, F. (2001). "Palaces of memory," in *Index for Free Expression, passim.*

La Guma, A. (1967). "From the Discussion," in *The Writer in Modern Africa,* Uppsala, The Scandinavian Institute of African Studies, 1968, p. 22.

La Guma, A. Report of the Acting Secretary-General, *Lotus,* Nos. 42/43/41, 79- 1/80/pp.72- 80, p. 75.

Mazrui, Ali A. (2012). "The Fiction, the Facts, the Poetry of Things Fall Apart," Library of Congress, Washington D C.

Family Obituary of Ali Mazrui, *www./Alimazrui.com_*

Joliso: East Africa Journal of Literature and Society. Editor, Chris L Wanjala, Vol. 1, (1, Nairobi: East African Literature Bureau.

Nazareth, P. (1972). The Trial of a Juggler, "a Review of The Trial of Christopher Okigbo by Ali Mazrui" in *Dhana, 1(2), Nairobi: EALB. This review was republished in Chris L. Wanjala, Standpoints On African Literature.* Nairobi, Kampala, Dar es Salaam: East African Literature Bureau, pp. 147-157.

Nazareth P. "Is A Grain of Wheat a Socialist Novel?" in Literature and Society in Modern Africa. Nairobi: *EALB.*

Ngugi, J. (1971). "The African Writer and His Past," in *Perspectives On African Literature,* Edited by Christopher Heywood. London: *HEB.*

Thiong'o, Ngugi wa. (1972). *Homecoming,* Essays on African and Caribbean Literature, Culture and Politics. London: Heinemann Educational Publishers.

_____. (1972). *Homecoming,* New Statesman, Vol. 84 (20th October), p. 562.

_____. (1972). *Homecoming, The Times Literary Supplement,* 3rd November, p.1344

_____. (1981). *Writers in Politics, Essays.* London: HEB.

_____. (1974). *Homecoming,* in *Choice,* Vol. 10, January, p. 1727.

_____. (1973). *Homecoming* in Book List, Vol. 70, 15th October, p.192.

_____. (1973). *Homecoming,* Library Journal, Vol. 98, 1st September, p. 2444.

Okigbo, C. (1971). *Labyrinths With Paths of Thunder.* Phillips, Adam.

Peter, C.B. (1994). *Dialogue between Christianity and African Traditional Religion (With Special Reference to Chinua Achebe's novels)* in *Saudia Missionalia,* Vol. 43.

The Africans: A Triple Heritage, The Institute of Global Cultural Studies website, *http://www2.binghamton.edu/igcs.*

Mazrui, Ali A. (1971). The Trial of Christopher Okigbo. London: Heinemann Educational Publishers.

www./AliMazrui.com

https://www.voutube.com/watch?V=SDQ434vsAZk

Wanjala, C. "Why the Attack On Mazrui Pains Me," *Daily Nation.*

Rethinking the Idea of *Afrabia* in Ali Mazrui's Political and Social Thought

Hamdy A. Hassan

Introduction

The issue of identity and language is key to the crisis of the modern state in post-independence Africa. Similar to other Afro-Arab borderland countries, such as Mali, Niger and Mauritania, the Sudan has experienced a sharp divide in identity. In some of these countries, the ruling elites tried to embrace Arabization and Islamization policies to attain national integration. It was not out of the ordinary for Sudan – amidst the escalation of the crisis of the South – to forge links with the Arab Nationalist Movement in the 1960s. This was manifested in its hosting of the Arab summit in the capital, Khartoum, in the wake of the Arab defeat in 1967. Within this intellectual and political context, Ali Mazrui presents his view for salvation and cultural development in the countries of the South.

In 1968, at the invitation of the University of Khartoum, he delivered a lecture on: "The Multiple Marginality of the Sudan". Mazrui (1985, p.240) was preoccupied with the question of identity; he viewed Arabs as Afro-Asians. Hence, he painted two contradictory images of the Sudan, as being the Afro-Arab Frontier. The first image reflects the multi-cultural reality that encompasses Arabism, Africanism and Islam. Mazrui may have developed this vision later, as part of the concept of the Triple Heritage (Hassan, 2014). The second image mirrors the identity crisis and inability to co-exist. He quoted one of the participants in the South Sudan Roundtable conference, when he emphasised that the Sudan had failed to form a united society. Mazrui labelled the Sudan's case as "Dichotomous Duality", and viewed it as a paradigm of the divided Arab-Islamic identity. Some years later he was able to produce a full-fledged vision of Afro-Arab relations from a cultural and historical perspective transcending all obstacles that evoked disunity and divide. He called this vision *Afrabia*.

This chapter seeks to reconsider this concept in the light of the new scramble for both the Arab and African worlds – which is reminiscent of the atmosphere of the Cold War. It is an attempt to capitalise on the legacy of Mazrui's political and social thought regarding the formation of a unified Afro-Arab front to face the challenges of the new world order.

Afrabia: Beginning and development

It is clear that Ali Mazrui made his biggest mark in the Arab cultural scene in 1976, the year in which the first symposium on Afro-Arab relations was held in Sharjah in the UAE (Sharawi 2014). The Sharjah ruler named the room, where Arab and African intellectuals came together, "Africa" – which has since then been a witness to the cultural heritage shared by both sides. Mazrui was engrossed in his intellectual project which was essentially based on African cultural and social dimensions. The project also reflected the complexities of the reality that exceeded the contrariety between the coloniser and the colonised, the local and the foreign, the civilian and the military, or the ruler and the ruled. Therefore, Mazrui believed that the future of Africa's political and social crisis was linked to its historical and intellectual context, in addition to the subsequent developments in the political and social thinking (Mazrui 2014). These intellectual convictions held by Ali Mazrui saw him clashing with the ideology of development that swept post-independence Africa.

At this point, we can recall his political diatribe against *Nkrumah and Nyerere,* and his opposition to the authoritarian form of government represented by the reign of Idi Amin in Uganda (Mazrui 1966: 9-17). That was not everything, as Mazrui also engaged in cultural battles with symbols of the leftist culture in Africa, such as Walter Rodney and Archie Mafeje (Campbell 2014). It seems that the television series presented by Mazrui in the early 1980s entitled: "The Africans: A Triple Heritage", was a vision of an alternative perspective to rewrite some aspects of African history. However, the Nigerian author, Wole Soyinka, who won Nobel Prize in literature in 1986, clashed on the Internet with Mazrui.[1] Soyinka argued that Mazrui's ideas had undermined the major contributions of African traditional religions and cultures for the sake of highlighting the role of the Islamic factor. Soyinka (2000: 12) has mockingly pointed out that Mazrui is not only culturally Arabised, but above all, is an Arab by both blood and passion. This debate reveals some negative views about the role of Islam in Africa, as can be found in the colonial literature: like saying that Islam is irrationally imposed on Africans by force (Lang 1991). Perhaps, most notably, that Soyinka discredited a senior researcher in African history because he is a Muslim (Adem 2014: 143).

Within this context, as reflected by the atmosphere of the Cold War and the emergence of Africa's economic crisis in the late 1970s, Mazrui has tried to adopt an authentic paradigm in order to deal decisively with the issues of identity and belonging in the construction phase of the national state. He opted to construct an analytical framework for the relations of power and culture, as part of Africa's Triple Heritage.

Consequently, the Sharjah conference – according to Helmi Sharawy (2014) – marked the real beginning of the Afro-Arab cultural dialogue. All the extremely sensitive issues were put on the table of discussion. These included slavery, petrodollar, Africa's affiliation to Francophonie, and its hesitation to support the Palestinian cause.

Mazrui presented a multi-sided cultural project, which he called *Afrabia*, through which all dimensions of the conflict, such as slavery and the Zanzibar Revolution, could be surmounted and a state of integration, reflecting Afro-Arab cultural interaction, could be created ((Mazrui and Wondji 1998: 243-244). Both Islam and Arabism are the most prevalent in Africa; moreover, the history of Africa's relation with Arabism and Islam has not seen any real confrontation, unlike its relation with the European West.

Mazrui argues that both Arabs and Africans had lived together on one continent before the geological split of Africa from the Arabian Peninsula as a result of the formation of the Red Sea. The separation between the two entities was completed in the 19th Century with the digging of the Suez Canal. However, the extent of interaction between the Arab and African peoples, throughout this long geological and historical epoch, overshadowed the physical split caused by the Red Sea. This suggests that the experience of interaction and co-existence for long historical periods and eras gave rise to *Afrabia* and Afro-Arab societies.

It is no secret that this phenomenon is not a novelty, given that the Europeans had tried to establish links with both the Asian and African worlds, despite the recentness of Europe's contact with them. In this regard, let us remember terminologies such as Eurasia and Euro-Africa. It seems that the *Afrabia* phenomenon is deeply rooted in the common history of the Arab and African peoples; it also has a real basis in the contemporary reality.

Mazrui identifies four types of Afro-Arab groups, based on four determining factors, as follows (Mazrui 2005: 66-67):

- *The cultural factor*: This encompasses the groups and peoples the cultures of which are a blend of African traditions and Arab-Islamic heritage. The most outstanding example of this is perhaps the Muslim Africa and Hausa and Swahili-speaking peoples.

- *The factor of descent and relationship by marriage*: This encompasses the groups with Arab and African lineage. The best example of this is perhaps the family of Mazrui himself.

- *The ideological factor*: This encompasses all the groups and individuals who believe in the need for Arabs and Africans to be united, regardless of the fact that they share cultural and religious heritage. President Kwame Nkrumah is considered to be the most prominent example of this type of groups.

- *The geographical factor*: This includes North Africa and other countries that are members in both the African Union and the Arab League such as Somalia and Comoro Islands.

While *Afrabia* is the outcome of geography and geology, the Afro-Arab societies are the product of history and mutual relationships and interactions. The materialisation of this cohesion between the peoples in the two Arab and African entities was contributed to by three key channels of communication.

The first was the Eastern Africa region, including the Great Horn of Africa, though relations between Arabs and Africans in this region expanded to include the entire region of the Indian Ocean. Arabs had traded in, and migrated to, the region of East African Coast since the pre-Christian era.

The second channel of communication was the Nile Basin, which represents the artery of life to many Arab and African societies, as evidenced by the fact that it led to the creation of an Afro-Arab country: The Sudan. The third channel of communication was the Sahel Sahara and West Africa region. The history of commercial relations between the Arabs and Berbers in the north of Sahara and the Africans in its south is long and well-documented (Mazrui 2002: 89-90).

Despite all this, *Afrabia* encountered serious challenges during the colonial era. Western countries persistently tried to tear apart the bonds of convergence and cohesion between the two Arab and African entities in all possible ways. These countries sought to eliminate the relations and heritage shared by both sides and re-direct Arab and African economies to be linked with them. Also, the West continuously attempted to sow the seeds of hostility and conflict between the region's peoples. This was quite evident in countries such as the Sudan, Mauritania, and Tanzania. These attempts were promoted on religious, ethnic and cultural grounds and pretexts.

Afrabia as a unifying cultural framework

Seeking to prove the importance of the role of intellectuals in the Pan-Africanism movement, Mazrui borrowed the idea of intellectual determinism from the legacy of Leninist socialism. In the same context, it can be said that *Afrabia* without intellectuals is a mere dead duck. Therefore, the task of re-Africanising the Arabian Peninsula should be undertaken by Arab and African intellectuals, before it can win the hearts and minds of people. Mazrui (2002: 85) argues:

> The tyranny of the sea is in part a tyranny of European geographical prejudices. Just as European map makers could decree that on the map Europe was above Africa instead of below ..., those mapmakers could also dictate that Africa ended at the Red Sea instead of at the Persian Gulf. Is it not time that this dual tyranny of the sea and Eurocentric geography was forced to sink to the bottom?

Mazrui presents the concept of *Afrabia* as a comprehensive analytical framework that underlines the deep cultural ties shared by the Arabs and Africans. This concept includes a conciliatory side that transcends the moments of hostility and factors of disunity, such as the memories of the Zanzibar Revolution and Arabs' involvement in the slave trade. For this reason, Mazrui refers to two models of reconciliation in contemporary history: the first is the Anglo-American model; the second, the American-Japanese model.

This intellectual and cultural proposal is important in the light of the African debate that is prevailing as a result of Afro-Arab tensions. Most of the intellectual works on the part of Africans still looks at the advent of Islam as an Arab or *Maghreb* invasion aimed at imposing Islamization and Arabization on the African peoples. Anthropologist Kwesi Prah goes as far as to say that Arabic is not one of the local African languages. Prah (2008) argues that the problem with the "African and Arab cultural divide is that historically it has been marked amongst many other things by domination, slavery and oppression of Africans by Arabs. Till today in the Afro-Arab borderlands Arabs enslave Africans. We must not pretend that this is not the case." He takes the strong view of a social and cultural divide.

The situation was not different in relation to the mutual negative images that prevailed because of the nation-state policies after independence. Many African writers such as Garba Diallo (1993: 32) argue for the importance of studying the cultural split and racial prejudices in the Afro-Arab borderland regions along the western coast of the African desert. There is a feeling of racial superiority from the White societies of Arabs and Moors towards the black societies of Fulani, Wolof and Tokolor along the Mauritania borders.

Also, the use of racial epithets and negative mental images about the other between the informal groups in Mali, such as the Tuaregs, Moors, Arabs, Songhai and Fulani, in fact, reflect the atmosphere of doubt, lack of confidence, and feeling of insecurity which obstruct development and renaissance in these societies. Diallo (1993: 26) argues:

> The history of Afro-Arab relations in the Sudan and Mauritania have mainly been characterised by brutal wars, slavery, forced Islamization and Arabization, the systematic destruction of indigenous cultures, values and civilisations coupled with insatiable territorial expansion on the part of the immigrants. As in the cases of South Africa and Zimbabwe, colonial powers left power firmly in the hands of the settlers in both Mauritania and The Sudan.

Mazrui refuses this artificial cultural divide between the Arabs and Africans, with the aim of forming a united front against what he called "Global Apartheid". The new world order has resulted in two clear strands: the first is the rise in the number of Arab and Muslim victims in the key flashpoints such as Palestine, Iraq, Syria, Libya, Afghanistan and Yemen. The second is the economic suffering of the black Africans as a result of the continued Western support for corrupt regimes in Africa, in addition to the unfair division of labour at the international level. Only then does *Afrabia* emerge as a part of the solution, to square up to the challenges of this inequitable world order.

The Afro-Arab cultural interaction involves mutual positive sides. The sacred texts written in Arabic (*Sorabe*) serve as evidence of the Arab influence on the ethnicities in south-eastern Madagascar, particularly the Antaimoro (Versteegh 2001: 177-187). According to this written traditional heritage, a group of Muslims migrated from Mecca in the Arabian Peninsula to the Comoros and from there they moved to Madagascar, where they settled on the banks of the Matitanania River. This sacred book is still held in high esteem and is used as a source of blessing by the people, despite the fact that its Islamic content is not clear. Members of the Antaimoro ethnic group still keep some links to Arabic in their chit-chats, through what is called *Kalamon anteditesy*, namely the language of the people of the sand – which are Arabic words as part of Malagasy lexicon.

Strikingly, this civilizational interaction, which has never reflected cultural hegemony, as some try to depict it, is also manifest in the traditional heritage of West Africa. The epic of the Mande people in West Africa, known as Sunjata, reflects a clear Arab-Islamic heritage (Wolny 2014: 14). The rise of Sundiata to power unveils the early history of the king of Mandingo. The epic also narrates the adventures of building the old kingdom of Mali and the story of the king going to and returning from the holy pilgrimage (Haj) journey. It is this cultural interaction, reflected by the mutual migration of people between the Arabian Peninsula and Africa (referred to by Mazrui in the concept of *Afrabia*) that is unveiled by the epic of Sunjata. According to the narrator, one of the sons of Bilal ibn Rabah, the *Muezzin* of the Prophet, moved from Mecca to West Africa.

On the part of the Arabs, in relation to African traditional epics, we find that that of Antarah, which corresponds to the epic of Homer in Western culture, bears a conciliatory meaning and expresses co-existence between the Arabs and Africans. The epic of Antarah ibn Shaddad in Arabic literature is about mixed race. His mother was an Ethiopian slave called Zabiba while his father was an Arab ethnic chief. Antara is considered one of the greatest Arabic poets in the pre-Islamic period (Heath 1996). Antara's poems reveal the spirit of tolerance and reconciliation in the old Arab heritage:

Enemies revile me for the blackness of my skin,
but the whiteness of my character effaces the blackness.

I endeavoured to be fair to my opponent,
However, he wronged me,
Resorting to mean, devious means.
Finally, my sword dealt him a fair blow.
Should others taunt me
On account of the blackness of my skin,
Let them keep in mind.

On the opposite side of the spirit of tolerance expressed by the epic of Antarah, we can find other cases of conflict and hegemony between the Arabs and Africans. The image of the black slave abounds in Arabic literature. The Arab clashes against Abyssinians in Yemen and *Najran* were one of the triggers for the first wave of African slaves in the Arabian Peninsula.

Challenges to *Afrabia* in a changing world

Any observer of how Afro-Arab relations have progressed over the past 50 years or so would notice that they always involve the problem of missed opportunities. This may be the result of the political side prevailing over the economic one in the strategic dialogue between the Arab and African worlds, or because of the continued international dogfight for resources and influence in the Afro-Arab environment (Landsberg 2009 and Auda 2012: 574).

The key themes of the strategic dialogue between the Arabs and Africans included the issues of colonisation, challenges to nation-state building, and the evoking of the spirit of non-alignment and Bandung. Other main themes were the Nile water economies and the problems of conflict and sustainable development in the light of the globalisation policies and the reproduction of the strategic hegemony policies at the international level. Therefore, the mistakes of the 1970s were a stumbling block to implementing the joint Afro-Arab action mechanisms adopted by the first Afro-Arab summit in Cairo in 1977. On the other hand, the personality of the late Libyan colonel Gaddafi and his desire to lead and control had turned the second Afro-Arab summit in Sirte in 2010 into a mere media platform that went no further than its symbolic and political connotation.

So, can it be said that the third Afro-Arab summit held in Kuwait in November 2013 represents a watershed in the common Afro-Arab consciousness? Ironically, and surprisingly, this summit was about 33 years overdue, for the second Afro-Arab summit was scheduled to be held in Kuwait in 1980, namely three years after the first Cairo summit.

On the other hand, Egypt – which sheltered the Pan-African movement and played a pivotal role in the adoption of the system of Arab-African cooperation by hosting the first Afro-Arab summit in Cairo – found itself attending the Kuwait summit as an Arab League member state after its membership of the African Union was suspended in the wake of the overthrow of the regime of President Muhammad Morsi in July 2013.

In any case, the special and important nature of the third Afro-Arab summit in Kuwait lies in a number of essential aspects, of which the key ones perhaps are the following:

> One, overwhelming changes have taken place in the Arab regional order in 2011 after the Arab Spring revolutions which set off in Egypt, Tunisia, Libya, Syria and Yemen, as well as other Arab countries. The greatest indication of this is perhaps the extent of the cohesion between the Arab and African countries in yearning for political, economic and social liberation. I believe that the African Spring, which started in the late 1980s, had preceded the Arab Spring – which suggests that the latter has possibly been inspired by some key African experiences and stories of success, such as Ghana, Botswana, Nigeria, South Africa, and Kenya.

Two, the big conflicts that pose a challenge to the Afro-Arab security system, such as Somalia, Darfur, and Northern Mali, highlight the importance of coordination and pursuit of Afro-Arab solutions to them without foreign parties' interference. I believe these tough security challenges necessitate a search for a joint Afro-Arab security system to intervene in the areas of tension and conflict with the purpose of keeping and making peace.

Three, the change in the nature of the balance of power in the Afro-Arab borderland regions, such as the two regions of the Horn of Africa and the Nile Basin, means that it is necessary that the Arab-African dialogue is based on new grounds and criteria. For example, the new geo-strategic formula of the Arab-African environment has seen a decline in the two roles of Egypt (after the fall of the Mubarak regime) and the Sudan (after the separation of the south); and Somalia has been ripped apart after the imposition of the international will on it in 2012. Meanwhile, Ethiopia and the East African countries have seen a noticeable development and have received clear international support, which means that it is necessary that the distribution of the Nile water is re-negotiated.

Four, Israel is trying to infiltrate the collective African security system through its endeavours to join the African Union as an observer state. Although Israel's attempts have fallen through, it is trying hard – through African mediators, mainly Nigeria, Ethiopia, and Kenya – to win a membership of the African Union in its next session (Oded 2010 and Fakude 2016: 4-5). It is clear, as shown by the incident of the attack in September 2013 on the Westgate shopping mall in Nairobi, that Israel holds sway in the Nile Basin countries.

Five, there is a new international dogfight for Africa's resources, and new policies have emerged to reproduce the international hegemony over Africa through new mechanisms and tools. The creation of the Africa Command (AFRICOM) in 2008 and the presence of American camps in Djibouti and Niger, as well as the direct French and Western military intervention in African conflicts, constitute a direct threat to the collective Arab and African security. Additionally, attempts by China, and some other rising powers in the world order, to gain influence and control in Africa, too, pose challenges to the Afro-Arab regional system.

If we take into account the nature of the economic, security and political challenges encountered by the Arab and African peoples, we would find that responding to the spirit of the African renaissance project, whose foundations were laid down by former South African President Thabo Mbeki, and the ambitions of the new initiative for development in Africa (NEPAD) in 2001, means that it is necessary to go for the choice of Afro-Arab cooperation based on the perspective of partnership and common interests.

What went wrong?

In the 1970s, it was hoped that *Afrabia* would take an institutional form, that is to move from the intellectual and ideological framework to a tangible reality through the 1977 Cairo conference. At the time, some talked of "the food basket strategy" whereby the African countries, rich in natural resources, would assist in achieving Arab food security, while the oil-rich Arab countries would help provide financial and developmental support necessary for the renaissance of Africa.

The enthusiastic tendency to support Afro-Arab cooperation at that foundational stage can be understood in the light of a number of considerations, mainly including: the mutual emphasis on the importance of collective self-reliance to face the development challenges in the Arab and African worlds, and Israel's occupation in 1967 of African territory which led many African countries to cut off their relations with it in the wake of the 1973 war.

President Sékou Touré says (Sylvester 1981: 199):

> Our support for the Arab causes springs from Afro-Arab solidarity which has always been a matter of principle to Guinea. This support does not depend on any financial rewards being paid to us by the Arabs. We have stood by the Arabs because we thought they were right, not because we expected any financial gain. Guinea broke off relations with Israel in 1967, the day when the Zionist state launched its aggression against the Arabs.

However, the most important variable in the relations with Africa during the 1970s was the Arab financial support, as manifested in the establishment of some funding and developmental institutions, such as the Arab Bank for Economic Development in Africa in 1974, and the Arab funds for financial and technical assistance delivered to African countries.

The first Afro-Arab summit in Cairo issued four important documents:

- A political declaration which emphasised the importance of cooperation being based on the charters of both the Arab League and the Organisation of African Unity (OAU), which meant supporting the struggle of the Palestinian people and facing South Africa's regime of racial segregation.

- A programme of action for Afro-Arab cooperation, particularly at the level of various sectors.

- Organisation and method for achieving Afro-Arab cooperation, as it was agreed to establish a joint ministerial council that would hold its sessions periodically every 18 months, while the council of heads of states would hold its meetings every three years. Additionally, the Permanent Commission for Afro-Arab Cooperation was formed, of 24 members: 12 from Africa and 12 from the Arab world. This commission was due to convene every 6 months to follow up the implementation of the resolutions on Arab-African cooperation.

- A resolution on financial and economic cooperation which, in effect, served as a declaration of intent on the part of the Arabs to provide financial and economic support to the African countries.

However, all these efforts failed and all Arabs and Africans missed a historic opportunity for a genuine strategic partnership. This can be attributed to prioritising political considerations, predominance of the concept of blackmailing, and inequality in the negotiations between the two parties. For example, the Arab aid to Africa was conditional, directly or indirectly, upon the stances of the African countries in support of the Arab causes, mainly the Palestinian issue. Additionally, the signing in 1979 of the Camp David agreement by Egypt and the suspension of its membership of the Arab League led to the absence of its central role in support of the course of Afro-Arab relations. From a third angle, the issue of Western Sahara between Morocco and Algeria, as well as Libya's military adventures in Chad, represented another stumbling block to supporting and implementing the programme of action for Afro-Arab cooperation adopted by the first Afro-Arab summit.

It is evident that the early 2000s and the major transformations witnessed by the OAU and its successor the African Union in 2002 had all prompted a restoration, once again, of Afro-Arab cooperation. This summit issued two important documents: The first was entitled "The strategy of Afro-Arab partnership", and it covered four fields: peace and security, investment incentives and trade exchange, food and agricultural security, and cultural and social cooperation. The dimensions of this strategy were explained in the second document, which was adopted by the conference under the title "Plan of Joint Afro-Arab- Action 2011-2016", and contained specific measures to boost mutual cooperation.

Based on the vision of *Afrabia*, the financial institutions connected with the joint Afro-Arab action reflect a wrong model that should be amended. The dominant perception is that the Arab side provides funding and aid to Africa. What is needed according to Mazrui (2002: 93) is to change the pattern "of Arabs always as donors and Africans always as recipients of foreign help". Afrabian institutions would collect funds from both relatively rich Arabs and Africans to alleviate poverty in its region.

Afro-Arab and crossing into the future

A wise reading of the challenges to Afro-Arab relations would suggest it is important to mull three essential aspects on the basis of which it is possible to establish a genuine Afro-Arab partnership and transition into the future, so that the 21st century can become an Afro-Arab century par excellence.

The first aspect is political bargaining, as the relation between the Arabs and Africans, in its most periods, has been built on the premise that, in return for Arab financial support, the Africans are expected to support the Arab causes in international forums. Doubtless, this political price does not reflect a real will from both sides to set up a strategic partnership based on equivalence and equality. The second aspect is the absence of balance, or more precisely, equality in the system of Afro-Arab relations. This may have led the Arab countries to adopt a dual approach in their relations with Africa, to ensure the achievement of their national interests away from the institutional framework of cooperation which resulted from the first Afro-Arab summit.

The third aspect is international parties' interference to obstruct the course of Arab-African cooperation. In addition to the traditional colonial powers, such as Britain and France, the US has come, after September 11, carrying the slogan of war on terror in Africa, which in essence means the blowing up of turbulent areas and flashpoints in the Arab and African worlds. Also, rising powers like China and traditional regional powers, such as Turkey, Israel and Iran, are trying through their Africa policies and their soft power tools to gain influence within the strategic Arab sphere in Africa, which represents a significant challenge to the implementation of the plan for Afro-Arab cooperation. In this context, we can point to the danger of the role of China and its provision of the necessary support and funding in the Nile Basin region in a way that conflicts with Egypt's water interests. Additionally, the presence of a state like Iran may mean the tearing apart of the Islamic bloc in Africa, by stirring up religious, sectarian sentiment. It is noticeable that the dimension of Islam has always represented one of the incentives for Afro-Arab cooperation (Hassan 2011: 60). However, the element of Islam has today become a cause for divide and infighting, which is manifested in the experience of Boko Haram in Nigeria, Al-Shabaab in Somalia, and Salafist Jihadism in northern Mali.

Conclusion: What can be done then?

I believe the reassessment of the concept of *Afrabia* as a unifying collective framework leading the renaissance of Arabs and Africa is tied to the adoption of three essential approaches. The first is the cultural approach, with the aim of overcoming the historical sensitivities that are embodied by the negative mental images and stereotypes prevailing between the Arabs and Africans. The problem of identity which stood as a barrier to an inequitable partnership between the two sides must be surmounted; regions such as Darfur, northern Mali, and Mauritania reflect a dichotomy in identity between the Arabs and Africans which was entrenched by the colonial legacies and wrong national policies. We need to adopt a new perspective that focuses on the importance of benefiting from the joint experience of the Arab and African peoples on an equal footing. The Afro-Arab culture, reflected by the Afro-Arab migrations and relationships of blood and marriage, represents a key approach to the removal of the effects of the past and proceeding towards the future.

The first Afro-Arab summit held in Cairo in 1977 realised the importance of this goal, so it decided to work towards entrenching cultural relations between the Arabs and Africans. This led to the adoption of the statutes of the creation of The Afro-Arab Cultural Institute in 1985, which was officially opened in 2002 in Bamako, Mali. However, this important cultural institution reflected the image of the general Arab weakness, by producing only a single work on "Arabic Letters in African Writings and Scripts (Ajami)", which was edited by Helmi Sharawy (2005).

It seems that those in charge of the institute saw in the character of Ibn Battuta a symbol of the depth and richness of the afro-Arab culture, so they were preoccupied with making a statue of the Arab traveller so that it could be placed in a public square in Bamako.

The concentration on the sources of the Ajami culture in the African heritage is considered one of the strategic approaches that can be built on. What is meant by this is the use of the Arabic alphabet in the writing of African languages. Any observer of the important African languages, such as Hausa, Wolof, *Soninke*, Jola, in West Africa and Swahili in East Africa would find that they have key historical sources written in Arabic script.

Mazrui wised up to the need to stick to the Arabic language as a unifying cultural factor, explaining that it is the language of Africa and that the writing of the Ajami letters exists in several African languages. This may concur with John Hunwick's statement that the Arabic language represents the Latin of Africa, in the sense that if the Latin alphabet was the common basis of the European languages of English, French and German, the Arabic alphabet was as well qualified to be the common basis of the African languages of Hausa, Fulani, Swahili, and Somali (Hunwick 2005: i). In his collective cultural vision, Mazrui concluded that the Arabs and Africans are one thing. He relied on the origins of Prophet Ibrahim which trace the Arabs back to their grandfather Ismail, and they are thus the children of Hajar, the Afro-Egyptian slave, while the Jews are the children of Sarah. That is why the Jews later headed towards the West and blended in, but the Arabs, the children of Hajar, mingled with their old African mother, driven by nostalgia for Africa.

The second approach is economic and developmental and it focuses on the perspective of common interests, and involves the establishment of a real partnership within the framework of the development of the countries of the South and collective self-reliance. The project to link Yemen to Djibouti through the creation of a bridge linking the two sides of the Bab el-*Mandeb Strait* perhaps represents a key step towards the restoration of the physical unity between the Arabian Peninsula and the eastern coast of Africa. It is useful to note the importance of this developmental perspective in overcoming many of the crises that obstruct Arab-African relations, such as Somalia, the Sudan, and the issue of the Nile Water.

Ali Mazrui (1975: 725-742) discussed the economic and historical links between the Arabs and Africa. The aid provided by Arab countries for liberation movements in Rhodesia and South Africa, as well as the diplomatic support for African countries, was aimed at influencing the African decision in relation to the Arab-Israeli conflict. Mazrui believes that the Arab aid, from the perspective of *Afrabia*, should come, as we mentioned, from wealthy Arabs and wealthy Africans to contribute to the renaissance of the Arab and African worlds. Therefore, such assistance differs from the "Dead Aid" which Dambisa Moyo (2009) talked about.

The third approach is related to the security issue. There are common threats from armed conflicts, cross-border smuggling operations, and religious extremism which necessitates security cooperation between the Arabs and Africans to tackle these serious challenges. Africa's success in formulating a new security perspective since 2002 perhaps represents a significant step to be benefited from in the reformation of the Arab region's collective security system.

The issues of rule and the failure to build a state which led to the Arab Spring in North Africa underlines once again the importance of the

Afrabia idea. Ali Mazrui sees that the right understanding of the events in Egypt, Tunisia, and Libya is to view them in the context of Afrabian uprisings. The Soweto events in 1976 and the uprisings of the Sudanese against the military rule in 1964 and 1985 represent significant African precedents for popular movements calling for democracy in the Arab world. Therefore, the reformulation of the concepts of security and rule from the *Afrabia* perspective constitutes a big starting point for overcoming the fragile situation and the dilemma of security in the Arab and African worlds.

The success in establishing a new strategic partnership between the Arabs and Africans is dependent on how far the two sides are successful in not politicising their mutual relations and in launching a new strategic dialogue that would discuss all issues of common interest on an equal footing. All this perhaps makes it imperative upon us to necessarily adopt the slogan of "heading southwards" towards Africa to set off together towards new horizons of renaissance and progress. So, are we going to learn from the mistakes of the past and tackle the present and future challenges to achieve the dream of *Afrabia*?

Endnotes

[1] Wole Soyinka's negative critique of Islam in Africa could be considered as part of the intellectual trend which might be called "Black Orientalism". It is a new Black paradigm which combines cultural condescension with paternalistic possessiveness and ulterior selectivity similar to that shown by Western scholars towards non-Western societies in Africa, Asia and the Middle East. The central issue here is Islam and the black African identity. Some Africans and black scholars reaffirmed that embracing Islam by Africans and Afro Americans is a form of cultural apostasy. This radical intellectual trend claims that all alien ideologies, such as Islam, have brought destruction and violence to Africa.

References

Adem, S. (2014). Ali A. Mazrui, the Postcolonial Theorist. *African Studies Review*, 57 (1), pp. 135-152.

Auda, A. (2012). An Evolution of the Afro-Arab Cooperation. In: Haseeb, K. *The Arabs & Africa*. London and New York: Routledge.

Campbell, H. (2014). *The Humanism of Ali Mazrui, Counter Punch*. Available at: http://www.counterpunch.org/2014/10/17/the-humanism-of-ali-mazrui/. Accessed on 16 August 2016.

Diallo, G. (1993). *Mauritania, the Other Apartheid?* Uppsala, Sweden: Nordiska Afrikainstitutet.

Fakude, T. (2016). Forty Years after Entebbe: A New Era of Israeli Relations with Uganda and Kenya, Doha: Al Jazeera Center for Studies. Available at: *http://webcache.googleusercontent.com/ search?q=cache:3QxxdNo3bJIJ:studies.aljazeera.net/mritems/ Documents/2016/5/31/6f2855174f3445fc8423cc735179760b_100. pdf+&cd=1&hl=ar&ct=clnk&gl=ae.* Accessed on 25 August, 2016.

Hassan, H. (2014). Ali Mazrui: The Pioneer of Afrabia, Al-Ahram, October 21, 2014.Available at: *http://www.ahram.org.eg/NewsPrint/332356.aspx. Accessed 22 March 2016.* Accessed on 20 May 2016.

Hassan, H. (2001). *Regional Integration in Africa Bridging the North-Sub-Saharan Divide.* Oxford: Africa Institute of South Africa.

Heath, P. (1996). *The Thirsty Sword: Sīrat 'Antar and the Arabic Popular Epic.* Salt Lake City: University of Utah Press.

Hunwick, J. (2005). *Arabic Literature of Africa: Project and Publication.* Northwestern University, Program of African Studies. Working Paper Series. Institute for the Study of Islamic Thought in Africa.

Landsberg, C. (2009). *New Afrabia: South Africa's New Agendas Towards Africa,* Arab World and The Middle East. Abu Dhabi: The Emirates Center for Strategic Studies and Research.

Lang, G. (1991). Through a Prism Darkly: 'Orientalism' in European-Language African Writing. In: Harrow, K. ed., *Faces of Islam in African Literature,* Portsmouth, NH: Heinemann, pp. 299-311.

Mazrui A. (1966). *Nkrumah: The Leninist Czar. Transition:* A Journal of the Arts, Culture and Society, 6(26), pp. 9-17.

Mazrui, A. (1985). The Multiple Marginality of the Sudan. In: Yusuf Fadl Hasan, (ed), Sudan in Africa, Studies Presented to the First International Conference Sponsored by the Sudan Research Unit, 7-12 February, 1968. Khartoum: Khartoum University Press.

Mazrui, A. (1992). AFRABIA: Africa and the Arabs in the New World Order. *Ufahamu:* Journal of the African Activist Association, 20(3), pp. 51-62.

Mazrui, A. and Wondji, C. (1998). *General History of Africa.* Vol. 8. Africa since 1935. Paris: UNESCO.

Mazrui, A. (2000). Black Orientalism: Further Reflections on 'Wonders of the African World', *West Africa Review,* 1(2), pp. 15-18.

Mazrui, A. (2002). *Africanity Redefined:* Vol. 1. Trenton: Africa World press.

Mazrui, A. (2005). Pan Africanism and the Intellectuals: Rise, Decline and Revival. In: Mkandawire, T. Ed., *African Intellectuals: Rethinking Politics, Language, Gender and Development*. Dakar: CODESRIA Books, pp. 66-67.

Mazrui, A. (2009). Black Africa and the Arabs. *Foreign Affairs*, 53(4), pp. 725-742.

Mazrui, A. (2014). African Thought in Comparative Perspective. Newcastle Upon Tyne: Cambridge Scholars Publishing, p. xi Available at: *http:// public.eblib.com/choice/publicfullrecord.aspx?p=1661251*. Accessed on 12 April 2016.

Moyo, D. (2009). *Dead Aid: Why Aid Is Not Working and How There Is a Better Way for Africa*. New York: Farrar. Straus and Giroux.

Oded, A. (2010). Africa in Israeli Foreign Policy-Expectations and Disenchantment: Historical and Diplomatic Aspects, *Israel Studies*, 15(3), pp. 121-142.

Prah, K. (2008). A Pan-Africanist reflection: Point and counterpoint, Pambazuka. Available at: *http://www.pambazuka.org/pan-africanism/pan-africanist-reflection-point-and-counterpoint*. Accessed on 20 May 2016.

Sharawy, H. (2005). Heritage of African Languages Manuscripts (Ajami), 1st ed. Bamako: The Afro-Arab Cultural Institute.

Sharawi, H. (2014). Ali Mazrui. An Afrabian Case, al-ithad Newspaper, Available at: http://www.alittihad.ae/wajhatdetails.php?id=82359. Accessed on 23 March 2016.

Soyinka, W. (2000). The Trouble With You, Ali Mazrui! - Response to Ali's Millennial "Conclusion". *West African Review*, 1 (2), Available at: http://www.africaknowledgeproject.org/index.php/war/article/view/422. Accessed on 12 January 2016.

Sylvester, A. (1981). *Arabs and Africans: Co-Operation for Development*. London: Bodley Head.

Versteegh, K. 2001. "Arabic in Madagascar". *Bulletin of the School of Oriental and African Studies*, University of London. 64(2), pp. 177-187.

Wolny, P. (2014). *Discovering the Empire of Mali*. New York, NY: Rosen Publishing.

Ali Mazrui and Verbal Combats

Macharia Munene

Introduction

In many ways Ali A. Mazrui was religiously and socially ecumenical and therefore had all the Gods looking after his welfare right from cradle to grave. God was so good to Mazrui that He allowed him overlapping attributes that led to intellectual greatness. He grew up in the context of kadhis and chief kadhis and received two types of high class education; Islamic, from his father and in Mosques, and British. His grand uncle and father were great Islamic scholars who had learned to balance British colonial desires with those of advancing Islamic interests. They instilled in young Mazrui the love of verbal engagements and being articulate.

Mazrui was scion of a prominent family that claimed the right to rule Mombasa and the coastal zone and was very resistant of others trying to do the same. Members could trace their dominance at the coast to the final ouster of the Portuguese from Mombasa, thereby portraying the family as liberator.[1] They, argued James de Vere Allen, became "swahilised" on assuming power in Mombasa and "learned to behave more like Swahili patricians than like Omanis." They "established a de facto if not de jure dynasty in Mombasa"[2] and, so argued Colonial Settler and Nakuru Ward Councilor Genesta Hamilton, "regarded Mombasa as their own property."[3]

In an effort to promote its perceived interests, the Mazrui family combined the ability to cooperate with and also challenge supposed authorities, and it often succeeded. In the 19th Century, for instance, the Mazrui often cooperated with and also defied the sultans of Zanzibar with their British supporters.[4] One of the Mazrui cousins, Mubarak Bin Rashid, was reportedly a slave dealer and attracts attention as a symbol of Mazrui resistance. Pioneer colonial administrators C.W.

Hobley, observed that "Mazrui chief of Gazi, Mbaruk bin Raschid" kept sending slaves "to the chief of Rombo on Kilimanjaro, with whom he had a standing arrangement to obtain slaves."[5] When he felt shortchanged by the British in matters of succession, he mounted resistance to the imposing of British rule. Eventually, Britain subdued Mbaruk and imposed its will on the coastal Muslims in 1895.[6] Mazrui probably inherited rebelliousness from grand uncle Mbaruk.

It was, however, the scholarly gene that he inherited from his biological ancestors that made him grow to world fame. His great grandfather, Shaykh 'Abdullah B. Nafi was a scholar who adopted and promoted the Shafi'i school of Islam at the Coast. His great great grandfather, Shaykh Ali bin Abdalla bin Nafi al-Mazrui, served as kadhi and travelled widely promoting scholarship. At the time of his death in 1894, he entrusted the raising of his four-year old son to his nephew, Shaykh Maamun bin Suleman Mazrui, who became Kadhi and Chief Kadhi.[7] Sulaiman taught his little cousin, Shaykh Al-Amin bin Ali bin Nafi al-Mazrui, how to be a good Islamic scholar that enabled Ali Mazrui's father to be very knowledgeable in Islamic studies.

The father also distinguished himself as an Islamic scholar, as well as, a socio-cultural reformer. He was a prolific writer in Arabic and Kiswahili on religious, political, social, and cultural challenges. He was the first to publish books on religion in Kiswahili, teaching materials for children on Islam titled *The Children's Guide*, and a newspaper in Kiswahili to address all types of issues. His fame as a scholar in East Africa spread far and wide. His crowning work was his incomplete book, *The History of the Mazru'i Dynasty of Mombasa*. He died in 1947 before he could analyze and write about his own grandfather, let alone his father and uncle.[8] At that time, young Mazrui was 14 years old but he inherited the scholarly bend.

The overlapping attributes that God allowed him enabled Mazrui, in his 81 years on earth, to succeed where many had not. He was an Islamic prince of the Swahili type, a keen student of his father in terms of scholarship and handling British authorities, and was fluent in languages that opened many doors. He thereafter succeeded in fulfilling three intertwined dreams; his father's, Governor Philip Mitchell's, and his own. His father, Chief Kadhi Sheikh Al-Amin B. Ali Mazrui had wanted to uplift coastal youth by establishing schools and academies where Muslim youth would be taught Western science and skills as well as receive religious education.[9] When Governor Mitchell founded the Mombasa Institute of Islamic Education (MIOME) in 1950, with dreams of uplifting Muslims to the 20th Century, it was as the Chief Kadhi had wished.[10] Among those present in 1950 was Mazrui. Mitchell zeroed in on Mazrui for uplifting into the 20th Century. And Mazrui's childhood dream was to become a verbal combatant.

In the young Mazrui, God/Allah granted the Chief Kadhi's and the governor's wishes to uplift Muslims. He had two types of high class education, being the grandson of the Kadhi of Mombasa and son of the Chief Kadhi of Kenya, as well as a British colonial subject. He received Islamic education from his father and in Mosques[11] and walked with his father almost everywhere "since my Dad wanted me to be around him most of the time."[12] That way, Mazrui toured different parts of Kenya, nephew Alamin M. Mazrui wrote, observing the performance of and learning about "judicial duties of his father as a roving court of appeal" for Muslims.[13] This on-hand training came to an end when the father died in April 1947 "rather pre-maturely".[14]

He survived the shock of the father's death and overcame the Cambridge deficit with Mitchell's help. Roughly 50 years after the founding of MIOME, Mazrui was the Chancellor of Jomo Kenyatta University of Science and Technology. He quipped: "The Lord does indeed operate in mysterious ways. Let us praise him. Amen!"[15] And he could praise the Lord for the fulfillment of his personal dream of becoming a verbal warrior by using English as a tool of verbal combat. For this, he said, "I have a soft spot for Sir Philip Mitchell for … changing the course of my career."[16]

This is the man that the world watched return to Fort Jesus in October 2014 to rest permanently next to his ancestors having made his father, Governor Mitchell, and himself blessedly happy. He had recovered from the Cambridge deficit, entered Makerere through Oxford, mounted anti-socialist crusades, and had "redesigned" himself when he relocated to the United States. He engaged in verbal combats with anyone who could throw verbal brickbats. He compares well with other giants of the intellect. God was good to him, and he enjoyed it.

Mazrui and his intellectual predecessors, Augustine and Khaldun

Although Mazrui's biological ancestors were scholarly, he reportedly modelled himself after Ibn Khaldun, the 14th Century Tunisian. He virtually became, Seifudein Adem Hussein claims, a "Postmodern

Ibn Khaldun".[17] It is therefore appropriate to compare Mazrui with Aurelius Augustine and Ibn Khaldun, two brilliant North Africans who preceded him as men of the pen. Both Augustine and Khaldun produced masterpieces in defense of their respective faiths. For Augustine, it was the defense of Christianity in his 426 The City of God against accusations of being responsible for the collapse of the Roman Empire. For Khaldun, in the Muqaddimah, the concern was over the declining Islamic empire.[18] Probably because Khaldun was a Muslim and son of an Islamic scholar,[19] just like Mazrui 600 years later, Mazrui identified more closely with Khaldun than with Augustine. He considered "St. Augustine … one of the most brilliant theologians in the history of Christianity," but, he believed, Khaldun was greater than Augustine as a theorist.[20]

While Khaldun's Muqaddimah was a master survey of all types of knowledge in what later became academic disciplines for Euro-scholars to distinguish themselves and get credit,[21] he ignored Christian writers. At the time, Islam was on the defensive as European Christians mounted Reconquista against "the infidels" to liberate Spain from Islamic dominance. After capturing Seville in Andalusia in 1248, Castilian King Ferdinand III turned it into his headquarters, converted the Mosque into a Cathedral, and the Cathedral was turned into a tomb in 1252 when he died.[22]

Among those Muslims kicked out of Seville, ordered to "empty the city", and given one month to "sell the things they could not take with them,"[23] were members of the prominent Khaldun family. They escaped and settled in Tunis, North Africa, where Khaldun was born in 1332.[24] Thereafter, Khaldun had little regard for Christianity, which he believed, did not have a universal mission or concept of holy war because it tended to separate the spiritual from the secular.[25] For Khaldun, only Muslims were believers and had a duty to convert others by force. Since Christians were non-believers, he wrote in the Muqaddimah, he did not want to "blacken the pages of this book with discussions of their dogmas of unbelief … It is (for them to choose between) conversion to Islam, payment of their poll tax, or death."[26]

Yet, despite his preference for Khaldun, Mazrui's intellectual temperament, training, and formative backgrounds were like Augustine. Augustine had trained in rhetoric at Carthage, engaged in philandering activities that distressed mother Monica, and had spent a lot of time studying with the Manicheans. He went through religious transformation and turned against Manicheans and delighted in destroying Manichean arguments in public debates.[27] However, in his disputes with Pelagius, Augustine had difficulties defeating the Pelagius challenge to his invention of the "Original Sin".[28]

Similarly, Mazrui had a brilliant and naughty youth. He attracted bottom thrashing from Mother Safia for making "a war-cry" to scare another little boy.[29] In England, he was "cheeky" and would sneak into the tutor's office to check his marks, lock out a "loud and silly" colleague, pee in "a milk bottle", and climb dormitory walls Romeo-like to pamper Molly Vickerman with words.[30] Like Augustine, he was trained to use language in combat but his Manicheans were initially socialistic opponents. He loved demolishing them. He too went through transformation in 1979-1980 and evolved into a sharp critic of the Western powers. Mazrui's confrontations with Wole Soyinka were similar to Augustine's confrontations with Pelagius.

Family background

Once the British subdued the Mazrui, both sides worked to reinforce each other. Credit goes to Arthur Hardinge who, had as the Coast Provincial Commissioner Charles Hobley commented, "an uncanny insight into the Arab character."[31] That insight enabled Hardinge, the first Commissioner of the British East Africa Protectorate, to reorganize Islamic religious administration using the Ottoman model of the *Wilayet*. He created a new post of *Shaykh al Islam* that evolved into *Chief Kadhi*[32] in order to, Ahmed Idha Salim wrote, "oversee the work of other kadhis."[33] Among the ultimate beneficiaries of this Islamic reorganization were members of the Mazrui family. Hobley made the case for Shaykh Maamun bin Suleman Mazrui as suitable to become Chief Kadhi mainly because he was an Islamic scholar.[34] Sulaiman was followed as Chief Kadhi by his nephew, Shaykh Al-Amin bin Ali bin Nafi al-Mazrui, who was Ali Mazrui's father. Then, in 1947, came Shaykh Mohammed bin Kassim Mazrui, son of Chief Kadhi Suleman and cousin to Ali Mazrui's father.[35]

The father knew how to ingratiate himself to the British and probably passed the genes of scholarship and being nice to the British to his son. Mazrui most certainly read his father's *The Children's Guide* and internalized some of the lessons. He also observed his father's way of argumentation including defending the British. The father wrote *The History of the Mazru'i Dynasty of Mombasa* in which he referred to, and used, many British sources to buttress his argument. It is not true, the father wrote, that the Mazrui were hostile to the British. They were instead, "the first of the 'Umani Tribes who sought friendship with the British... names of the outstanding personalities of the Mazraia ... took important positions under the authority of the British Government... All these contradict those who say that they were noted for adopting an attitude of hostility to the British Government... When the Government called for volunteers for service in this past War of 1939, the Mazari'a were the first to answer the call... Is this not proof enough of their friendship to the British Government?"[36]

Mazrui went beyond Islam into acceptability by members of other faiths. Having grown up in Mombasa under British Christian colonial rule, he learned from his father how to combine the dictates of Islam and those of Christianity as projected by the British colonial masters. He twice married Christian women, let them continue to practice their faith, and still remained a devout Muslim.[37] His flexibility of mind allowed him to engage widely so much that he became a global man. By then, as Hedley Bull put it, Mazrui had become "one of the few contemporary writers to have thought deeply" about the question of "justice" in the world[38] and was the "most illuminating interpreter of the drift of world politics" handling "global" issues.[39] Mazrui appreciated and felt flattered that three organs of that world recognized his ability and name him as one of the most influential public intellectuals or one of the most influential Africans.[40]

The rebooted man

Young Mazrui had two types of high class education. He received Islamic education from his father and in Mosques[41] and walked with his father almost everywhere.[42] Touring different parts of Kenya and, nephew Alamin M. Mazrui wrote, observing the performance of and learning about "judicial duties of his father as a roving court of appeal" for Muslims.[43] He also observed how the father handled the British even as he received British education beyond Islam. He was fascinated by the English language as "a medium of debate" and dreamt of going to Makerere College to study English "as a tool of verbal combat". He impressed teachers with his ability to weave and deliver ideas in debates and in writing, a talent he inherited from his grand uncle and father, as men of the pen who became Chief Kadhi.[44] The school made him skip certain classes, which probably explained his poor performance in Cambridge School Certificate.

Despite Cambridge, his verbal wizardry still opened doors for him to jump over other people. He became a print and radio journalist, an after-dinner speaker for Mombasa high society and in such public places as the Mombasa Institute of Education.[45] This opened his doors to England, the real home of the English language, where he re-bloomed intellectually and jumped over all the others academically in effort to exorcise the ghost of Cambridge. He thus "entered the Western game with such gusto," he wrote, "that I did it brilliantly at Manchester emerging with a bachelor's degree with Distinction."[46] He then went to Columbia University and thereafter became an object of Anglo-American competition, receiving doctoral scholarships from Princeton University in the United States and University of Oxford in England. Britain was not willing to lose Mazrui to the Americans the way it had lost Tom Mboya.

Oxford's success was the work of two dominant British academics, Margery Perham and John Plamenatz. Perham, the first director of the Oxford Institute of Colonial Studies, had long worried about American anti-colonialism and had, on occasion, to "correct the distorted view of the character of the British Empire."[47] The first woman to give the BBC Reith lectures, she had talked of "Colonial Reckoning" and advised Britons to groom potential African leaders.[48] Having helped to groom Mboya only for the Americans to snatch him, she was not willing to watch the Americans "steal" another brilliant African mind. On his part, Plamenatz was a leading political philosopher at Nuffield who also acted to ensure that Mazrui landed at Oxford in 1961.[49] Plamenatz was also one of those scholars that were, as Jan Vansina put it, "retooling".[50]

Mazrui found other brilliant minds at Oxford, staff and students. "We were all intellectually influenced," Mazrui wrote of Isaiah Berlin's lecture on "'Two Concepts of Liberty' but I was ideologically to his left on the kind of liberty worth pursuing."[51] There was also Kenneth Kirkwood, the Rhodes Professor of Race Relations[52] arguing that on balance British colonialism was positive for Africans and Britons.[53] He wanted Britain to develop a Lugardian "dual partnership" using the "bridgeheads available to Britain in Commonwealth African states". [54] He and Mazrui remained close till Kirkwood's death in 1997.[55] His fellow Oxford students included Yash Pal Ghai and Okot p'Bitek, who entered Oxford in 1960 to study social anthropology [56] and Yash Pal Ghai studying law.[57]

Subsequently Oxford, the citadel of the British Empire, won the bout in the battle for Mazrui. In its decolonization strategy, Britain had planned to "capture the academic princes like Mazrui[58] who was, Mazrui later wrote, slated to become the first African professor of political science in the same way that Mwai Kibaki was slated to become the first African professor of economics. Kibaki had deviated into practical politics. Mazrui became Makerere's first African professor of political science in East Africa.[59] Thus Britain not only ensured that Mazrui landed at Oxford in 1961,[60] it also went out of its way to clear his path to enter Makerere "through the roof," as Okello Oculi put it,[61] and to jump stages in academic ranks.

In the British project to make Mazrui the first African professor, Oxford man Colin Leys virtually became academic *chaperon*, or John the Baptist, in preparing the way for Mazrui at Makerere. And Mazrui, having learned from his father to be friendly to the British wishes, did not mind being British chaperoned. It started with Makerere hiring Colin Leys from Oxford as professor and Chairman of Department of Political Science in 1963 and Leys quickly returning to Oxford to hunt for Mazrui. Britain then waived a bond requirement that Mazrui return to work in Kenya for five years by arguing that Mazrui would be teaching Kenyans at Makerere. Within two years, in 1965, Leys left the professorship and the chairmanship to Mazrui, who was yet to get his PhD. For Mazrui, Oxford was expunging the ghost of Cambridge.[62] For that to happen, Britain reportedly pressured Vice-Chancellor Yusuf Lule to appoint Mazrui, if Makerere was to receive funds.[63] In 1967, Leys had capped his chaperoning act by declaring that his protégé, Mazrui, was intellectually incapable of writing dullness.[64]

Stirring intellectual trouble at Makerere

At Makerere, Mazrui astounded students and faculty, mesmerizing people with his command of the Greeks, Romans, and other Euro-icons.[65] In the process, as Alamin pointed out, Mazrui "repeatedly borrowed from English literature to point an African moral or adorn an Islamic tale."[66] At Makerere, Ngugi wa Thiong'o wrote, Mazrui was "the new wonder kid ... He shone: he dazzled: he enlightened."[67] When Julius Nyerere first met him at Makerere, Mazrui later wrote, Nyerere "made my day" with simple Kiswahili greeting "*Tunasikia sifa tu!*"[68] (We hear your praises).

And the dazzling was partly by mudding intellectual waters. This was at a time that the African intelligentsia was claiming to be socialistic. He told a Makerere audience in 2006, "Intellectuals and academics thought they could be effective agents of economic change by the ideology they adopted. In the 1960s and 1970s socialism and even Marxism were popular on many campuses in Africa... Marxism became the opium of the post-colonial intelligentsia. Addiction to Marxism and socialism was at its height on the campuses of the University of Dar es Salaam and Haile Selassie I University in Addis Ababa ... The Makerere campus was the least intoxicated by socialism and Marxism, resisting the opium of the rest of the African intelligentsia."[69]

Mazrui was at the forefront of that resistance and distinguished himself as an avid advocate of the ability of capitalism to smother socialism.[70] He set out to de-intoxicate the universities by attacking the political icons of that Marxist-socialist opium: Ghana's Kwame Nkrumah and Tanzania's Julius K. Nyerere. He termed Nkrumah a Leninist Czar and given that both Lenin and the Czar were synonymous with epithets in Western circles, the effect was to portray Nkrumah as a confused man who happened to be an African leader.[71] He made sure that Nkrumah received a copy of *Transition* but Nkrumah refused to be provoked into response[72] to Mazrui's "trash ... in *Transition*".[73] Mazrui then turned the snub into a positive by publicizing the non-response.[74]

Mazrui also accused Tanzania's Nyerere of being "a traitor to his class", the class of intellectuals.[75] He castigated Dar es Salaam for losing focus and being saddled with "the white Marxist burden" in which "white Marxists" contrived to "'socialize' the University College." He zeroed in on "a group of radical academics ... products of distinguished Western universities" and accused them of hypocrisy and not having faith in the concept of universities. While welcoming debates on reforms in East Africa, he wrote, "there is no room for a weird, hybrid creature from the womb of the nineteenth century – a poet-ideologue called 'Karl Kipling'"[76]

The article made Leys, by declaring that "Ali Mazrui is incapable of writing a dull paragraph",[77] some kind of authority on Mazrui and he subsequently became a reference point on assessing Mazrui's brilliance. Critics thought otherwise. Taban Lo Liyong dismissed Mazrui as one of the "captured princes of the West" whose "intellectualism" was "sterility" with inability "to grapple with issues."[78] James Karioki observed that while other African intellectuals "may be tickled by

Mazrui's skilled linguistic twists, they are profoundly disenchanted by his overall insensitivity to the phenomena that affect Africa... the disagreement is ... largely over a scenical attitude that runs below what on the surface may appear to be logical and true."[79] Mazrui took such criticism in stride, and responded to some of them.

The image of a captured Mazrui was reinforced in May 1970 when he met more than his match in what amounted to a debate of the "radicals". Broadcast live on the Ugandan radio and television, it featured Dar es Salaam historian Walter Rodney on the "left" and Makerere's political scientist Mazrui on the "right". Moderated by Makerere student leader Peter Anyang' Nyong'o, the debate placed Mazrui in the neo-colonial camp[80] and pricked his intellectual balloon, and he knew it. Mazrui sounded as if he was regurgitating Kirkwood's argument about the balance on colonialism being positive.[81] That enabled Rodney to charge: "Professor Mazrui has argued that colonialism was good, that on the one hand this and on the hand that. Colonialism had only one hand: the hand of oppression, the hand of exploitation. Exploitation was mainly a means to oppress and exploit African brothers and sisters."[82] Mazrui later admitted to Willy Mutunga that he had lost the debate to Rodney.[83]

Those that were impressed by Mazrui's intellectual prowess included General Idi Amin Dada who in 1971 overthrew Obote. Amin had ideas of his own on how to use the intellectuals at Makerere with Mazrui at the top. Having asserted that an intellectual was a person who enjoyed playing games with ideas effectively,[84] Mazrui was attractive to Amin's dreams of playing on the world stage. Fascinated by the relationship between US President Richard M. Nixon and Henry Kissinger, Amin wanted a Kissinger of his own and Mazrui fitted the bill. When Mazrui demurred using delaying tactics to avoid decision making, Amin developed a more exciting role for Mazrui than playing Kissinger. He wanted Mazrui to be an exhibit in confronting South Africa with evidence that Africans had brilliant minds. Unsure of what to do, Mazrui prayed to his Gods who then smiled on him and, he wrote, "my prayers were answered" by South Africa turning down Amin's suggestion. In rejecting Amin's idea of intellectual confrontation between black and white minds, the Boers saved Mazrui from the opprobrium of apartheid apologia.[85] Mazrui's days at Makerere, however, were numbered as Amin clamped down on free thinking and Mazrui found it necessary to escape to the United States where he drifted to Rodney's intellectual side.

Mazrui Redesigned, turning on theimperialists

In the United States, Mazrui was forced to "redesign" himself. He underwent internal redesigning to discard his previous image at the intellectual, personal and family levels. At home, he separated from Molly while he was in Michigan and then moved to SUNY Binghampton in 1982. He also found special appointment at the University of Jos, Nigeria, and found his heart throbbing towards the direction of Jos, where Pauline captured it and he married her. This symbolized completion of Mazrui's triple heritage of Arab, European, and African blood flowing in the veins of his family members.

No longer predisposed to pamper, and to be defensive about, the British or the Conceptual West, he increasingly took on an intellectual attitude that was akin to that of his previous critics. These were people who had problems with the portrayal by Mazrui's teacher at Oxford, Kirkwood, claiming that on balance Euro colonialism was fundamentally positive for Africa, a position that Mazrui initially espoused. These included James Karioki, Walter Rodney, Ngugi wa Thiong'o, Julius Nyerere, and Kwame Nkrumah. Some of them became his intellectual buddies. He also became vocal in defense of Islam almost in proportion to his criticism of the Conceptual West.

The intellectual redesigning of Mazrui took time to be noticed. He angered former admirers with his increasing Euro-criticism. In his 1979 Reith Lectures on "The African Condition", he aroused furious debate by suggesting that Third World countries should have nuclear capacity, if nuclear proliferation was to be limited.[86] Connor Cruise Obrien, Editor-in-Chief of *The Observer* in England, furiously dismissed the entire Lecture series as "nonsense" and wondered why BBC allowed Mazrui to air such nonsense. Economist Peter Bauer complained that Mazrui's lectures were meant to "diminish or undermine the West" and to exonerate the Arab slave trade. Bauer's message was that Mazrui should quit blaming the West for the woes in Africa.[87]

He also aroused anger with his PBS television series labeled "*The Africans: A Triple Heritage*" that was contrary to the expectations of the sponsors. The Triple Heritage was visual/television continuation of the radio/audio Reith Lecture series. In them, he shifted intellectual camp to that of Walter Rodney with whom he had reconciled. Most Africans commended the new Mazrui while sponsors and some opinion makers were furious. Lynne Cheney, Director of the sponsoring National Endowment for Humanities, fumed that *The Africans* "frequently degenerates into anti-Western diatribe" and "moves from distressing moment to distressing moment" in blaming "all the moral, economic and technological problems of Africa on the West."[88] *Chicago Tribune* TV/radio critic Clifford Terry considered Mazrui to be "a man with ... maddening" opinions. Despite being "maddening", Terry concluded "'The Africans' deserves to be seen, flaws and all. And whatever one thinks of Mazrui, it is obvious, through it all, that here is a man who deeply cares about what he likes to call 'a remarkable continent.'"[89]

Several well-known Africans accused Mazrui of soft-peddling Arab slave trade and atrocities in Africa. Among them was Wole Soyinka. Thereafter, Mazrui wrote, he and Soyinka "brutalized each other in the pages of the newly revived *Transition* magazine."[90] Besides American officialdom, Mazrui also attracted the wrath of Kenyan political leaders. His 1993 suggestion that Kenya's President Moi relinquish office and the claim that Moi was "guilty of neglect, verging on criminal neglect"[91] displeased Moi. In turn, Moi dismissed Mazrui as "that strange man"[92]

Bethwell A. Ogot had low opinion of Mazrui, dismissing Mazrui as arrogant and an Arab slave trade apologist.[93] Both were beneficiaries of British educational largesse and became prominent Kenyan academics. Before going to Britain, Mazrui was already a local celebrity as journalist, radio presenter and Kiswahili story-teller in "Sauti Ya Mvita", and in high demand as an after-dinner speaker in English for the Mombasa elite clubs.[94] Ogot was an established mathematics teacher at Alliance and had been a student at Makerere, which Mazrui missed courtesy of Cambridge. The two were in the same plane, BOAC flight BA 176 from Nairobi to London on September 5th 1955. Mazrui, wrote Ogot, was going "for his high school education"[95] at Huddersfield Technical College, a kind of pre-university programme, before being admitted to Manchester University.[96] In contrast, Ogot went to a prestigious Scottish university, St. Andrews University, and switched to study history.[97]

Both men had unique sense of self-awareness and could not resist trumpeting their brilliance. Each complained about neglect by post-colonial governments of people in their biological neck of the woods which made them sound as if they were romanticizing colonialism.[98] Ogot did not shy from pronouncing his brilliance, mainly in his writings where he pointed out his achievements and the shortcomings of the others.[99] Mazrui, though he refrained from passing intellectual judgments on others, was also good at blowing his trumpet and tended to discuss his rare achievements in rising to the top of the intellectual world.

Mazrui, however, was uneasy engaging Ogot, who questioned Mazrui's reparation crusade. Debating Ogot, "perhaps Kenya's most distinguished historian", Mazrui wrote, made him "uncomfortable". Ogot, Mazrui commented, initially complained that "Africans were making too much of the issue of slavery" and then seemingly "decided that Africans were not making enough of the Arab slave trade." Still, Mazrui was uncomfortable engaging Ogot in "the verbal exchanges in the Press [that] were sometimes heated and acrimonious."[100]

While uncomfortable with Ogot, Mazrui was angry at Ogot's star student, William Robert Ochieng'. Unhappy that Ogot, his mentor, repeatedly seemed to be intellectually shortchanged when compared to Mazrui or even novelist Ngugi wa Thiong'o. Ochieng made it his business to belittle and ridicule Mazrui as being very good in English and over-rated in terms of international reputation.[101] The climax of the mutual dislike between the two was in July and August 1996 when Ochieng questioned Mazrui's intellectual alertness and patriotism to Africa. He then negatively compared Mazrui to his chosen heroes. "He lacked," claimed Ochieng' "the youthful reflexes of age mates like Professors B.A. Ogot and T. R. Odhiambo". He dismissed "this guy" Mazrui as "simply another harmless coastal chatterbox" and, literary critic Chris Wanjala observed that Ochieng was "boorish" in attacking Mazrui.[102]

Mazrui threw the gauntlet at Ochieng'. He called for a public debate on university education in Africa in a public university of Ochieng's choice. Ochieng then displayed unexpected intellectual cowardice by declining the challenge,[103] fearing Mazrui's command and use of English as a tool of verbal combat. "I cannot agree to such a debate," Ochieng told William Mayaka, when the two met in Kisumu, "the man would finish me."[104]

Conclusion: Back to Fort Jesus, Mombasa

When in October 2014, Mazrui passed on, he returned to Fort Jesus a world famous and globally revered man. God had been so good to him that he managed to fulfill dreams and his father's dream of empowering the coastal youth. He actually inherited his father's genes for scholarship and being friendly to the British. Among the Britons to whom he was grateful was Mitchell whose dream of uplifting an African Muslim to the 20th Century was seemingly fulfilled in Mazrui. Finally, he fulfilled his own dream of becoming a verbal combatant.

Mazrui came close to Augustine and Khaldun whose attributes he tended to combine. He was like Augustine in the love of verbal combats and like Khaldun in Islamic upbringing. While he adored Khaldun's intellect as the "man of the pen",[105] he was not bound by Khaldun's anti-Christianity. In the *Al'Muqadidimah*, Mazrui believed, Khaldun displayed an "imaginative concept of *asabiyah,* which is often translated as '*social cohesion.'* He went on to link *asabiyah* to modern "nationalism" and "globalization" as "post-modern *asabiyah.*"[106]

Mazrui was part of the 20th Century phenomenon that overlapped into the 21st Century as Africans sought liberation from all types of colonialism, giving rise to African intellectual warriors.[107] By then Mazrui had redesigned himself into an anti-imperialist intellectual warrior, who tended to address the three issues of slavery, colonialism, and imperialism. Mazrui was a post-colonial writer and generated more than his share of controversy for he liked to provoke his contemporaries. There was Kwame Nkrumah of Ghana whose *Neo-Colonialism: The Last Stage of Imperialism* popularized the dilemma confronting emerging post-colonial African States as that of neo-colonialism or the continuation of colonialism in ways that were not territorial. Nkrumah and Mazrui had their differences although Mazrui's were more public than those of Nkrumah. It also included Walter Rodney, the historian whose *How Europe Underdeveloped Africa* ended up challenging claims by Europeans. Mazrui admired the two anti-imperialists and redesigned his scholarship along their logic.

Mazrui liked mending fences with almost anyone he had a fight with and could not resist entertaining and hosting his critics. In Manchester, he would climb ladders Romeo-style to plead with Molly after they had had a lover tiff. Moving to Nkrumah's and Rodney's anti-imperialist positions, he adopted Nkrumah's Triple Heritage and Rodney's underdevelopment arguments and combined them in the television series, *The Africans: A Triple Heritage.* The series had led to verbal altercations between Mazrui and Wole Soyinka but, Mazrui once commented that despite the feud, "The pity of it: I still like the guy."[108]

His intellectual "unflagging adversary", Wole Soyinka, could return the favor and declare Mazrui to be a reconciler and a "perfect host", having made General Yakubu Gowon and Wole Soyinka sit next to each other during his 70th birthday celebrations. The two Nigerian rivals eased tensions when Gowon "confessed" that he was Soyinka's jailer and Soyinka disagreed by "insisting that I had been merely his fortuitous guest at Kaduna and Kirikiri Prison." Mazrui's passing, concluded Soyinka, "is a great loss to us. I already feel his absence. I miss him."[109] And Soyinka, a great verbal combatant himself, is not the only "guy" who misses Mazrui's verbal combats. I am sure there are many globally who also miss the verbal combats.

Endnotes

1   J. McL. Ritchie, translator and annotator of Shaykh Al-Amin Bin 'Ali Al Mazru'i, "Introduction," *The History of the Mazru'i Dynasty of Mombasa.* (Oxford: Oxford University Press, 1995), pp. 1-5.

2   James De Vere Allen, *Swahili Origins: Swahili Culture & the Shungwaya Phenomenon.* (Nairobi: EAEP, 1993), pp. 243- 244.

3   Genesta Hamilton, *In the Wake of Da Gama: The Story of Portuguese Pioneers in East Africa, 1497-1729.* (London: Skeffington and Son Limited, 1951), p. 168.

4   Ritchie, translator and annotator of Shaykh Al-Amin Bin 'Ali Al Mazru'i, pp. 3-5.

5   C.W. Hobley, *Kenya: From Chartered Company to Crown Colony, Thirty Years of Exploration and Administration in East Africa*, Second Edition with an Introduction by G.H. Mungeam. (London: Frank Cass & Co. Ltd, 1970), p. 29.

6   See J. McL. Ritchie, "Epilogue: The last Chapter of the Saga of the Mazai'a," in Shaykh Al-Amin Bin 'Ali Al Mazru'i, *The History of the Mazru'i Dynasty of Mombasa*, pp. 121-122.

7   Shaykh Al-Amin Bin 'Ali Al Mazru'i, "Introduction," in *Ibid.*, p. 1.

8   *Ibid.*, pp. 2-3

9   Randall L. Pouwels, "Sh. al-Amin Mazrui and Islamic Modernism in East Africa, 1875-1947," *International Journal of Middle East Studies*, Vol. 13, No. 3 (August 1981), pp. 329-345.

10   Ghalib Yusuf Tamim, *Maisha ya Sheikh Al-Amin Bin Ali Mazrui (1891-1947)* (Nairobi: Signal Press, 2006), p. 63.

11   Michael O. West, "Kwame Nkrumah and Ali Mazrui: An Analysis of the 1967 *Transition* Debate," *The Journal of Pan-African Studies*, Vol. 8, No. 6, September 2015, p. 134.

12   Ali Mazrui, "Death, Destiny and Coincidence," *Mazrui Newsletter.* No. 27, early 2003, pp. 34-35.

13   Alamin M. Mazrui, Chapter One, "The African Impact on American Higher Education: Ali Mazrui's Contribution," in Parviz Morewedge, editor, *The Scholar Between Thought and Experience: A Biographical Festschrift in Honor of Ali. A. Mazrui* (Binghamton, NY: Institute of Global Cultural Studies Global Publications, Binghamton University, 2001), p. 5.

14   Ali Mazrui, *Annual Mazrui Newsletter: Between Global Africa and the World of Islam*, No. 22, Early 1998, pp.2-3, 21-22; Mazrui, "Death, Destiny and Coincidences," pp. 36-37; Mwapachu,, "A Rich Legacy."

[15] Ali A. Mazrui, "A Chancellor in Circulation," *Annual Mazrui Newsletter*. No. 31, Spring 2007, p. 24.

[16] Ali A. Mazrui, "From MIOME to Huddersfield," *Annual Mazrui Newsletter*. No. 26, Early 2002, p. 13.

[17] Jack Kalpakian, "Ibn Khaldun's influence on Current International Relations Theory," *The Journal of North African Studies*, Vol. 13, No. 3, 2008, pp. 364, 367; Seifudein Adem Hussein, "Ali A. Mazrui: A Postmodern Ibn Khaldun?" *Journal of Muslim Minority Affairs*, Vol. 23, No. 1, April 2003, pp. 127-145.

[18] Vernon J. Bourke, editor, An Abridged Version of Saint Augustine, *The City of God*, Abridged for Modern Readers (London: Doubleday Image Books, 1958); Ibn Khaldun, *The Muqaddimah: An Introduction to History* as translated from the Arabic by Franz Rosenthal and edited and abridged by N.J. Dawood (Princeton: Bolingen Series, Princeton University Press, 1967).

[19] Charles Issawi, "Ibn Khaldun," *Britannica Online Encyclopedia http://www.britannica.com/ print/article/2807* accessed June 11, 2016.

[20] Ali A. Mazrui, "The Re-inventing of Africa: Edward Said, V.Y. Mudimbe, and Beyond," *Research in African Literatures*, Vol.e 36, No. 3 (Fall 2005), pp. 73-74; also reproduced in Ali A. Mazrui *African Thought in Comparative Perspective* (New Castle upon Tyne, England: Cambridge Scholars Publishing, 2014), pp. 283-284.

[21] Seifudein Aden, "Ibn Khaldun as a Modern Thinker," *Area Studies Tsukuba*, 24, 2005, pp. 129-152.

[22] J.H. Elliott, *Imperial Spain, 1469-1716* (New York: Meridian Books, 1963), pp. 26, 55-56; Ballandalus Crescat Scientia Vita Excolatur, "The Tomb of Ferdinand III (d. 1252) in Seville: Emblem of Convivencia or Symbol of Reconquista," *http://ballandalus.wordpress. com?2015/04/22/7657 accessed June 19*, 2016.

[23] Quotes in Manuel Gonzalez Jiminez, "Seville in the Lower Middle Ages," in M* Jesus VigueraMolins, Coordinator, *IbnKhaldun, The Mediterranean in the 14th Century: Rise and Fall of Empires* (Seville: Fundacion Jose Manuel Lara and Fundacion El Legado andalusi, 2006), p. 390.

[24] *Ibid.* ; Marnie Hughes-Warrington, " Ibn Khaldun," in *Fifty Key Thinkers in History* (London: Routledge, 2015), p.163; Issawi, "Ibn Khaldun,"

[25] Olivier Mongin, "Recognising the Importance of Ibn Khaldun: Interview with Abdesselam Cheddadi," *La Revue des Revues de l'adpf, selection de mars 2006* as translated by David Macey originally published in Espirit, n*11, Novembre 2005.

[26] Ibn Khaldun, *The Muqaddimah: An Introduction to History* as translated from the Arabic by Franz Rosenthal and edited and abridged by N.J. Dawood (Princeton: Bolingen Series, Princeton University Press, 1967), p. 188.

[27] Richard Lim, *Public Disputation, Power, and Social Order in Late Antiquity* (Berkeley: University of California Press, 1995) as retrieved from http://ark.cdlib.org/ark:/13030/ ft0f59n6vv/

[28] Herbert McGonigle, "Augustine v. Pelagius on Original Sin," *European Exploration in Christian Holiness*, 2, Summer 2001, pp. 41-54; Stephen N. Filippo, "St. Augustine and Pelagianism," *Ignatius Insight*, *http://www.ignatiusinsight.com/features2008/sfilippo_ augustinepeleg_jan08.asp* accessed June 9, 2016; Farley, "The Great Pelagian Controversy."

[29]   Ali A. Mazrui, "The Making of an African Political Scientist," *International Social Science Journal*, Vol. XXV, No. 12, 1973, pp. 108-109.

[30]   Burjor Avari, "Recollections of Ali Mazrui as an Undergraduate," in Omari H. Kokole, editor, *The Global African A Portrait of Ali A. Mazrui* (Trenton, NJ.: Africa World Press, 1996), p. 295.

[31]   C.W. Hobley, *Kenya: From Chartered Company to Crown Colony, Thirty Years of Exploration and Administration in East Africa*, Second Edition with an Introduction by G.H. Mungeam (London: Frank Cass & Co. Ltd, 1970), p. 34.

[32]   Hassan Mwakimako, "Conflicts and Tensions in the Appointment of Chief Kadhi in Colonial Kenya 1898-1960s," in Shamil Jeppie, Ebrahim Moosa & Richard Roberts, editors, *Muslim Family Law in Sub-Saharan Africa: Colonial Legacies and Post-colonial Challenges* (Amsterdam: Amsterdam University Press, 2010), pp. pp. 110-111; Sandy Prita Meier, *Swahili Port Cities: The Architecture of Elsewhere* (Bloomington: Indiana University Press, 2016), pp. 75-76; Susan F. Hirsch, *Pronouncing and Persevering: Gender and the Discourses of Disputing in an African Islamic Court* (Chicago: University of Chicago Press, 1998), footnotes 8 and 10 on p. 312.

[33]   Ahmed I. Salim, "Sheikh Al-Amin bin Ali Al-Mazrui: His Career and Impact on East Africa", paper presented at UN function, n.d.

[34]   Mwakimako, "Conflict and Tensions," pp. 120-121.

[35]   *Ibid.*, pp. 120-126.

[36]   Quotes in Ritchie, translator, Shaykh Al-Amin Bin 'Ali Al Mazru'i, *The History of the Mazru'i Dynasty of Mombasa.* (Oxford: Oxford University Press, 1995), pp. 27-28.

[37]   J. Isawa Elaigwu, *Mwalimu Ali A. Mazrui, From Palo Auto to Plateau: My Personal Reflections* (Jos, Nigeria: Institute of Governance and Social Research [IGSR], 2012), pp. 14-15.

[38]   "Chapter 8 : Hedley Bull in his Own Words, Three Essays, 'Order Vs Justice in International Society,'" in Carol Bell and Meredith Thatcher, editors, *Remembering Hedley Bull* (Canberra: Australian National University, 2008), p. 83.

[39]   Quote in Seifudein Adem, "Ali A. Mazrui, Postcolonialism and the study of International Relations," *Journal of International Relations and Development*, Vol. 14, 2011, p. 506.

[40]   Ali A. Mazrui, "Between Secular and Religious Intellectual," *Annual Mazrui Newsletter No. 30*, Spring 2006, pp.2-4.

[41]   Michael O. West, "Kwame Nkrumah and Ali Mazrui: An Analysis of the 1967 *Transition* Debate," *The Journal of Pan-African Studies*, Vol. 8, No. 6, September 2015, p. 134.

[42]   Ali Mazrui, "Death, Destiny and Coincidence," *Mazrui Newsletter* No.27, early 2003, pp. 34-35.

[43]   Alamin M. Mazrui, Chapter One, "The African Impact on American Higher Education: Ali Mazrui's Contribution," in Parviz Morewedge, editor, *The Scholar Between Thought and Experience: A Biographical Festschrift in Honor of Ali. A. Mazrui* (Binghamton, NY: Institute of Global Cultural Studies Global Publications, Binghamton University, 2001), p. 5.

[44]   Ali A. Mazrui, "The Making of an African Political Scientist," *International Social Science Journal*, Vol. XXV, No. 12, 1973, pp.102-104, pp. 102-104, 108-109.

45   Ali Mazrui, "From MIOME to Huddersfield," *Annual Mazrui Newsletter*, No. 26, Early 2002, p. 12.

46   Ali Mazrui, "The Bonds of Friendship," p. 38.

47   Roger Owen, "The Dark Continent: The Colonial Reckoning, by Margery Perham; and Africa for Beginners, by Melvin J. Lasky," *Commentary*, July 1, 1963 *https://www. commentarymagazine.com/article/the-colonial-reckoni.....* accessed June 21, 2015

48   *Ibid.*

49   Chaly Sawere, " Scholar, Ideologue," p. 270.

50   Jan Vansina; *Living With Africa* (Madison, Wisconsin, 1994), p. 117; Macharia Munene, *Historical Reflections on Kenya: Intellectual Adventurism, Politics& International Relations* (Nairobi: University of Nairobi, Press, 2012), p. 37

51   Ali Mazrui, "The Bonds of Friendship and the Menace of Time," *Annual Mazrui Newsletter*, No. 22, Early 1998, p. 37.

52   *Ibid.*, p. 36; Ali Mazrui, "The British Connection," p. 21.

53   Kenneth Kirkwood, *Britain and Africa* (Baltimore: Johns Hopkins Press, 1965), pp. 13-14.

54   *Ibid.*, pp. 204, 208.

55   Ali Mazrui, "The Bonds of Friendship and the Menace of Time," *Annual Mazrui Newsletter*, No. 22, Early 1998, p. 3; Ali Mazrui, "The British Connection," p. 21.

56   Okot p'Bitek, *African Religions in Western Scholarship* (Nairobi: Kenya Literature Bureau, 1970), p. vii.

57   Ali Mazrui, "Between Campus and Career" *Annual Mazrui Newsletter,* No. 19, Early 1996, p.9.

58   Taban Lo Liyong, "Let the Intellectualism of Ali Mazrui Die," *Daily Nation*, February 14, 2006 as reproduced in *https://natna.wordpress.com/2014/10/14/let-the-intellectualism-of-a....* Accessed June 18, 2015.

59   Ali Mazrui, "Mazuriana Africana," *Newsletter*, No. 27, Early 2003, pp. 7-8.

60   Chaly Sawere, "Scholar, Ideologue, Philosopher, Artist" in Omari Kokole, editor, *The Global African: A Portrait of Ali Mazrui* (Trenton, NJ: Africa World Press, 1998), p. 271.

61   Okello Occuli, " 'Counter-penetration', and other tantalizing images of Ali Mazrui," *Mail and Guardian*, October 17, 2014.

62   Chaly Sawere, "Scholar, Ideologue, Philosopher, Artist", p. 271; Mazrui, "The Making of a Political Scientist"

63   Okello Occuli, " 'Counter-penetration', and other tantalizing images of Ali Mazrui."

64   Colin Leys, "Inter Alia- or Tanzaphilia and all that," *Transition*, No. 34 (December 1967-January 1968), p. 51.

65   Ambassador Juma V. Mwapachu, "A rich legacy: The life and times of Ali Mazrui," October 16, 2014 *http://mobile.thecitizen.co.tz/opinion/A-rich-legacy--The-life-and-ti...* Accessed June 20, 2015.

66 Alamin Mazrui, "The African Impact on Higher Education," p. 7.

67 Ngugi wa Thiong'o, "How Ali Mazrui, the global Kenyan, charted my path," *The Standard Digital News* , Thursday, October 23, 2014, *http://www.standardmedia.co.ke/ article/2000139170/ngugi-wa-thio...*

68 Ali A. Mazrui, *The Titan of Tanzania: Julius K. Nyerere's Legacy* (Binghamton: Institute of Global Cultural Studies, Global Publications, Binghamton University, 2002), p. 4.

69 Ali Mazrui, "The Role of the Academy in Politics and Economic Revival: Uganda in Comparative Perspective," Presentation at Makerere University to mark 40th anniversary of the Bank of Uganda, August 15, 2006.

70 James N. Karioki, "African Scholars verses Ali Mazrui," as reprinted in Seifudin, Willy Mutunga, and Alamin M. Mazrui, editors, *Black Orientalism and Pan-African Thought: Debating the African Condition, Ali A. Mazrui and His Critics, Volume III* (Trenton, NJ: Africa World Press, 2013), pp. 100-102

71 Macharia Munene, "Politics and the African Intellectuals: Perspective From East Africa," in Gbemisola Adeoti and Mabel Evwierhoma, editors, *After the Nobel Prize: Reflections on African Literature, Governance and development* (Lagos: Association of Nigerian Authors, 2006), pp. 191-192

72 Quote in Michael O. West, "Kwame Nkrumah and Ali Mazrui: An Analysis of the 1967 Transition Debate," *The Journal of Pan African Studies*, Vol. 8, No. 6, September 2015, p. 125.

73 *Ibid.,* p. 126.

74 *Ibid.,* p.132.

75 Paul Bonahene Adejei, "Review Essay: Mazrui and His Critics," *The American Journal of Islamic Social Sciences*, Vol. 22, No.2, 2005, p. 93.

76 Ali Mazrui, "Tanzaphilia: A Diagnosis," *Transition*, Volume 6, No. 31, June-July 1967, pp. 20-26.

77 Colin Leys, "Inter Alia- or Tanzaphilia and all that," p. 51.

78 Taban Lo Liyong, "Let the Intellectualism of Ali Mazrui Die," *Daily Nation*, February 14, 2006 as reproduced in *https://natna.wordpress.com/2014/10/14/let-the-intellectualism-of-a....* Accessed June 18, 2015.

79 Karioki, "African Scholars verses Ali Mazrui,", p. 96.

80 Peter Anyang' Nyong'o, "Appreciating Ali Mazrui," *Daily Monitor*, October 19, 2014.

81 Kirkwood, *Britain and Africa*, p. 14.

82 Quotations in Peter Anyang Nyong'o, "Appreciating Ali Mazrui," *Daily Monitor*, October 19, 2014.

83 Willy Mutunga, "Kenya's Chief Justice Mutunga reflects on renowned African scholar Mazrui-and how he lost a debate with Walter Rodney," *Mail and Guardian*, October 17, 2014 *http://mgafrica.com/article/2014-10-17-growing-up-with-mjomba-ali....* accessed june 7, 2016.

84 Ali Mazrui, "What is an intellectual? What is his role in the African revolution?" *East African Journal*, April 1969, p. 11

[85]   *Ibid.*

[86]   Ali Mazrui, "Nuclear Proliferation and I," *Annual Mazrui Newsletter: Special Chancellor's Edition*, Early 2004, pp. 4-6; ------- "The Expansion of Western Technology," *Annual Mazrui Newsletter* No. 29, Early 2005, p. 19.

[87]   Peter Bauer, "Ali Mazrui, A Prophet out of Africa: Broadcasting the Liberal Death-Wish," *Encounter*, August-September 1980 as reprinted in Seifudein Adem, Willy Mutunga, and Alamin M. Mazrui, editors, *Black Orientalism and Pan-African Thought: Debating the African Condition, Ali A. Mazrui and His Critics, Volume III* (Trenton, NJ: Africa World Press, 2013), pp. 61-81.

[88]   Irvin Molotsky, "U.S. Aide Assaults TV Series on Africa," *The New York Times*, September 5, 1986.

[89]   Clifford Terry, "Pbs' Maddening, Moving 'Africans' Deserve to be seen," *Chicago Tribune*, October 6, 1986.

[90]   Ali Mazrui, "Summary of a Year," *Mazrui Newsletter(Abridged)*, Eve of 1992, p.2; --------- "The Shadow of Soyinka," *Mazrui Annual Newsletter*, No. 17, Eve of 1993, pp. 11-12.

[91]   Kevin J. Kelley, "Mazrui: 'Prophet' who is least honoured at home," *Daily Nation*, November 16, 1993.

[92]   William Ochieng', "Intellectual Achievement: Ali Mazrui is proof that few heroes are respected in life," *Daily Nation*, September 16, 2009, p. 13.

[93]   H.H Waru, "Attack on Mazrui Unfair," *Sunday Nation*, Nairobi, June 20, 1993 as reproduced in Alamin M. Mazrui and Willy Mutunga, editors, *Debating the African Condition: Race, Gender, and Culture Conflict, Mazrui and His Critics* (Trenton, NJ: Africa World Press, 2004) p.317.

[94]   Ali A. Mazrui, "From MIOME to Huddersfield," *Annual Mazrui Newsletter*, No. 26, Early 2002, p. 12.

[95]   Bethwell A. Ogot, *My Footprints on the Sands of Time: An Autobiography* (Kisumu: Anyange Press, 2003), p. 74.

[96]   Mayaka, "Ali. A. Mazrui: Profile of a Scholar," pp. 124, 128; Chaly Sawere, "Scholar, Ideologue, Philosopher, Artist" in Omari Kokole, editor, *The Global African: A Portrait of Ali Mazrui* (Trenton, NJ: Africa World Press, 1998), p. 270.

[97]   Bethwell Ogot, *My Footprints on the Sands of Time*, pp.75-77.

[98]   Ali A. Mazrui, "Paradox of the jewel that never shone," *Sunday Nation*, July 7, 1996, p. 7; B.A. Ogot, "The Siege of Ramogi: From National Coalition to Ethnic Coalition, 1960-1998," in Bethwell A. Ogot, *Building on the Indigenous: Selected Essays, 1981-1998* (Kisumu: Anyange Press, 1999), pp. 277-288.

[99]   Bethwell Ogot, *My Footprints on the Sands of Time*, passim.

[100] Ali Mazrui, "The Reparation Crusade," *Annual Mazrui Newsletter*, No. 18, Eve of 1994, p. 4.

[101] Ochieng' Interview in the *Nation*, "Professor William Robert Ochieng" (date?)

[102] Chris Wanjala, "Mazrui's fertile pen let best ideas win," *The Standard*, October 18, 2014, p. 20.

[103] Ochieng Interview in the *Daily Nation*, "Professor William Robert Ochieng': Ngugi is a tribalist, Tabaan a con and Mazrui overrated," November 30, 2013 as reproduced in Kenya Today__*www.kenya-today.com/news/professor-william-robert-ochieng-ngugi-tribalisttaban-con-mazrui-overarated* ...

[104] Interview with William Mayaka, October 5, 2015 at Villa Rosa Hotel, Nairobi.

[105] Ali A. Mazrui, "The Re-inventing of Africa: Edward Said, V.Y. Mudimbe, and Beyond," *Research in African Literatures*, Vol. 36, No. 3 (Fall 2005), p. 73.

[106] Ali A. Mazrui, "Ibn Khaldun Modernized: Between Nationalism and Globalization," Paper prepared for presentation in Istanbul, Turkey, September 27-28, 2013.

[107] Macharia Munene, *Historical Reflections on Kenya: Intellectual Adventurism, Politics, and International Relations* (Nairobi: University of Nairobi Press, 2012), p. 60.

[108] Ali A. Mazrui, "Wole Soyinka as Television Critic: a Parable of Deception," *Transition*, No. 54, 1991, p. 177.

[109] Wole Soyinka, "Remembering Mazrui," *Transition*, Issue 117, 2015, pp. 192-193.

Ali Mazrui's Islamic Studies: Defending Oppressed Muslims, Reforming Islamic Thought

Ahmed Ali Salem

Introduction: Ali Mazrui Whom You May Not Know

Professor Ali Mazrui was a giant sage of multiple faces. Many recognize him as a scholar of Africa, while others identify him as a scholar of Islamic studies which, in the American academic tradition, broadly include not only Islamic religion and theology but also Islamic history, society and politics (Ahmad *et al.* 2012, especially chaps. 2 and 3). However, while the latter group is well aware of Mazrui's scholarship in African studies, the former group is hardly familiar with his Islamic studies achievements, some of which are in order.

Mazrui's highly esteemed contributions to Islamic studies earned him a special status in the Islamic studies circles and Muslim communities in the West where he lived most of his life. Thus, he was appointed the Ibn Khaldun Professor-at-Large and a Board member at the Graduate School of Islamic and Social Sciences, Virginia, USA (1997-2001); the President of the Association of Muslim Social Scientists (AMSS – later renamed the North American Association of Islamic and Muslim Studies) for two terms from 2007 to 2011; and the Editor-in-Chief of the American Journal of Islamic Social Sciences (AJISS) from 2009 till his death in 2014. He also served as the first Chairman of the Washington-based Center for the Study of Islam and Democracy; a member of the Board of Trustees of the Oxford Center for Islamic Studies, UK, from 2009 till his death; and a member of the academic council of the Prince Alwaleed Bin Talal Center for Muslim-Christian Understanding at Georgetown University, USA. In 2011, he received the International Institute of Islamic Thought (IIIT) Distinguished Scholar Award for his lifetime, distinguished contributions to scholarly work on Islam and Muslim world affairs and his outstanding service to the American

Muslim community as an engaged public intellectual and a strong voice – with unrivalled courage – in defense of the oppressed and the pursuit of justice. He also received the AMSS (UK) first Lifetime Achievement Award in 2000 (Nyang 2015: 24-29; IIIT.org, October 2014).

In a previous work (Salem 2001: 63-101), I counted more than a hundred of Mazrui's publications on various Islamic issues in Africa and globally, and in a recent article (Salem 2016: 44-60), I established that Mazrui's interest in studying Islam was originally part of his general exploration of post-colonial Africa. Though trained in mainstream political science which emphasizes materialism, he quickly realized that culture is a powerful key to understand politics. It was from this cultural optic that Mazrui began to interpretatively revive Islam as a powerful factor in African politics and highlight Islamic values as capable of improving African conditions. His most celebrated work, namely, the 1986 television series *Africa: The Triple Heritage*, was in part a call to reconsider Islam as a major foundation of African societies. His cultural studies helped him gain new constituencies among the larger Muslim *Ummah* (i.e. global community). His global studies upheld Islam against both Marxism and racism, and helped him escape the narrowness of Afrocentrism and broaden his concept of Pan-Africanism to include not only sub-Saharan Africans but also their Arab neighbors to the North and the East and diasporic Africans. In the West, Mazrui attempted to correct many misunderstandings of Islam and demonstrate its closeness to, and impacts on, Western civilization and modern societies in several ways: Islam is a monotheist religion like Judaism and Christianity, has preserved and added to the Greco-Roman legacies, preceded Mercantilism and Capitalism in hailing free trade and hard work, and modelled the Western view of a tripartite world in the second half of the twentieth Century.

In this chapter, I focus on other aspects of Mazrui's Islamic scholarship, namely, his analysis of the tensions between Muslims and the West, and his efforts to reform Islamic thought and rid it of the social traditions that do not conform to true Islamic teachings.

Understanding Muslim-Western tensions

Mazrui believed that the current tensions between Muslims and the West are not inevitable. He once dreamed of an international religious order based on economic cooperation between Muslims and the West. Muslims are oil-producers and technology-consumers, while the West is the vice versa, and therefore an international religious order would be based on the exchange of Muslim oil and Western technology (Mazrui 1978: 129-145; Mazrui 1988: 145). However, several factors resulted in the current tensions between Muslims and the West.

According to Mazrui, Muslims have been victims of the West both politically and culturally. In terms of politics, Muslim states have been targets of Western colonialism and neo-colonialism throughout the twentieth century. Mazrui (1996c/1998: 55) noted that most Muslim countries were subjected to 'the collective empire of the West,' officially in the first half of the twentieth century and informally later on. Informal subjugation was no more benign, though, as Muslims were the West's first military victims after the Vietnam War. According to Mazrui (1994a: 531):

> About half a million have been killed by the West or Western-subsidized initiatives since the Vietnam War. Palestinians, Libyans, Iraqis, and Lebanese are among the casualties. Since World War II, far more Muslims have been killed by the West than have citizens of the former Warsaw Pact, from the Suez War of 1956 to the Gulf War of 1991."

Western aggression against Muslims has not always been direct. Mazrui (1996d: 95-99) noted a clear example of indirect aggression, that is, the Western unconditional support to Israel. While Britain sponsored the partition of Palestine that gave birth to the Zionist state, France assisted it in building its nuclear capabilities, and the United States continued to provide it with all sorts of economic, political and military support. Another indirect aggression has been through the United Nations, which Mazrui considered as a main international organization that the West uses for its own interests, particularly for legitimizing its 'informal collective empire'. This is not unexpected, given that the United Nations represents the West more than the entire globe. Mazrui (1998a: 7-8) wrote:

> The UN, as a supposedly global institution, represents states and regions, but does not try to represent civilizations. Six out of the past seven UN secretaries-general have come from Christian traditions, yet the Christian world contains only about one-fifth of the world population. … The UN was formed primarily by the victors of World War II, all of whom belonged to one and one-half civilizations. Britain, the United States, France, and the European part of the Soviet Union all belonged to Western civilization. …one major function of the UN was to help keep the peace according to the principles of international law. The law of

nation was itself a child of European diplomatic history and statecraft. It once used to be the law of Christian nations.

From a cultural point of view, Islam is seriously misunderstood by many Westerners, thus leading to Islamophobia. Mazrui (1997a: 102) found one of the Eurocentric biases of Islamophobia is the *harem* bias because Islam is believed to be a sexist culture. However, he argued, only a small fraction of total Muslims may be sexist. On the other hand, Pakistan and Bangladesh have taken the lead in empowering Muslim women to the highest political offices in the land. As Mazrui (1997b: 122) noted, they are ahead of the United States in this regard:

> The United States, the largest and most influential Western nation, has never had a female president. In contrast, two of the most populous Muslim countries, Pakistan and Bangladesh, have had women prime ministers: Benazir Bhutto headed two governments in Pakistan, and Khaleda Zia and Hasina Wajed served consecutively in Bangladesh. Turkey has had Prime Minister Tansu Ciller. Muslim countries are ahead in female empowerment, though still behind in female liberation.

Another example of misunderstanding is the case of Salman Rushdie's Islam-defaming novel of *The Satanic Verses*. While the West celebrated the novel in the name of freedom of expression and creativity, Muslims protested, sometimes violently, against it. For Mazrui (1994: 83), this debate was a classic case of the dialogue of the deaf between Westerners and Muslims. Westerners were bewildered by the depth of Muslim anger, and Muslims were shocked by Western insensitivity. While Westerners failed to realize that the most sacred in Islam is the religious, Muslims failed to realize that the most sacred in the West is the political.

This novel was also a classic case of Western double standard in dealing with cultural rights and responsibilities. While the West defended freedom of expression, and therefore protested against the many Muslim countries that banned the novel, the practice of censoring was not unknown in modern Western societies. Mazrui (1997b: 123) reminded us that:

> Western intellectuals argued that as an artist, Rushdie had the sacred right and even duty to go wherever his imagination led him in his writing. Yet until the 1960s *Lady Chatterley's Lover* was regarded as morally repugnant under British law for daring to depict an affair between a married member of the gentry and a worker on the estate.

Mazrui himself was a victim of such practice when his metaphorical description of Karl Marx as the last of the great Jewish prophets in the 1986 television series *The Africans* was censored in the United States.

The West also betrays its own doctrine of pluralism and, in Mazrui's (1997b: 120) words, fails to live up to its liberal mythology when it persists in Westernizing the world. He (1990a: 219) indicated that:

> Although in doctrine Western culture favors pluralism and diversity... its impact on the cultures of the world has been homogenizing; it has been anti-pluralist in consequence. Cultures are enfeebled by the impact of the West upon them and some are actually dying away.

Mazrui (1996c/1998: 84-86) noted that Westernization in the Muslim world in particular was so intensive that it affected many aspects of Muslim societies, including the adoption of European-modeled nation-states; the increasing use of Western technology and languages; the Western-styled educational system that successfully replaces traditional schools; the Western media that overwhelmingly distributes news, information and entertainment; and the Christian calendar and Western men dress that have become very common in the Muslim world.

Muslims in the West in particular are increasingly persuaded or forced to Westernize and abandon their cultures. They sometimes have to support Islamic-hostile values as a part of a larger value package. Mazrui (1996a: 498; 1996b: 246-247) gave the example of elections in the United States where Muslims have to choose between the Republican values, which are socially Islamic-friendly but politically Islamic-hostile, and the Democratic values, which are politically Islamic-friendly but socially Islamic-hostile:

> While American secularism (separating church from state) is good news for Muslims, American libertarianism (such as the latest debate as to whether same-sex marriages should be legally recognized countrywide as they already are in Hawaii) is bad news for Islam. The Democratic Party in the United States is more insistent on separating church from state, including opposition to prayer in schools. This draws some Muslim parents towards the Democrats, since Muslim parents do not want their children to be under peer pressure to attend Christian prayers. On the other hand, the Republicans are stronger in support of traditional family values and in opposition to sexual libertarianism. This draws many Muslims (especially immigrant Asians) to the Republican Party.

Westernization continues currently under the new attractive title of globalization, in whose name the West homogenizes and hegemonies the world. Mazrui (1990b: 2-3) articulated:

> Homogenization is increasing similarity. The second accompanying characteristic of globalization is hegemonization, by which I mean the paradoxical concentration of power in a particular country or civilization … With globalization, there has arisen an increasing similarity between and among different societies. However, this trend has been accompanied by a disproportionate share of global power among a few countries.

Mazrui (1990a: 224-225) called upon Muslims to stop the West from destroying pluralism and diversity while singing tribute to them.

> There is a heavy responsibility on the shoulders of Islam as the one culture that clearly produces rebels against Western hegemony … It is the vanguard against Western cultural hegemony. Whenever we complain about Muslim fundamentalists, let us remember that that is a term which describes a rebellious mood against being assimilated by this majority culture in the world.

But the West hardly listens to Muslim protests against its cultural and political colonialism as it hardly listened to Marxist protests against its economic colonialism. Disappointed of the West's cultural insensitivity, Muslim rage sometimes explodes, such as in the popular revolution in Iran which shocked the deaf West (Mazrui 1990b:116, 126-128). Mazrui (1993: 527-531) found Muslims increasingly willing to stand up to the West. While they were objects of history in the first half of the twentieth century, they emerged as shapers of history in the second half of the twentieth century. He gave two clear examples of Muslims shaping history: the first is Algeria's independence war (1954-1962) which resulted in a new constitutional order in France and thus a new history of Europe, and the second is Afghanistan's independence war (1979-1990) which resulted in the collapse of the Soviet imperial will, followed by the Soviet Union and the old world order along with it.

Muslim resistance to Western colonialism and Westernization is not always that obvious; rather, it is sometimes very subtle. For instance, Muslim "pro-fertility" is partly a distrust of the forces of Westernization in the Muslim world. Mazrui (1994b: 125-126) explained:

> Modern forms of contraception like condoms and intrauterine devices are identified as part of the Western culture of family planning. The financial and moral support that family planning clinics in Africa receive from sources deepens fundamentalists' distrust of Western-style contraception. The international family planning campaign, especially when backed by such citadels of Western power as the World Bank, may

be perceived as a subtle invasion of the sanctity of the harem. In the eyes of the militant, contraception becomes a meeting point between the forces of cultural imperialism and the forces of preemptive genocide.

Although Mazrui generally appreciated Muslim resistance to Western cultural and political colonialism, he called upon Muslims to learn from certain Western values to reform and renew their understanding of true Islamic teachings. In a recent article (Salem 2016: 44-60), I gave examples of Mazrui's insights on polygamy, slavery and economy. In the next section, I discuss his insights on punctuality, mobility, and liberty in gender relations and governance.

Liberating Islam from social traditions

Mazrui's efforts for reforming Islamic thought can be traced to three distinct but related origins: his Islamic faith which calls for reform as a continuous process necessary to understand and implement God's revelation in new contexts, his family's scholarly and practical efforts to reestablish Islamic practices in East Africa in the face of then dominant social customs deemed un-Islamic, and his eclecticism which synthesized and utilized Islamic and Western values.

According to God's revelation in the Quran, reform is highly valued as the mission of old prophets, and reformers will be surely rewarded (S. 7:170, S. 11:88). Prophet Muhammad once said, "God will send to this *ummah* (i.e. Muslim community) at the head of each century those who will renew its faith." Renewal is needed to bring about a regeneration of authentic faith because, over time, Muslims depart from the Straight Path of the Quran and the Prophet's sayings and actions (Voll 1983: 33). This prophetic saying should not be understood as restricting the renewal process temporarily to the head of a century because faith must be rejuvenated whenever it seems obsolete. If renewal was necessary every century in old generations, due to the relatively slow pace of social changes, which make established religious practices appear outdated, renewal is now needed more frequently, perhaps every generation, because social changes occur more rapidly. Similarly, the above-mentioned prophetic saying does not make renewal a concern of only Muslims, because it should be interpreted in light of the Qur'anic verses that treat all prophets and their followers as belonging to one community: "Verily, this *ummah* of yours is a single *ummah* and I am your Lord" (S. 21: 92; S. 23: 52). Thus, renewal is expected to impact all believers and people of faith. In this sense, all prophets, having delivered the same message, "Serve Allah and eschew evil" (S. 16: 36), might be considered revivalists of God's one and true religion (Salem and Khafagy 2000: 1).

At the core of reform and renewal is a call for individual and communal efforts to return to the basic fundamentals of Islam as presented in the Quran and the Prophet's sayings and actions (Voll 1983: 32-33). Other sources for judgement and guidance may be helpful but do not have to be followed, especially if they are associated with un-Islamic practices. In this case, they must be rejected or at least ignored. Hence, reformers are unbound by the views and rulings of earlier teachers or the ideas and interpretations that emerged after the time of the Prophet and his companions. This process of independent and informed analysis of the Islamic authentic sources is called *ijtihad* (Voll 1983: 37-38), and aims at applying the basic fundamentals of Islam, which were ignored or misunderstood over time, in addressing the particular issues of each community. Thus, Islam is reintroduced as relevant for each generation (Salem and Khafagy 2000: 4).

Muslim reformers practiced *ijtihad* with varying degrees of success and effectiveness, until it became badly needed with the increasing modernization of Muslim societies in the nineteenth century and onward. A discussion of reform and renewal erupted as never before in all Muslim metropoles, bringing to the fore issues of identity, women, the state, social traditions, text and reason, and Islam and the West (Nafi 2004: 28). According to Saeed (2006: 134), "the modern context demanded a reappraisal of the intellectual heritage of Muslims and this meant giving up the blind imitation of early scholars." Some Muslim reformers went even further to reformulate Islam and reinterpret its texts "in ways that are supportive of the tenets of modern life" (Kamrava 2006: 15). In the African context, a prominent but tragic example is the Sudanese intellectual Mahmoud Muhammad Taha whose interpretation of Islam was not confined to the literal meanings of its texts, which he contended less sacred than human dignity and freedom (Hamrour 2016: 76). Under Numeri, he was convicted of blasphemy and sentenced to death (Al-Jazouli 2016: 71).

Mazrui's ancestors were among the foremost advocates of reform in East Africa. For example, his patrimonial grandfather, Sheikh Ali bin Abdalla Mazrui (1825-1894), was the pioneering role model of the East Africa Muslim reformers (Baalawy 2013: 9-19). He spent nine years with his father, sheikh Abdalla bin Nafi Mazrui, studying in Mecca where they converted to the *Shafi'i* mainstream school of jurisprudence. Upon his return, Sheikh Ali imparted the knowledge he had acquired to as many people as possible and as far as he could reach, making mosques institutions of learning. He visited many urban and rural centers from the Kenyan coast to Zanzibar and Pemba, thus spreading *Shafisim* in East Africa. He embarked on a reform agenda with zeal and "created a paradigm shift in practice and understanding of Islam [that] was virtually a total shift in approach from the conservative mode of earlier scholars of the East African coast." For example, unlike most scholars who tolerated local traditional beliefs, including those against the fundamentals of Islam, hoping not to attract the wrath of the elite in their respective societies, Sheikh Ali challenged "the status quo of both the Sultanate's creed of *Ibadhism* and the local traditional norms of Islamic practice." In addition, he neither confined his classes to a select group nor segregated students according to their racial or ethnic backgrounds which was then a prevalent tradition. Therefore, he was able to attract many students and produced scholars who later became reformers in their own rights.

One of those scholars was Mazrui's matrimonial grandfather, sheikh Suleiman bin Ali Mazrui (1867-1937), who became the judge of Mombasa (1910-1932), then the Chief Judge of Kenya (1932-1937). Through him, Mazrui's father, sheikh Al-Amin bin Ali Mazrui was raised, trained, then became the trainer of the next generation of reformers in East Africa. He articulated reformist ideas in booklets and a weekly pamphlet that carried the Arabic title *Al-Islah*, which literally means reform, and replaced his mentor and father-in-law as the chief judge of Kenya till his death in 1947 (Baalawy 2013: 21-24; Baalawy 2005). Mazrui greatly admired his father's original thinking, intellectual prowess, courage of conviction, and power of will. He noted with appreciation his father's role as a social reformer, including his efforts to abolish certain practices of East African Muslims, such as the excess in religious rituals and extravagance in such social traditions as weddings. Nevertheless, Mazrui was not at ease with other elements of his father's reform, such as his harsh attack on the "heresies" of the then growing Ahmadiyya movement, and intolerance towards homosexuality. Perhaps, that is why Mazrui described his father as "both a modernist and traditionalist" (Mazrui 1999). Indeed, the difference between the father's and the son's ideas lies in that buzzword of modernism. While the father's model of reform was purely Islamic, the son's was hybrid: Islamic and Western.

Modernity provided Muslims with not only a challenge and a stimulation to change as discussed earlier, but also an alternative route to reform based on modern Western philosophies, ideologies and experiences, not basic Islamic fundamentals. Consequently, in the context of Muslim societies, the term reform is sometimes ambiguous and needs a qualification: Islamic or Western. Hence the dichotomy between Islamic revivalism and Western modernization (or Westernization). However, Mazrui attempted to demonstrate this dichotomy as unnecessary because at least some Islamic and Western values are perfectly compatible. His position is based on eclecticism, which he defined as "synthesizing and utilizing values from different traditions" (Makinda 2016).

Take for example the Islamic and Western values encouraging punctuality and mobility. Mazrui (1985: 823-833) noted that, "strictly speaking, Islam was all set to inaugurate a revolution in time among its converts [but] the revolution in the discipline of time succeeded strictly within the religious domain." Islam's discipline of time is related to Islamic rituals, such as the five prayers of the day, which are spaced out across the twenty-four hours with a good deal of precision; the fast of Ramadhan, which is also prescribed with precision from the hours before dawn to sunset; and the pilgrimage to Mecca, which has a precise week in the year and its different steps are carefully tamed within the rituals of the *Hajj*. However:

> "Both the Arab world and Africa have had to await the greater impatience of Western civilization before the ethos of punctuality could be secularized. Even then, the West has failed to make Africa observe the clock with the same attentiveness with which it observed the clock under Islamic stimulation."

On mobility, Mazrui (1998b: 18-20) was confident that the new technology of the Internet and the World Wide Web will give Muslims a chance to realize Islam's original aim of killing distance. Islam is a religion which has always celebrated both movement and direction, and each of its three holy cities signifies different levels of the death of distance: Mecca is the direction of the daily five prayers and the city of the annual pilgrimage; Medina was the destination of Prophet Muhammad's momentous migration from Mecca; and Jerusalem is the city to which the Prophet moved from Mecca in a single night in the age of travel by camel, and the city from which he ascended from Earth to the heavens during the same night.

Another area of convergence between true Islamic and modern Western values is women's right to work and accumulate wealth freely. Mazrui (1993: 515) noted that:

> Prophet Muhammad's first wife was not only 'a working woman' but also his employer. Muhammad happily worked for a woman, sought her advice, and she was the first person to whom he brought his doubts about the revelation he had in the cave.

Mazrui (1997b: 121) also asserted that "Islamic law has always allocated shares from every inheritance to both daughters and sons. Primogeniture has been illegal under the sharia for fourteen centuries." On the other hand, Mazrui (1998b: 22-23) condemned "the tradition of the harem which has been in existence since the Abbasid dynasty in many Muslim societies," but was again confident that it will not survive the information technology which will revive egalitarian Islamic values:

> More and more information may refuse to be susceptible to gender-discrimination ... The traditional forms of seclusion of women will not long survive a technology in which women can declare their presence and in time assert their rights.

Islam, he stressed, promotes freedom, which is necessary for human dignity, but at the same time opposes the immoral excesses of libertarianism. (Mrani 2016: 79-94). Mazrui's call for applying true Islamic teachings to liberate women from social traditions echoed the efforts of such renown reformers as sheikh Muhammad Abdu and Rasheed Reda of the early twentieth-century Egypt. Reda, for example, confirmed that Islamic law treats men and women as equal human beings and urges women to take part in all social and political activities of their communities (Salem 2014: 18-20).

Governance is another, though more controversial, area where Mazrui (1990b: 23-25, 35-36) found modern Western experiences helpful in ridding Islam from traditions. He believed that Islamic polity turned into a theocracy, or a God-focused system, because the thorough Islamic monotheism was "translated into an earthly quest for Muslim solidarity and a distrust of dissent among believers." He thus urged Muslims to learn from the English experience of democratizing a theocracy, or converting it into a people-focused system. "What the English have demonstrated is that theocracy can be democratized first by making democracy stronger and later by making the theocracy weaker". In a democratic Islamic polity, Mazrui (1993: 531) argued, governments should be accountable to not only God but also the people, the concept of *Ummah* should be localized in an electoral constituency rather than a diffuse one billion Muslims in different states of the world, and Muslim women should be full participants.

While Mazrui's observation on the impact of Islamic monotheism on distrust of dissent is accurate, as evident in the writings of such distinguished scholars of Islam as Al-Faruqi (1982, chap. 10), the English model of democratizing a theocracy implies more than making rulers accountable, constituencies local, and women full participants; it also means secularization, which hardly has a solid basis in Islam's authentic sources (Salem and Khafagy 2002), thus eliminates the possibility of what Mazrui (2009: 49-51) called *Shariacracy*, or rule of Islamic law. Nevertheless, a closer look at Mazrui's view proves that he did not oppose Islamic law; rather, he was against upholding obsolete and fallible interpretations of God's infallible law. He called explicitly for reopening the door of *ijtihad*:

> What is crucial is that human interpreters should not act as if they are in direct communication with Allah. Humans should always allow for their fallibility while interpreting the Shari'ah. For the Shari'ah to survive ..., the door of *ijtihad* (judicial review) would have to be reopened.

Mazrui's reference to the two divine and human levels of Islamic law resembles to some extent the contemporary Turkish reformer Fethullah Gulen's (2006: 100) distinction between Islam's immutable fundamental principles and changing worldly aspects, and hence his conviction that Islam only orients "a government general character, leaving it to the people to choose the type and form of government according to time and circumstances."

Conclusion

Ali Mazrui was a full-fledged scholar of Muslim world affairs. He addressed its social and political concerns, with an eye on reforming Muslim thoughts and practices and improving conditions of Muslim interactions with the West. This twofold mission might seem self-contradictory, as it implies that Muslims should resist Westernization and, at the same time, accept certain Western values, especially those which help revive true Islamic teachings. However, this view ignores the principled and ethical foundation of Mazrui's standpoint, which can be described, in the Qur'anic words (S. 3:102), as commanding good and forbidding wrong – a duty entrusted by God to all Muslims to the extent of their capacities (Cook 2003: 11-12). Hence, Mazrui called for justice and condemned injustice regardless of the identities of the oppressed and the oppressor, thus adhering to fairness as prescribed in the following the Qur'anic verse: "O you who believe! stand out firmly for Allah, as witnesses to fair dealing, and let not the hatred of others to you make you swerve to wrong and depart from justice. Be just: that is next to piety: and fear Allah. For Allah is well-acquainted with all that you do" (S. 5:8).

Mazrui did not only prescribe certain Western values to Muslims but also the vice versa. Indeed, he invited Westerners to take advantage of certain Islamic teachings in order to rid themselves of moral evils and social crises. For example, Islam provides avenues of sobriety that can minimize drunkenness and drug addiction – two main ills of Western societies. He stressed the importance of this value in the light of predominant individualism that prevents the state from infringing on individuals' rights, even if they pose a danger to themselves or to others (Mazrui 1993: 533). Mazrui (1998b: 8-9) alerted Westerners to the Islamic values which restrained Muslims and prevented them from committing some of the worst crimes in modern history:

> Muslims are often criticized for not producing the best, but they are seldom congratulated for having standards of behavior which have averted the worst. There are really no Muslim equivalents of systematic Nazi extermination camps, nor Muslim conquest by genocide on the scale perpetrated by Europeans in the Americas and Australia, nor Muslim versions of rigid apartheid once approved by the South African Dutch Reformed Church, nor Muslim equivalents of the brutal racism of Japan before the end of World War II, nor Muslim equivalents of Pol Pot's killing fields in Cambodia, nor a Muslim equivalent of the racist lynching culture of the old South in the United States, nor a Muslim version of Stalinist terror in the name of Five Year Plans. Nor can Islam be blamed for the only world wars in human history.

References

Ahmad, M., Bukhari, Z. and Nyang, S., eds. (2012). *Observing the Observer: The State of Islamic Studies in American Universities*. London and Washington, D.C.: The International Institute of Islamic Thought.

Al-Faruqi, I. (1982). *Tawhid: Its Implications for Thought and Life.* Wyncote, PA: International Institute of Islamic Thought.

Al-Jazouli, M. (2016). (in Arabic) Mahmoud and Mahmoud: Two Strangers in Two Worlds. *Al-Hadatha* [*Modernity*], 2, pp. 70-72.

Baalawy, G. (2005). *Sh. Al-Amin b. Ali Mazrui (1891-1947): His Life and Times.* [online] Available at: *http://www.academia.edu/9317317/Sh._Al-Amin_b._Ali_Mazrui_1891-1947_-_His_Life_and_Times* [Accessed 4 August 2016].

Baalawy, G. (2013). *Sh. Ali bin Abdalla bin Nafi' Mazrui (1825-1894): The Pioneering Role Model of the East Africa Muslim Reformers.* Nairobi: Signal Press Ltd.

Cook, M. (2003). *Forbidding Wrong in Islam.* New Jersey: Princeton University.

Gulen, F. (2006). A Comparative Approach to Islam and Democracy. In: M. Kamrava, ed., *The New Voices of Islam: Rethinking Politics and Modernity – A Reader.* Berkeley: University of California Press, pp. 99-104.

Hamrour, Q. (2016). (in Arabic) A Reading of the Republican School and Its Leader. *Al-Hadatha* [*Modernity*], 2, pp. 74-76.

IIIT.org, (October 2014). *IIIT Newsletter: Special Issue on the Late Prof. Ali Mazrui.* [online] Available at: *http://archive.constantcontact.com/fs142/1102818738102/archive/1118769540060.html* [accessed 2 Aug. 2016].

Kamrava, M. (2006). Introduction: Reformist Islam in Comparative Perspective. In: M. Kamrava, ed., *The New Voices of Islam: Rethinking Politics and Modernity – A Reader.* Berkeley: University of California Press, pp. 1-27.

Makinda, S. (2016). Eclecticism as a Theoretical Approach: The Pillar of Ali A. Mazrui's Intellectual Legacy. Paper presented at *Ali A. Mazrui International Symposium*, Nairobi, Kenya, 14-17 July.

Mazrui, Ali A. (1978). Christian Power and Muslim Challenge in Africa's Experience. *Indian Journal of Politics*, 12(3), pp. 129-145.

_____. (1985). Religion and Political Culture in Africa. *Journal of the American Academy of Religion*, 53(3), pp. 817-839.

_____. (1988). African Islam and Competitive Religion: Between Revivalism and Expansion. *Third World Quarterly*, 10, pp. 499-518.

_____. (1990a). The World of Islam: A Political Overview. *Journal Institute of Muslim Minority Affairs*, 11(2), pp. 218-225.

_____. (1990b). *Cultural Forces in World Politics*. London: James Currey; Portsmouth, NH: Heinemann; Nairobi: Heinemann.

_____. (1993). Islam and the End of History. *American Journal of Islamic and Social Sciences*, 10(4), pp. 512-535.

_____. (1994a). Global Apartheid? Race and Religion in the New World Order. In: T. Y. Ismael and J. S. Ismael, eds., *The Gulf War and the New World Order: International Relations of the Middle East*, 1st ed. Gainesville, FL: University Press of Florida, pp. 521-535.

_____. (1994b). Islamic Doctrine and the Politics of Induced Fertility Change: An African Perspective. In: J. L. Finkle and C. A. McIntosh, eds., *The New Politics of Population: Conflict and Consensus in Family Planning*. New York: The Population Council, pp. 121-134.

_____. (1996a). Between the Crescent and the Star-Spangled Banner: American Muslims and US Foreign Policy. *International Affairs*, 72(3), pp. 493-506.

_____. (1996b). Islam in a More Conservative Western World. *American Journal of Islamic and Social Sciences*, 13(2), pp. 246-249.

_____. (1996c). The Imperial Culture of North-South Relation. In: B. Parrott and K. Dawisha, eds., *The International Politics of Eurasia, vol. 9: The End of Empire? The Transformation of the USSR in Comparative Perspective*. New York: M.E. Sharpe. (Translated into Arabic in: Mazrui, Ali A. (1998). *Intellectual Issues: Africa, Islam and the West*. Cairo: Center for African Future Studies, pp. 53-88.)

_____. (1996d). The Nuclear Option and International Justice: Islamic Perspectives. In: N. H. Barazangi, M. R. Zaman and O. Afzal, eds., *Islamic Identity and the Struggle for Justice*. Gainesville, FL: University Press of Florida, pp. 95-116.

_____. (1997a). Islam and Islamophobia: Conflicting Images in a Eurocentric World. In: M. A. Choudhury, M. Z. Abdad and M. S. Salleh, eds., *Islamic Political Economy in Capitalistic-globalization: an agenda for change*. Kula Lumpur: Utusan Publications and Penang: International Project on Islamic Political Economy, Universiti Sains Malaysia.

_____. (1997b). Islamic and Western Values. *Foreign Affairs*, 76(5), pp. 118-132.

_____. (1998a). Globalization, Islam, and the West: Between Homogenization and Hegemonization. *American Journal of Islamic and Social Sciences*, 15(3), pp. 1-14.

_____. (1998b). *Islam, Western Democracy and the Third Industrial Revolution: Conflict or Convergence.* Abu Dhabi: The Emirates Center for Strategic Studies and Research.

_____. (1999). Preface: My Dad, Al-Amin Aly Mazrui: The Man, the Legend and the Moralist. In: G. Baalawy (2005). *Sh. Al-Amin b. Ali Mazrui (1891-1947): His Life and Times.* [online] Available at: *http://www.academia.edu/9317317/Sh._Al-Amin_b._Ali_Mazrui_1891-1947_-_His_Life_and_Times* [Accessed 4 August 2016]. First draft, courtesy of the author.

_____. (2009). *Shariacracy* and Federal Models in the Era of Globalization: Nigeria in a Comparative Perspective. *American Journal of Islamic Social Sciences* 26(3), pp. 41-55.

Mrani, M. (2016). Values and Gender Equality between Islam and the West: Mazrui's struggle for a system of universal values. *American Journal of Islamic and Social Sciences*, 33(3), pp. 79-94.

Nafi, B. (2004). The Rise of Islamic Reformist Thought and Its Challenge to Traditional Islam. In: S. Taji-Farouki and B. Nafi, eds., *Islamic Thought in the Twentieth Century*. London: I.B. Tauris, pp. 28-60.

Nyang, S. (2015). Ali A. Mazrui: A Global African Muslim. *Islamic Horizon*, 44(1), pp. 24-29.

Saeed, A. (2006). *Islamic Thought: An Introduction*. London: Routledge.

Salem, A. (2001). The Islamic Heritage of Mazruiana. In: P. Morewedge, ed., *The Scholar between Thought and Experience: A Bibliographical Festschrift in Honor of Ali Mazrui*. Binghamton, NY: Institute of Global Cultural Studies, pp. 63-101.

_____. (2014). (in Arabic) *Ijtihad, Irshad*, and *Ittihad* in Sheikh Mohammad Rasheed Reda's Reform Thought and Movement. *Rakaiz Marefia [Knowledge Bases]*, 2(1), pp. 1-32.

_____. (2016). Localizing Islam in the West: Mazrui's Journey from the Study of African Politics to Global Cultures. *American Journal of Islamic and Social Sciences*, 33(3), pp. 44-60.

Salem, A. and Khafagy, R. (2000). Islamic Rejuvenation: An Endless Process. *CIMIC Newsletter*, 2(3), p. 1, p. 4.

Salem, A. and Khafagy, R. (2002). (in Arabic) Islamic Political Thought between Reform and Exploitation: Reviewing the Debate on "*Islam and the Bases of Governance.*" *Roua* [*Perspectives*] 23-4, pp. 96-101.

Voll, J. (1983). Renewal and Reform in Islamic History: *Tajdid* and *Islah*. In: J. Esposito, ed., *Voices of Resurgent Islam*. Oxford: Oxford University Press, pp. 32-47.

Who is an African? Reflections on Ali Mazrui's notion of the African

Jideofor Adibe

Introduction

Who is an African? At the face value this will seem like a naive question. Certainly all of us know who the African is, it would seem. However, the answer to this apparently elementary question becomes less obvious once other probing qualifiers are added. How is the African identity constructed in the face of the mosaic of identities that people of African ancestry living within and beyond the continent bear? For instance, is Barack Obama, the 44th President of the United States who has a Kenyan father but a white American mother, African? Is Jerry Rawlings, the former military ruler and former President of Ghana whose father was Scottish and his mother a Black Ghanaian, truly an African? Was the late Bob Marley who passionately sang many redemption songs about Africa but whose father, *Norval Sinclair Marley, a White Jamaican, was originally from Sussex, England,* and his mother, a Black Jamaican, an African? Are all who proclaim themselves Africans accepted as such? Are there levels of Africanness (or Africanity as Mazrui preferred to call it)? And by the way who allots this 'Africanness' and why? How does African identity interface with other levels of identity?

The above are some of the questions one inevitably encounters when one tries to academically delineate who is an African and who is not. How did Mazrui try to grapple with these questions?

My interest in Mazrui's notion of who is an African

As a young undergraduate student at the University of Nigeria, Nsukka, in the 1980s, we were exposed to the works of Ali Mazrui. One of our lecturers, Professor Okwudiba Nnoli, was at the University of Dar-es-Salam when Mazrui was at the University of Makerere. Professor Nnoli would tell us of Mazrui's epic debate with the late Walter Rodney of *How Europe Underdeveloped Africa* fame (Rodney 1972). Most of us admired Mazrui for his firm grasp of the English language and for the fact that it was impossible to read any of his works without coming out with several memorable and quotable quotes.

While we admired Mazrui, many of our lecturers were very critical of his works. They were especially critical of what they called his weakness in theory construction and the fact that he often shied away from staying long enough on a theme to mature with the discussions in that field. For this reason, some also called his writings journalistic or polemical while others rejected him as a political scientist. We thought they were jealous of his global stature and command of the English language. When, in my later years as an undergraduate, I read Mazrui's satire, *The Trial of Christopher Okigbo* (1972) where Mazrui, in a fictional Hereafter, found Okigbo guilty of sacrificing his art as a poet to fight with his people in the short lived Biafra, I felt Mazrui got it all wrong. I believed and still believe that to subordinate your community to your art is to celebrate art for art's sake. A writer's community is precedent to his art. The late Christopher Okigbo died fighting for Biafra.

I later found that while non-academics and non-political scientists were fascinated by Mazrui's works, several political scientists and Africanists were dismissive of him as at best an aloof polemicist with questionable commitment to Africa (Karioki 1974). Other critics accused him of being excessively defensive of the Arabs, including their role in the trans-Saharan slave trade. For instance Pana Press in a report on August 19, 2001, entitled "Kenyan scholar downplays Arab role in slave trade", wrote of him as follows:

> Kenyan historian, Ali Mazrui, has reiterated the view that Africans cannot make a strong case against their enslavement by Arabs in the past centuries because it was not a commercial venture. "You cannot compare the magnitude of the Trans-Saharan trade that involved Arabs with the Atlantic slave trade", Mazrui said in a comment reproduced by Kenyan media ahead of the World Conference Against Racism in the South African port city of Durban. "The latter (Atlantic slave trade) was motivated by capitalism as opposed to the former (Arab slave trade) that was for domestic purposes," he added.

Mazrui was said to have made the statements at a time that Africans were pushing for compensation for both the Trans-Saharan slave trade (which lasted from the 8th to the early 17th century) and the Trans-Atlantic slave trade (15th – 19th centuries). David Horowitz, a conservative American author and policy advocate, had also listed Mazrui among the 101 most dangerous academics in America (Horowitz 2006).

In the United Kingdom in 2004, I founded a journal called *African Renaissance* which, surprisingly, attracted the interest of respected Africanists. It was at a time of talks of African renaissance and a section of the British press was sneering and asking contemptuously on when Africa ever had its 'naissance'. I was introduced to Mazrui by the Ethiopian scholar Mammo Muchie. Mazrui became the editorial adviser to the journal while my publishing company, Adonis & Abbey Publishers, (*www.adonis-abbey.com*) set up a year earlier, became one of his European publishers. In 2009, Mazrui contributed three chapters in a book I edited titled: *Who is an African: Identity, Citizenship and the Making of the Africa-Nation*. The book also included contributions from some of Mazrui's harshest critics such as Bankie Forster Bankien and Kwesi Prah. Most of my discussions of Mazrui's notion of the African will come from his contributions to the book.

Mazrui's notion of Africa

Obviously one cannot talk of the African without a prior conception of what Africa is all about. In the documentary, *Africa: A Triple Heritage*, written and narrated by Ali Mazrui in the early 1980s and jointly produced by the BBC and the Public Broadcasting Service (WETA, Washington) in association with the Nigerian Television Authority, Mazrui argued that Africa (or Africa's identity as we know it) is formed by a triple heritage - an indigenous heritage borne out of time and climate change; the heritage of eurocentric capitalism forced on Africans by European colonialism and the spread of Islam by both jihad and evangelism. The documentary was subsequently published as a book (Mazrui 1986). The implication, for Mazrui, is that since what we call Africa is influenced by a 'triple heritage', African identity could be a mosaic of combinations from these heritages.

In one of the three chapters he contributed to my book (Adibe 2009) entitled: "On the Concept of We are All Africans" Mazrui reflected more on the notion of Africa. He accepted the argument by Herskovits (1960), whom he quoted approvingly, that Africa is a mere geographic fiction, noting that Africa is diverse climatically, ethnically and racially.

As he put it:

> Climatically the range in Africa is from arid deserts to tropical forests; ethnically from the Khoisan to the Semites; linguistically from Amharic to Kidigo. What have all these in common apart from the tyranny of the map maker? (Mazrui 2009a: 35).

In another chapter in the same book, 'Who are Africans?' Mazrui (2009b: 30), elaborated further on this. He argued:

> If Africa invented man in places like the Olduvai Gorge and the Semitic invented God in Jerusalem, Mt. Sinai and Mecca, Europe invented the world at the Greenwich Meridian. It was the Europeans who named all the great continents of the world, all the great oceans, many of the great rivers and lakes and most of the countries.

For Mazrui, Africa and the noun African were mere European inventions. He argued that Europe created the African or consciousness of being African through two processes – the triumph of European cartography and through racism and its related imperialism and neo-imperialism. He further argued that following the triumph of European cartography, which decided on which countries should be lumped together and called whichever name they chose, it was the "humiliation and degradation of Black Africans across the centuries, which contributed to their recognition of each other as 'fellow Africans' (2009b: 30). He equally argued that it was European racism that convinced sub-Saharan Africans that "one of the most relevant criteria of their Africanity was their skin colour" (2009b: 30) because, as he argued, until the coming of the Europeans in the areas of Africa that would later be called sub-Saharan Africa, Blackness was taken relatively for granted. Mazrui also argued that related to racism are imperialism and colonialism which created a sufficient sense of shared identity for the movement of pan Africanism to be born (2009b: 31).

Following from the above, Mazrui believed that what we call African identity or the notion of 'African' is largely a fiction created by European cartography, colonialism, racism and imperialism. The implication of this for him is that any attempt to define Africa, and by extension delineate the African, will inevitably bring one into the tension between Africa being an "accident of history" (different people being lumped together on the say-so of the European powers at the Berlin Conference of 1884-85) and "geographical facts" (because the European cartographers arbitrarily made the choice for groups that are today located in the African continent). As Mazrui (2009a) puts it:

> Geographical facts are as much 'accidents' as historical accidents are facts. In the politics of Africanism, which aspects are really important? (2009a: 36).

Here Mazrui introduced another important element that is often overlooked in the discussion of who is an African – namely that there is often politics in such delineations. Given that Africa and African identity is largely a fiction as Mazrui would argue, it would seem that the question of who allots this Africanness and why has not been given sufficient attention in the discourse on African identity. For instance, in January 2008, the British newspaper, *Guardian Unlimited* proposed a list of the six best African footballers of all time and ranked the Portuguese hero Eusebio at No.1, arguing that though he was a Portuguese international, this was only because it was not feasible for him to represent his "native Mozambique". A blogger Ayo Akinfe immediately begged to differ and challenged any suggestion that Eusebio was African. He argued that though Eusebio was born in Mozambique, that fact alone was not enough to make him an African. As Akinfe (2008) put it:

> I love Eusebio to death and still vividly recollect those mazy runs of his in the 1966 World Cup and his breath-taking displays for Benfica but the fact remains that he is not an African. Yes, Eusebio was born in Maputo but then so too were Carlos Queiroz, Manchester United's assistant manager and Abdel Xavier, the Portugal and LA Galaxy defender who once played for Middlesbrough, Everton and Liverpool...Accident of birth does not make you an African. Nothing in Eusebio's mannerism, interests, charitable activities or community programmes gives the slightest indication that he is vaguely interested in Africa.

Read between the lines, Ayo Akinfe challenged Eusebio's ascribed Africanness not only because of his skin colour but also allegedly because he was not known to have displayed the necessary consciousness of being an African. However, the fact that *The Guardian* considered him an African at all while Akinfe (who probably saw himself as the 'authentic African') begged to differ, clearly illustrates the contentious nature of African identity and the ambiguous role of race in delineating such an identity. An important question here though is whether the decision by *The Guardian* to call Eusebio an African was political? There is also the related question of whether identity is an imposition. For instance, did Eusebio see himself as African?

An insight into how politics could play a role in the formation or imposition of African identity was Mazrui's approving quotation of what Gamal Abdel Nasser, the second President of Egypt, (1956-1970) who supported the anti-colonial movements in sub-Saharan Africa was said to have told his countrymen to justify his support of the African freedom fighters:

> ... we cannot in anyway stand aside, even if we wish to, from the sanguinary and dreadful struggle now raging in the continent between five million Whites and two hundred million Africans. We cannot do so for one principal reason, *we ourselves are in Africa* (Quoted in Mazrui 2009a: 38, emphasis mine).

It is interesting to note that in the above quote, Nasser did not say they could not stand aside from the raging anti-colonial struggles because "we are Africans" but because "we ourselves are in Africa", implying that the Egyptians perceived themselves to be non-Africans despite being located in Africa.

We can further argue, following from the above, that the use of consciousness to delineate the African – as Nasser seemed to have done in his message to his fellow countrymen to justify his support of the anti-colonial movements- recreates the African both as an ideology and as a geographic fiction. Nasser felt compelled to support the liberation movements in sub-Saharan Africa because "we ourselves are in Africa". Does this affinity with Africa make Nasser an African on the same level of Africanity as, say, the late Kwame Nkrumah from Ghana, who famously popularised the notion of "we are all Africans?" Mazrui's answer to this question was:

> Nasser was an Egyptian in a deeper sense historically than Nkrumah was a Ghanaian but he was an African in a shallower sense emotionally than Nkrumah was an African. The continental feeling built up by colonialism was more emphatic in Africa south of the Sahara than it ever was either in north of the Sahara or Asia (Mazrui 2009a: 39).

If both Nasser and Nkrumah were Africans by different parameters, does it mean that there should be a hierarchy of Africans based on the parameter that qualifies one most to be called African? Here Mazrui seems to answer this in the affirmative by arguing that "the very term 'Africanism' seems to imply that geography matters more since "Africa is a geographic designation", which made the people who inhabit that geographic space to develop a new consciousness of "geographical contiguities." He further argued that when people who are manifestly dissimilar in ethnicity and race proclaims "we are all Africans, it may be no more than recognition of geographical fact" (2009a: 37).

In other words, for Mazrui, anyone from a country which European cartographers determined to be in Africa is by that fact alone, of a higher Africanity than possessors of other taxonomies for delineating the African. This position obviously contradicts Mazrui's position on another paper, 'Comparative Africanity: Blood, Soil and Ancestry' (Mazrui 2009c), which we shall discuss later.

Africa: A geographic fiction?

It may be germane to interrogate Mazrui's notion that Africa is a fiction created by European cartography, racism, imperialism and neo-imperialism. While Mazrui may have been factually right, his notion of Africa in this sense is static. One could argue that if Africa is a fiction, so also are several successful modern nations like Germany and France which at different points in their history were made up of different peoples and principalities. Essentially, therefore, Mazrui's notion of 'Africa' and the 'African' as fictions created by Europeans appears to have ossified history in time and space because several countries that are today successful were once diverse and geographic fictions. On the other hand, groups that are culturally homogenous such as Somalia have not exactly shown the sort of cohesiveness that such homogeneity ought to bring. In essence, therefore, Mazrui's emphasis on the differential influences on Africa gives the wrong impression that cultural and linguistic homogeneity are prerequisites for successful nation-building.

Mazrui's delineation of the African

From his theoretical notions of Africa and the African, Mazrui in an article on 'Comparative Africanity: Blood, Soil and Ancestry', (Mazrui 2009c), sought to move into the more empiric exercise of how to delineate or identify the African. Here Mazrui tried to identify different types of Africans. He identified the following:

Africans of the blood: Mazrui argued that these are defined in "racial and genealogical terms" and are identified with the Black race.

Africans of the soil: These are, according to him, defined in geographical terms and are "identified with the African continent in nationality and ancestral location" (Mazrui 2009c: xi). Following from this Mazrui argued that most Diaspora Libyans, Egyptians and Tunisians are Africans of the soil but not necessarily of the blood. He also argued that most Diaspora Africans in the United States, the Caribbean or Brazil are Africans of the blood but not of the soil and that most Ghanaians, Nigerians or Ugandans are both Africans of the blood (genealogically belonging to the African race) and Africans of the soil (geographically located in or belonging to the African continent).

Largely because Mazrui believed that there are different types of Africans, he posed the question of who should be called the first African Secretary-General of the United Nations – Kofi Anan, a Black Ghanaian or the late Boutros Boutros-Ghali, a fair skinned Egyptian? Mazrui argued that Boutros-Ghali was an African of the soil but since he was descended from the Copts, he was as indigenous to Africa geographically as Kofi Annan. However, he argued that Boutros-Ghali could not qualify as an African of the blood since he was not racially Black. For Mazrui, therefore, Kofi Annan was the first Black Secretary-General of the United Nations from any country while Boutros-Ghali was the first African Secretary-General of the United Nations.

An interesting question here is: since Kofi Annan is both African of the soil and of the blood while Boutros Ghali is only African of the soil, does that mean that in the hierarchy of Africanity, Kofi Annan is more African than Boutros-Ghali?

Africans of the soil by adoption: Mazrui regarded White Africans such as F.W. de Klerk as 'Africans of the soil by adoption'. He said this also applied to East Africans of Indian or Pakistani ancestry.

African-Americans and American-Africans: Mazrui made a distinction between African-Americans and American-Africans: He argued that when you talk of African-Americans, the noun is on American, and then to the question, "what kind of American?" the answer becomes, "African-American". In the same vein, he argued that when you talk of American-Africans, the noun is on African and refers to African immigrants in the USA. He argued that unlike the African-American, the 'American-African', is conscious of his indigenous Africanity, is aware of his immediate continental ancestry, is in contact with relatives in Africa, is bilingual (speaking at least one African language) and is at home with much aspects of indigenous African culture such as cuisine (for instance foo-foo for West Africa, matoke for Uganda, sima or ugali for Tanzania and Kenya, and so forth).

Mazrui argued that unlike the American-Africans, most African-Americans are descendants of the Middle Passage, are not in contact with relatives in Africa, are not native speakers of the African language and are seldom socialised into African cuisines even when they are pan African (Mazrui 2009c: xi).

Following from the above, Mazrui argued that Barack Obama has an intermediate identity between being an African-American and American-African. He argued that the young Barack Obama did not know his Kenyan father well because he last saw him when he was about ten years old. However, Obama established contacts with the village of his father's birth and with his Kenyan half siblings and other African relatives. In this sense, Mazrui argued that Obama was closer to the identity of American-Africans but because he has no command of either Luo or Swahili languages and has not been socialised into indigenous African cuisines, he is culturally "almost totally American except for his considerable exposure to multiculturalism in both Indonesia and Hawaii. In this sense, he is a well-travelled African-American rather than an American-African" (Mazrui 2009c: xii).

Afrabians: Mazrui talked about the remarkable history of convergence between the Arabs and the Africans and noted that when the Arab conquest of Egypt occurred in the 7th Century, Egyptians were neither Arabs nor Muslims and their mother tongue was not Arabic and their religion was not Islam. He argued that today there are more than 100 million Arab Muslims in North Africa, which has created a new identity he called 'Afrabians'. He defined this group as "Africans of the soil in North Africa who are Arab without intermarriage with Africans of the blood ("Black Africans" (2009c: xiii).

Mazrui argued that if a "Diaspora Black like Obama is a bridge between Africans of the blood in Africa and those in the Diaspora", a new identity, "Afrabians", has developed in Africa as "a bridge between Africans of the soil of Arab lineage (like Boutros-Ghali and Muammar Qaddafi) and Africans of the soil who are Black (like Kwame Nkrumah and Kofi Annan" (Mazrui 2009c: xii-xiii).

For Mazrui the forces which created Afrabians across the centuries included the spread of the Arabic language into Africa, the spread of the Islamic religion across Africa, the migration, inter-marriage and intermingling between Arab and African peoples across time and the trade and economic integration between the Arabs and Africans as well as the political penetration of Africa by the Arabs. He talked about the silent convergence between African peoples and the Arabs slowly transforming two populations, which were once distinct into a newly integrated force in world affairs. "Africans of the soil and Africans of the blood were converging into more and more comprehensive identities" (Mazrui 2009c: xv).

Mazrui identified different types of Afrabians:

Geographical Afrabians: Africans of the soil in North Africa who are Arab without intermarriage with Africans of the blood (Black Africans).

Genealogical Afrabians: Products of intermarriage between Arabs and Black Africans such as the majority of Northern Sudanese, half of Mauritanians, "Swahilized dynastic Afrabian families like the Mazrui of Kenya and Tanzania and famous Arabs of mixed racial descent like the late President Anwar Sadat of Egypt, whose mother was Black" (Mazrui 2009c: xiii).

Ideological Afrabians: Mazrui defined this category as Africans who refuse to recognise the Sahara as a divide and insist that all people indigenous to Africa (be they Arab or Black) are one people. According to Mazrui, the late Kwame Nkrumah typified ideological Afrabians. He argued that by marrying an Egyptian woman, Nkrumah's children through that union became genealogical Afrabians.

Cultural Afrabians: These are, according to Mazrui, Black Africans who have no Arab blood whatsoever but are highly Arabised culturally. He argued that many Sudanese – both Northern and Southern - are deeply Arabised in speech and values without being Arab genealogically.

Mazrui posed the question of where to locate the Hausa and Hausa-Fulani of Nigeria and answered it rhetorically: "Indeed, are not the majority of Islamised Africans of the blood (Black Muslims) automatically cultural Afrabians? That is a defensible categorisation" (2009c: xiii).

Was Mazrui an African?

For some, the answer to this is obvious: Mazrui was generally regarded as a leading African intellectual. But there are several Africanists (such as the Nobel laureate Wole Soyinka and the Nigerian social critic Chinweizu) who questioned Mazrui's Africanness and even his commitment to Africa. Among the reasons for this were Mazrui's Arab ancestry, his excuse (if not defense) of Arab slavery of Africans during the Trans-Saharan slave trade (Panapress 2001) and his strong condemnation of nationalism in Africa as a mask for dictatorship in the early years of his career. Many Africanists also did not forgive Mazrui for his critical article on Kwame Nkrumah shortly after he was overthrown as the President of Ghana. The article, entitled: 'Nkrumah: The Leninist Czar' was published in the now defunct magazine, *Transition* (Mazrui 1966). Mazrui also suggested the re-colonization of some African countries (Mazrui 1994); a suggestion that did not go well with several Africanists (Alamin Mazrui and Willy Mutunga 2003).

He was regarded by many as a leading African academic, who would have been a good candidate for a Nobel Prize in political science if there was one. He was also called a Kenyan, so obviously he was an African. But did Mazrui see himself as an African on the same level of Africanity as, say, an average Ghanaian or Nigerian? This brings us back to the question of whether identity should be a choice or an imposition – or both.

As we saw earlier, Mazrui identified his family and himself as part of genealogical Afrabians, who according to him, are bridge builders between Black Africans and Arab Africans. A related question is whether Mazrui saw his Africanity as a 'belonging of a different type' as Steven Friedman (2009) chose to define the Africanity of White South Africans? Or did he see it as a category in the hierarchy of Africanness? If it is a category in the hierarchy of Africanness, where did Mazrui place himself in relation to those he called Africans of the blood? Was he below or above them in the hierarchy? Did he invent a new category – the Arabians - solely to show that as a bridge builder he was morally superior to his critics, mainly Africans of the soil, who questioned his Africanness or commitment to Africa? Or did he invent it to give identity to several Africans who have both Arab and African ancestry such as himself and several people in Sudan, Mauritania, Somalia and elsewhere in Africa?

Critique of Mazrui's delineation of the Africans

How true was Mazrui's typology of Africans? Does De Klerk for instance see his Africanness as arising from adoption or naturalisation? Are the second and third generation of children born to African immigrants in the United Kingdom British by adoption or simply Black British? De Klerk's ancestors may have adopted Africa but did De Klerk play any role in that adoption process? (p. xi)

Mazrui's assumptions about 'American–Africans' is also problematic because there are several in this category who cannot speak any indigenous African language. Also where would Mazrui put second or third generation African immigrants in Europe and America, many of who may fail his test of being bilingual and in contact with relatives in Africa?

Additionally, Mazrui's notion of the African is so universalist and elastic that virtually anyone could fit into one of the categories or a category created for the person. Mazrui's universalist conception of the African, in fact, reminded one of the 'cosmopolitans' whom Rousseau accused of trying to "justify their love of their country by their love of the human race and make a boast of loving the entire world in order to enjoy the privilege of loving no one" (Quoted in Mazrui 2009: 46).

In his discussion of Afrabians, it was not clear if he saw them as a different set of Africans or what Steven Friedman (2009) called 'belonging of a different type' or simply people who were neither fully Arab nor fully Africans. It was also not clear from Mazrui's discussion of 'Afrabians' whether he meant them to be a group super-Africans who would be bridge builders between the African Arabs and Black Africa.

It is possible that Mazrui deliberately chose a highly elastic notion of the African so that the continent would eschew any temptation to believe that unity could only be achieved through cultural, linguistic and religious homogeneity. Mazrui was acutely aware that such a system of nation-building in the West was mostly achieved through ethnic cleansing.

Conclusion

We have interrogated Mazrui' notion of who is an African, beginning with his notion of 'Africa'. We argued that Mazrui believed that Africa was a fiction created by European cartographers and racism and its related imperialism and neo-colonialism. We also noted that Mazrui believed that Africa (or African identity) as we know, is a product of three influences - an indigenous heritage the heritage of eurocentric capitalism and the spread of Islam by both Jihad and evangelism. For Mazrui, since what people call "Africa" is a fiction influenced by 'triple heritage', African identity could only be a mosaic of combinations from these heritages.

From a theoretical notion of Africa, Mazrui went into a more empiric delineation of Africans. He identified several types of Africans – Africans of the blood, Africans of the soil, Africans by adoption, African-Americans and American-Africans. He also invented a new category he called "Afrabians" whom he regarded as bridge builders between Black Africans and Arab Africans.

We critiqued Mazrui's notion of Africa for being too static. We also critiqued his empiric delineation of the African for being so universalistic that virtually anyone could become African.

References

Adibe, J. (ed. 2009). *Who is an African? Identity, Citizenship and the Making of the Africa-Nation.* London: Adonis & Abbey Publishers.

Ayo, A. (2008). 'Eusebio is not African', in *The Guardian, https://www. theguardian.com/football/2008/jan/20/sport.comment5* (accessed July 10, 2016).

Friedman, S. (2009). 'Belonging of a Different Type: Whiteness and African Identity' in J. Adibe, pp. 79-83.

Herskovits, Melville J. (1960). "Does Africa Exist" Symposium on Africa, Mass, cited in Mazrui (2009a).

Horowitz, D. (2006). *The Professors: The 101 Most Dangerous Academics in America.* Washington DC: Regnery Publishing.

Karioki, J.N. (1974). 'African Scholars versus Ali Mazrui', *Transition*, pp. 55-63.

Mazrui, Alamin A. and Mutunga, W. (eds. 2003), *Race, Gender, and Culture Conflict: Debating the African Condition: Mazrui and His Critics, Volume One.* New Jersey: Africa World Press.

Mazrui, Ali A. (2009a) 'On the Concept of "We are all Africans"', In Adibe, Jideofor (ed.), pp. 35-55.

_____. (2009b). 'Who are Africans?' in Adibe, Jideofor (ed.), pp. 29-33.

_____. (2009c). 'Comparative Africanity: Blood, Soil and Ancestry', in Jideofor Adibe (ed.), pp: xi-xv.

_____. (1994). "The Message of Rwanda: Recolonize Africa," *New Perspectives Quarterly*, fall, pp. 18-21.

_____. (1986). *The Africans: A Triple Heritage*. Boston: Mass, Little Brown & Co.

_____. (1972). *The Trial of Christopher Okigbo*. London: Heinemann African Writers series.

_____. (1966). 'Nkrumah: The Leninist Czar', *Transition,* No. 26, pp. 8-17.

PanaPress (2001). 'Kenyan scholar downplays Arab role in slave trade', *http://www.panapress.com/Kenyan-scholar-downplays-Arab-role-in-slave-trade--12-550112-34-lang2-index.html* (accessed July 2, 1016).

Rodney, W. (1972). *How Europe Underdeveloped Africa*. London: Bogle-L'Ouverture Publications.

Ali A. Mazrui and Turkish Interests

Mohamed Bakari

Introduction

I would like to divide Ali A. Mazrui's academic oeuvre into three broad chronological periods. The oeuvre can be meaningfully categorized into the following phases: The 1960s to 1980s, when Ali Mazrui paid attention entirely to African issues; the 1980s to 2000, and the post 9/11 period. These periods coincide with the shifting interests in the political phenomena that he studied and tried to understand. At the core of his understanding of global events was his focus on Africa. He looked at unfolding political events and their implications in their relation to the African continent. He understood very early that the second half of the mid-20 century and early 21st century was most probably going to be Africa's long century. It was going to be as much Europe's long century as it was going to be Africa's. Here we borrow Eric Hobsbawm's characterization of European history in the 20th century as its longest century because of the cataclysmic events that shaped the nature of European society.[1] Not only did Europe go through such traumatic events of gigantic proportions, yet these events implicated in a direct way the other continents, and not least, Africa. For it was in the 20th century that Africa came under the firm grip of European colonization and at the same time embarked on a sustained attempt to extricate itself from that imperialism.

The young Scholar

The 20th century witnessed two great wars, the First World War 1914-1918, and the Second World War 1939 – 1945; which wars not only had political, but also social, technological, and intellectual ramifications.

It was only recently that scholars had begun to pay attention to the impact of the changing political scene. The transformations that took place during this century created what Peter Watson has called "the modern mind". The modern mind was willed into being by the men and ideas that shaped the contemporary 20th and 21st first centuries. This period saw the cross-fertilization of ideas emanating not from only Europe, but also Africa, Asia and the Americas. The world became intellectually united and globalized in an unprecedented way.[2]

As a young scholar, Mazrui owed his intellectual formation almost entirely to the Western liberal tradition, and especially his own personal humanistic education. His political science background was fortified by his reading of the English canon as articulated by F.R. Leavis and his disciples.[3] It was this background in liberal education that turned him into a quintessential liberal in his politics and outlook in life.[4] He tended to problematize African within the Western liberal tradition. However, this background has to be qualified by noting that Mazrui only immersed himself mostly in its political / philosophical thought, rather than its whole gamut, including appreciation of not only its political thought, but also its arts and its music, for example. It does not appear that he appreciated, for example, the Renaissance in its entirety, including not only Machiavelli, but also its great painters and artists, its literary pathfinders like Boccaccio[5] and Dante,[6] and Rabelais,[7] among others. What was true of Ali Mazrui's humanistic education background was generally true of other African intellectuals, as will be noted. Mostly products of missionary schooling, other African intellectuals were fed on the staple of Christian literature, starting with the Bible and then taken through Morality Plays, down the path of Buchan's *Pilgrim's Progress*, the kind of reading that Ngugi wa Thiong'o particularly excoriates as a staple of Christian indoctrination in his recent memoir.[8] Interestingly, way back in the 1972, Chinua Achebe was intrigued by what African intellectuals read, and asked the same question, of course quietly aware, that they actually read little outside their own narrow professional interests.[9]

The western intellectual formation of Ali Mazrui must also be buttressed by his formative madrassa education where he acquired a reading fluency in Arabic through his immersion in the Qur'an and Hadith as a young man growing up in Mombasa in a locally intellectually distinguished family of the Mazrui. For one, his father was the 1930s Kenyan Islamic reformer Sheikh Al Amin Bin Ali Al

Nafi' Al Mazrui, who held the important juridical position as a Chief Kadhi of Kenya during the colonial period. Most of Ali Mazrui's engagement with Islam draws from this fount. This kind of background is almost identical to other African Muslim intellectuals and men of letters, from Cheik Hamidou Kane to Mariama Ba to Nuruddin Farah.[10] This point is important to belabor because after 2001, Mazrui came under unwarranted criticism from colleagues in academia, especially in America, as having increasingly veered to the extreme right as a Muslim apologist. This was not the first time that Mazrui had addressed Islamic issues and in particular political Islam. Those familiar with his oeuvre know that he was aware of the role of Islam in the contemporary world and especially on his focus on Africa. In a 1991 paper he addresses directly the place of Islam in African history, culture and politics.[11] In the early phase of his career, Mazrui concentrated on Africa South of the Sahara (the so-called sub-Saharan Africa) – defined by colonial scholarship to draw a wedge between the then perceived 'Arab Africa' and the so-called 'Black Africa'. Clearly, Mazrui's engagement with Africa was determined by his research at the time. Although he had already been appointed to a full professorship at Makerere, he was still working on his D. Phil at Oxford. This was an anomalous situation then for an African university, although in British universities, dominated by scholar gentlemen, did appoint leisured aristocrats to professorship on the basis of their publications. In fact, at Oxford, there were tutors, like his own at Nuffield College, John Plamenatz, an East European whose doctoral thesis was rejected, but still remained there as tutor.[12] The other interesting case was that of Elie Kedourie, whose thesis on nationalism was also rejected by Oxford dons but who went on to carve a distinguished career in the University of London, as a serious theorist of nationalism as an ideology.

That this first phase was dominated by African preoccupations, as noted above, was mostly a pragmatic strategy; one to find a niche in which to specialize, before he ventured into the wider world. His major publication, *Towards Pax Africana* had formed the bulk of his doctoral dissertation and many of the ideas there he was to develop later into articles he submitted to key journals in political science in the United States of America and in Britain and Europe. At this time, like all the then young pioneering and budding African scholars, he was charting new territory and implicitly defending the much-denigrated continent as part of their intellectual contribution to decolonization. Most of these budding scholars were writing works of historical provenance, especially after the ill-considered remarks of Trevor Roper, the Regius Professor of History at Magdelene College, Oxford in his BBC Reith Lectures in which he dismissed Africa's role in World History as irrelevant and inconsequential. Political thought in Africa was virgin territory, in that most African scholars were divided between history and anthropology. Historians like Bethwell Ogot from Kenya, Isariah Kimambo and Temu at Dar es Salaam, Adu Boehen and D.O. Dike at Ibadan and Nsuka respectively, were reconstructing African history through oral sources, while young anthropologists like Kofi Busia and the contemporary generation of Jomo Kenyatta at LSE were working under prominent British Functionalist anthropologists like Bronislaw Malinowski, Evans-Pritchard and later, Jan Vansina. Anthropology was itself under greater scrutiny because of its perceived association with the European colonial project. As early as 1973, questions had already been raised about the relationship between the practicing anthropologists and their uneasy relationship with colonial administrators. This prompted the convening of a special conference to address the issue.[13] Ali Mazrui's interest in African politics can only be understood within the context of this intellectual engagement and its surrounding euphoria.

To fully assess Mazrui's contribution and appreciate the role he played as the most high profile African political scientist in Africa, one has to go back to his intellectual background to meaningfully grasp the success he made of his vocation. This can be gleaned from his intellectual preparation early in life. Although he did not do well in high school, he did have one very useful habit that was going to put him in good stead. Both in high school and outside, he had developed a reading habit. He read voraciously, although he was not catholic or eclectic in his reading. But as fate would turn out for him, he impressed those he met as a bright young lad who could be helped to realize his full potential. As recorded in numerous of his autobiographical-cum-political essays, he graduated from Manchester and then Columbia Universities. It was in these institutions that he immersed himself in the Western canon, whether in political thought, literature, history, or general culture. He did not wear his learning lightly. Scattered in his writings are references to the Great Books, to political philosophers, literary figures and intellectuals spanning the whole gamut of the Western intellectual tradition, as noted above, with qualification. Even the titles of his essays refer to these intellectuals of the liberal tradition. Titles like *Edmund Burke and Reflections on Revolution in the Congo*, and *On Heroes and Uhuru Worship* are just two examples of his obeisance to European masters of political thought. One has to read outside political science to discover one of the most important British intellectuals of the 19th century, Thomas Carlyle, whose controversial lectures delivered in the middle of the 19th century shook complaisance out of the comfort zones of hidebound conservatives who were unprepared to concede any originality to non-Western peoples and cultures. Mazrui, as an intellectual of Muslim background, must have applauded Carlyle in his spirited defense of Prophet Muhammad in one his lectures entitled "The Hero as Prophet", in his collected essays published as *On Heroes, Hero-Worship, and the Heroic in History*.[14] No African intellectual was as versatile as Ali Mazrui, or of his breadth of knowledge of the western canon. Carlyle was a master of English prose and to read him, even today, is to experience a rare aesthetic immersion in the best prose that the nineteenth century had to offer. All great prose stylists, including Carlyle himself, have been influenced by the mellifluous cadences of the prose of Edward Gibbon's *Decline and Fall of the Roman Empire*.[15] By imitating the prose styles of the 18th and 19th century masters of English style, like Carlyle, Gibbon and Dr. Samuel Johnson, Macaulay, among others, Ali Mazrui was defining a new written style all his own, and brought humor and excitement, in the otherwise austere prose of social science. He was in the good company of later prose stylists like V.S. Naipaul, James Baldwin, Ralph Ellison, and George Orwell. Many Africans went searching for the next Ali Mazrui article just for the sheer delight of reading his distinctive prose. No other African social scientist wrote with the same literary finesse as he did, and political science as articulated in the issues that Mazrui addressed gained popularity as a people's political science as much as it was the scholars'.

Mazrui's intellectual sparring with Mwalimu Julius Nyerere, Milton Obote and the particular nemeses like of Akena Adoko and the acrimonious manner in which they took place, imperilled his position as a public intellectual and political theorist,[16] must be understood within the formative period of African self-government. This was a period when African leaders behaved as if they came from a long tradition of experience in statecraft, whereas the reality was that they had greatness thrust upon them by virtue of their colonial education and the historical material time of their own lives. Their political skins were still very thin, easily irritated, and being the gadfly that Mazrui was and remained throughout his life, that was easy for him to provoke the new power elite and the emergent political class.

There are key milestones in Western intellectual culture and these include the development of Greek philosophical and scientific culture, Medieval Christianity, the Renaissance, the Reformation, the Enlightenment, and the Industrial Revolution. Having come from the British liberal tradition, Mazrui demonstrates his command of these key epochs in some of the essays that he penned. A lengthy 54-page introductory essay, entitled "From the Semites to the Anglo-Saxons: Culture in Changing Communication" (1986) in his volume on *Africa and other civilizations: Conquest and Counter - Conquest*[17] provides the historical background to the collected essays, and acts as a guide through the events that had far-reaching effect on African societies. He was situating Africa within the larger canvass of world stage and the emergent globalization. On the whole Mazrui was far better read than most of the intellectuals of his generation, although he was not quite a renaissance man that he could have been if he had broadened his intellectual interests.

The move to the United States and global politics 1980 – 2000

Ali Mazrui never intended to leave Africa.[18] It was only the unfolding events and circumstances in East Africa, and especially Uganda, that forced him into involuntary exile. Makerere gave him an intellectual and academic base from which he could thrive. Besides, years spent in Britain and the United States and his isolation from his African roots made those places less appealing to his restless mind. He saw Africa as a new laboratory for political experimentation where he could test the hypotheses of the great European political thinkers like Machiavelli, Rousseau, and Karl Marx, among those he often evoked in his political studies. He married literary style to political science; his literary interests he put in the service of his academic discipline, as reflected in his only novel that had a political theme: the role of intellectuals in society.[19] He immersed himself in literary issues as much as he did in political issues. He lauded, for example, Makerere for being a beacon of a new literary beginning by noting that: "The Department of English at Makerere can still claim to have produced more creative writers in English in East Africa than any other Department, at home or abroad."[20] His ability to immerse himself in literary debates also attests to his wide reading in the literary field, quite apart from his own discipline. He was a great fun of whodunits.[21] Another dimension least known to the public was Mazrui's interest in Hollywood movies. I discovered this when I tried to find out whether he had interests outside political science and politics. It turned out he had least interest in music and the genre he ever paid attention to was the Swahili music of the 1950s by the likes of Ali Mkali, of Mombasa, Kenya, and Bakari Abedi of pre-revolutionary Zanzibar.[22]

Somehow, too, he had become some kind of political celebrity himself, an academic rockster by debating the most charismatic African politicians like Thomas Joseph Mboya and radical leftist academics like Walter Rodney. He also attracted notoriety by his critiques of the socialist policies of Nyerere, Obote and Nkrumah, all of which were familiar to the readers of *Transition* during its heydays in Kampala. If he had not been keeping abreast of debates in leading journals and other publications, he would not have been able to mount the kind of robust analyses that he became famous for.

When his enforced exile appeared irreversible, he began to shift interest from continental politics to global politics. It was here that he began to argue about the centrality of culture in the relations between nations, because culture shaped their worldviews and then that becomes the source of mutual misunderstanding or misrepresentation of political positions. This was of course long before Samuel P. Huntington came up with his thesis about the clash of civilizations. We can also see that it was around the same time that he also began to focus on the relationship between language and politics. Around this time he began to collaborate with his linguist nephew Dr. Alamin Mazrui, then at Ohio State University, Columbus, to address the political importance of issues of language in African and global politics. It was astonishing for a political scientist with no formal training in sociolinguistics to come up with incisive observations on the role of language in shaping the politics of nations.[23] For him to have brought himself to the level required to contribute meaningful ideas in discussions on language required of him extensive reading in contemporary thinking in the sociology of language.

There has been one sided criticism of Mazrui as an apologist for Islam by both his critics and his detractors on the Left. Although they have been careful not to point directly at his faith in order not to be seen as open bigots, it is quite clear that some of those criticisms reflect the religious bias of the critics themselves. For one, virtually all the critics from the Left have been Christian renegades. Many of these have been invariably Africans, more often than not themselves products of missionary institutions. They seemed to have carried their biases into their new found ideologies. Their criticisms appeared to Muslims not only as attacks on Mazrui as a scholar, but Mazrui as a Muslim.[24] This is the most ironic of Mazrui's relationship with his political detractors. Anyone who knew Mazrui would vouch for his complete liberal philosophy of inclusiveness in his dealings with people from all walks of life and backgrounds. He had a complete lack of vanity, let alone racist or sectarian inclinations. Virtually all those he shared his life with were of Christian background, from the women he married to his students, and to his colleagues. It can be argued that although he was Muslim, he spent the greatest part of his long life with non-Muslims. He saw himself as a secularist Muslim and some of his political and spiritual positions infuriated Muslims even more. They went against the orthodox and mainstream Sharia positions. For example, his stances on capital punishment or on gay rights or even on *hudud* punishments were to the extreme Muslim left. He was not only a political theorist but also a man of conviction. He took not only a scholar's distance but also a principled position in any of the issues he ventured to articulate. For non-Muslims, their Christian backgrounds were taken for granted when articulating ideological positions.

Paradoxically too, what were assumed as liberal, Western ideological positions, in fact, had their genesis in Christianity or pagan ancient antiquity. One has only to read Carl Schmitt's *Political Theology* to confirm the Christian antecedents of much Western 'liberal' thought. I do not think Mazrui, given his extensive early readings of Western Great Books, would have escaped his attention. He not only quoted liberally from William Shakespeare, but the Bible too. Rare indeed was that African intellectual from a Christian background who had opened, let alone read, the Qur'an. In an interesting essay on this very issue, Thomas Hodgkin, an English Marxist historian and one time professor at the University of Ibadan, once had occasion to remark that West African students seemed to know more about the writings of H.G. Wells than that of his immediate contemporaries writing in Arabic in West Africa.[25]

Of course as a Muslim, one expects Ali Mazrui to have been interested in aspects of Muslim societies, and as a political scientist, in the politics of Muslim societies, as an inevitable product of his own triple heritage background. It must be remarked here that apart from Ibn Khaldun, Mazrui does not seem to have paid much attention to Muslim political thought, both medieval or contemporary, although there is much there that could have interested him. He was more obsessed with Western and African political thought. The entire intertextuality in Mazrui's work is predicated on the Western canon in the broadest sense, as we had indicated earlier. Yet, at the same time, he recognized that Islam and Muslim societies were part of the interconnected globalized world. He had the epiphany that in this new world, stitched together by the worldwide web, culture mattered. That there was really no one center but multiple centers with their own cultural axis. The move to the US increased pressure on his academic performance. The competitive nature of American academia meant that he had to be even more productive than he had ever been in order to rebuild a new life from his shattered life that he had left behind in Kampala, after threats on his life from Iddi Amin. Mazrui became even more indefatigable in his efforts to interpret political phenomena that he was constantly observing, in his publications and ceaseless travel. It was around this time that one observes that there was now left out the previous allusions to other texts and his writing becomes increasingly inward looking, and impressionistic. His work began to be less focused on particular issues that demanded attention in terms of theoretical orientation and background knowledge. In other words, his writing increasingly took on the coloring of journalism. In fact, most of the articles that he published in the 1990s and 2000s also appeared as columns in newspapers and were subsequently collected in anthologies and published as books.

The highbrow Mazrui now began to be increasingly recognized as as middlebrow, as a public intellectual, as someone who was sought to make public statements on pressing issues of the day. This role attracted more lowbrow and non-specialist readers, thus broadening the audience base but at the same time diminishing the attention of the more serious and scholarly readers. It is ironic that Mazrui in the late 1960s and early 1970s had defined an intellectual as someone who is "fascinated by ideas and has acquired skills to handle those ideas effectively". On his part now, Mazrui became more of an interpreter of the new politics of Islam and a critical analyst of ideological Islamism, that it was around this time that Islam gained more public attention, and notoriety through its vulgarization and sensationalization by the global media after the events of 9/11 in 2001. This demand led him to give simplistic answers to complex problems, because the write-ups lacked theoretical rigor and watertight methodology and argumentation, while mainstream political science was increasingly veering towards mathematical and quantitative models, much to Mazrui's dismay.[26]

In many ways, Mazrui's approach to academic scholarship overlapped that of the other famous postcolonial theorist, Benedict Anderson, of the *Imagined Communities* fame. Reviewing Anderson's recent posthumous autobiography, Joshua Kurlantzick noted attitudes towards scholarship that could easily be ascribed to Mazrui himself. He notes that:

> "Anderson always disdained the classism (and racism) of his schooling in the 1950s, and yet he celebrates that classical education's broadness, its lack of professional utility, its dedication to language, its independence from modern technology and its resistance to quantitative analysis was always a champion of the informal, approachable, interdisciplinary style of writing, and so his autobiography often makes leaps in time and from location to location. He disdains the idea that "serious" academic writing should avoid asides or personal comments or even jokes, that professors' work must speak in "prose [that] should reveal immediately the guild to which they belong … a prose style that is often much worse" in readability than the style those same academics used when they were students. He condemns the narrowness of modern academia, the segregation by discipline and the proliferation of journals whose articles are read by a tiny group of fellow scholars rather than by the general public. He is particularly skeptical of the idea that universities, funded by states and companies, must serve as a kind of professional preparatory school helping students get ready for a job."[27]

We will demonstrate this more extensively when we look at his treatment of Turkey in his writings.

Political Islam: 2001-2014

Ali Mazrui began to take an interest in the relationship between Islam and politics early on in his career. After all, his increasing specialization on African politics required that he address the role and place of Islam in African societies both historically and contemporaneously, since Islam had a firm hold on the continent. Clearly then, Islam as a cultural system, and a source of values that shape their politics too, does play a role in the political formation of the state. One of his earliest articles addressed precisely this issue. In his "Egypt's Three Circles" he looked critically at Gamal Abdel Nasser's role in Africa, as an Arab leader and as a Muslim. Mazrui noted thus:

In his *Philosophy of the Revolution* Gamal Abdul Nasser envisioned Egypt as the center of three circles – that of the Arab world, that of the Muslim world, and that of Africa. His involvement in African affairs, ranging from serving as guardian to Lumumba's offspring to active membership of the Casablanca group of States has led to the suspicion in some quarters that it is at best in the President's "African Circle" that Egypt's hope of leadership might lie. At least, until the Yemen exploded in the Arab world, it was argued that Abdul Nasser had become a pathetic figure of frustration both in the Muslim world and the Arab circles, and had to turn his attention instead to Africa."[28]

Looking at Egypt's foreign policy, he was approaching the theme from a scholarly, and not a sectarian view, although his Islamic background would help in elucidating aspects of the policies that might have been influenced by religious factors. There have been places where he robustly defended Islamic positions in instances where he found what had been written was not even-handed. A classic example is the 1997 essay, *Islamic and Western Values*,[29] that appeared in the prestigious journal *Foreign Affairs*. He intervened only in situations he felt duty bound as a seeker of truth to explain or defend or describe views he thought needed to be articulated in order to disabuse people of blinkers or prejudice. He may have been prompted to do this as a scholar of Muslim heritage, but most certainly as a controversialist political scientist challenging common pieties. This may also partly explain his interest in other Muslim societies, especially important ones, for a variety of reasons, in countries like Egypt and Turkey.

Ali Mazrui and Turkey

Ali Mazrui, in fact, wrote only one piece on Turkey. There was the earlier version that was commissioned by UNESCO for a symposium on education and culture conflict.[30] What was then dubbed culture conflict has now come to be accepted as identity crisis or identitarian politics or politics of identity or even what we now have come to recognize as a discourse of the politics of recognition. A number of philosophers, political scientists and sociologists, and historians have exercised their minds on issues of identity.[31] Mazrui wanted to look at the conundrum of African modernization without technological development, and looked at the experiments in modernization in Japan and Turkey and tried to theorize the reasons behind African technological backwardness without substantive development. He tried to show that Africa's modernization was some kind of a halfway house between the successful Japanese modernization that borrowed Western technology without losing its cultural soul. The Turkish experiment, Mazrui averred, stopped at cultural imitation without the technological back up. The problem here, again, assumes that modernization is something that comes suddenly and that modernization cannot be described on its own terms without being followed by Westernization.

Following this argument, then, Turkey, under Mustafa Kemal Ataturk, according to Mazrui, merely took the trappings of Western society without acquiring the intended development in the sciences and technology. This is also another example where Mazrui looked at a complex issue and tried to give a simplistic answer. In the case of both Japan and Turkey, the processes of westernization were driven by a core of political elites in each case, who had come into contact with western culture and society. There must have been deeper reasons as to why modernization was stunted, if indeed it had been, in the case of Turkey, and why on the other hand Japan made a success of their experiment. In both cases, it appears that Mazrui had only superficially made himself acquainted with the full story of experiment in their modernization. This is, first of all, reflected in the references that Mazrui uses, which are too sparse to do justice to this important subject. There is enormous literature on modernization in both countries that Mazrui was clearly unaware of. Most scholars interested in aspects of Turkish society and politics mostly depend on English language literature by students of Turkish affairs writing in English. Until very recently, writing on Turkey in European languages was very sparse, people tending to rely on writers like Bernard Lewis. His *The Emergence of Modern Turkey*[32] seems to be the to-go-to text for most English readers trying to inform themselves about Turkey. On closer examination, however, for those who have explored other sources and those who are familiar with the writings Turkish historians writing in Turkish, one immediately discovers that Bernard Lewis was totally reliant on indigenous Turkish historians and does a good job of paraphrasing in English work that had already been done by those historians, but which had not been translated into English. What he succeeds in doing is to give those facts his own slant and couch them in palatable language. For one, he supported in its entirety the whole Kemalist project of coercive modernization. Indeed, the *modus operandi* of the Kemalist elite who presided over the modernization, was Jacobin in its spirit and imposition. The almost three quarters of a century of Franco–Turkish relations had brought in some of the most radical aspects of French culture and alien worldview into Turkish culture.

First, modernization is a contentious term, and currently sounds passé and rather quaint. At least in the case of Turkey, literature is legion, in history, politics, literature and economics, just to cite a few examples.

Turkey, by geography and culture has always been part of Europe. In fact, without Turkey's otherness as defined by Europe, there would not have been a European identity as it has come to define itself. Turkey was Europe's first "Other". The Ottoman Empire was a far advanced civilization compared to Europe during the medieval and early Renaissance periods. It was only in the 19th century that we see the decline of the Ottoman Empire, as a result of both internal and external factors. The Ottoman Empire only shrunk into its current remnant only in the 20th century, but before this it was very active in the European arena, manipulating and itself getting manipulated in the process. In both the medieval period and early modern period, the Ottoman Empire was relatively more technologically advanced than Europe and was busy inventing and making things, and these advances range from technology to medicine. And as noted earlier, most of the seminal events identified with European history, from politics to mythology were played out in what is today Turkey. Thinkers that we have come to think of as European, like Herodotus and Diogenes were born in what is today Turkey. Aristotle got his wife from Assos, an ancient city in the Turkish side of the Aegean. In relatively more recent history, starting with the decline and fall of the Roman Empire, we know that among the Ottoman Sultans, many had Byzantine mothers and spoke Greek too.[33] The Ottoman Empire impacted Europe on the road to modernization as Europe impacted the Ottoman Empire and later, Turkey.

Although all the credit in the West goes to Mustafa Kemal Ataturk for his enforced westernization of Turkish society, in reality, Ataturk himself was a by-product of the efforts of the Ottoman Sultans to modernize through westernizing. These changes in the 19th and early 20th centuries were like rapid fire, starting with the military and then percolating to the intellectual and political elite. The acceleration for the Ottoman modernization through westernization, interestingly, came from Mamluk Egypt, which was a renegade Ottoman province led by an Ottoman military notable of Albanian European extraction. Muhammad Ali sent missions to France in order to acquire what was at the time the state of the art military technology and at the same time set in motion the process of transforming the Egyptian education system by setting parallel schools that used French as the medium of instruction. This was the acknowledgement of the increasing superiority of European military technology, medicine and science. Egyptian students did not only pick the French language and technology, but many of them came back with subversive ideas in politics, literature and morality. An identical process took place in the capital of the Ottoman Empire. Europeans who visited Istanbul were amazed by the degree of cleanliness and general culture of the Ottomans, a truly cosmopolitan culture that was built collectively by Muslims, Christians and Jews under the stern eye of the autocratic Ottoman Sultans. Many European visitors were infatuated with Turkish culture, many opting to stay and even converting to Islam, despite centuries of the demonization of Ottoman Islamic culture and society.

From the foregoing, it is clear that Mazrui was spreading himself too thinly when he chose to write on such sexy topics as modernization and westernization in non-European societies. Mazrui's busy schedule left him very little time to go over the vast literature that addressed the same issues he attempted to address, but without enough background to do justice to them. He ruffled feathers in a public lecture he gave at the then Fatih University, now part of Istanbul University, when he berated the Turks for not turning former enemies in the Balkans and the Arab world to friends after the collapse of the Ottoman Empire, a la British Commonwealth. He was probably unaware that the Ottoman divorce was one of the most traumatic events in that part of the world.[34] The Ottomans were undermined by the combined forces of the Christian communities all over the Balkans, the Arabs and European states, in particular Britain, France and Russia, all keen to scavenge on the disintegrating Ottoman Empire. Turkey was the only part left after the dismemberment of the vast ramshackle Empire already on its death throes. Modern Turkey is a complex place with a long and fraught history that cannot be reduced to its Republican period only. As the young Turkish political scientist Kerem Oktem (Oktem 2011: 1) noted, mere metaphors are not adequate to capture this complexity. He notes the reductionist tendency among some scholars to treat his country as a place that can be captured simply by the use of binaries:

"Imagine a country that is known more for the metaphors with which it is described than for its rather complex politics, society and history

– a country that is unfailingly described as 'Bridge between East and West', a passage which links Europe and Asia, combines tradition and modernity, and raises hopes for the coexistence of Islam and democracy. This Country, is of course, Turkey, the modern state on the Asia Minor landmass, which stretches out into the Aegean Sea and also include a small part of Europe in its Thracian west. This is a country that has a mostly Muslim population, shares borders with some of the most feared dictatorships of the Middle East as well as with the European Union, and an economy with one of the fastest growth rates in the world. Few places are so often alluded to in world historical debates on the 'clash of civilizations' or the 'future of Europe', and few countries are so frequently misread and misunderstood. The metaphors of bridges are often euphemisms that seem to obfuscate conflict between binaries that the metaphors celebrate: conflicts between East and West, between Europe and Asia, between Islam and secularism. And yet these simple binaries are inappropriate if we want to understand the startlingly complex, but also intriguingly dynamic, country which is Turkey today, and the historical processes that have brought it about.[35]

It is through a grasp of the intricate forces that over hundreds of years shaped modern Turkey that one can understand how it ticks. It is certainly not enough to make categorical statements for a complex a place as Turkey.

Conclusion

This chapter has tried to show how the Mazrui of the 1960s to the 1980s had truly contributed important insights into African politics and society precisely because he had intellectually prepared himself through extensive reading of the western canon. His classic essays on Nkrumah,[36] Nyerere,[37] and on the emerging African political culture,[38] were vintage Mazrui. But as his reading of other intellectual traditions foundered, so did his insights into those other societies. This is ironic for an intellectual who had dedicated himself to explaining the Rest to the West. We have specifically addressed Mazrui's fascination with Turkey because in his declining years, through acts of harassment by right wing forces and Islamophobes in America, he became disillusioned by the double standards of American society and its categorical demonization of global Muslims on account of a segment of the religion crazed ideologues hell-bent on polarizing Muslims and non-Muslims. Ali Mazrui was a model African and Muslim intellectual who tried to reach out across sectarian and ideological divides and this is reflected in his entire oeuvre. His academic contributions were trailblazing and enriched much of our intellectual outlook.

Endnotes

[1]   *See* Eric Hobsbawm's writings on Europe : *The Age of Revolution*, 1789 – 1848. Penguin Books. *The Age of Capital. 1848 -1875.* Penguin Books *The Age of Empire. 1875 – 1914.* Penguin Books. *The Age of Extremes 1914 - 1991.* Penguin Books. See also Peter Watson: *The Modern Mind* (Also published as *A Terrible Beauty. The People and Ideas that Shaped The Modern Mind.* Phoenix Press. 2000). See also Tony Judt: *Post War. A History of Europe Since 1945.* Penguin Books 2005.   See Jean–Paul Sartre: *We Only Have This Life To Live.* New York Review of Books Classics. New York. 2013. See Richard Lizzard: *The Crisis of the European Mind.* New York Review of Books Classics. New York. 2014.

[2]   Watson, *The Modern Mind.*

[3]   F.R. Leavis: *The Great Tradition.* Penguin. See also David Ellis: *Memoirs of a Leavisite.* Liverpool University Press. 2013.

[4]   See Mazrui, Ali A. *The King, The king's English and I.* Transition No. 38 (Jun.- Jul; 1971), pp. 57-66.

[5]   Boccaccio: Decameron. Penguin. 2008; Giorgio Vasari: *Lives of the Painters, Sculptors and Architects.* Everyman library. 1996.

[6]   Dante Alighieri: *Divine Comedy*

[7]   Rabelais: *Gargantua and Pantagruel.* Penguin. 2007.

[8]   Ngugi wa Thiong'o: *In the House of the Interpreter.* Anchor. 2014.

[9]   Chinua Achebe. What do African Intellectuals Read? In Chinua Achebe: *Morning Yet On Creation Day. Essays.* Heinemann Educational Books. 1975.

[10] See for example Cheik Hamidou Kane: *Ambiguous Adventure.* African Writers Series; See Nuruddin Farah's acceptance speech at the Neustadt Prize ceremony, at the University of Kentucky. Farah had memorized the entire Qur'an like many ethnic Somalis at an early age. References to the Qur'an and Hadith are legion in the fictions of African writers of Islamic background. It is paradoxical that the Christian and Biblical backgrounds of Euro-American and European writers is taken for granted while that of writers of Muslim background are not given the benefit of their formal religious education as informing their writing. On the issue of the impact of the Bible on Western literature, see Melvyn Bragg: *The Book of Books.* The Radical Impact of The King James Bible 1611 – 2011. Hodder & Staughton. 2011. See also William Hazlitt: *The Bible, Shakespeare and English Literature.* Penguin. On a relatively recent discussion see Christian Joppke: The Strange But Necessary Suppression of Europe's Christian Roots. *The Hedgehog Review.* Vol. 16. No. 1. Spring, 2014.

[11] Ricardo Rene Laremont & Fouad Kalouche (editors) *Africa and Other Civilizations. Conquest and Counter-connquest. The Collected Essays of Ali A. Mazrui.* Africa World Press, Inc. 2002.

[12] Personal communication, Ali A. Mazrui, Nairobi circa 1992.

[13] See Talal Asad (editor): *Anthropology & the Colonial Encounter.* Humanity Books. New York. 1973.

14 Thomas Carlyle: *On Heroes, Hero-Worship, and the Heroic in History. Forgotten Books.* 2012.

15 Edward Gibbon: *The Decline and Fall of the Roman Empire.* Everyman. 1910.

16 For a perceptive analysis of Ali A. Mazrui as a political science theorist and as a major but marginalized theorist of International Relations, see the important work of Seifudien Adem: *Paradigm Lost, Paradigm Regained. The Worldview of Ali A. Mazrui.* Global Scholarly Publication. 2002.

17 Ali Mazrui: *Africa and Other Civilizations*, 2002.

18 Personal communication, (circa) April, 1973. Malindi, Kenya. He had just been offered a year's Fellowship at the Stanford Center of Advanced Study.

19 This novel was *The Trial of Christopher Okigbo,* African Writers Series. Heinemann. 1971. See also James Currey: The Novel as Political Science, in James Currey: *African Writers Write Back. The African Writers Series and the Launching of African Literature.* James Currey, Oxford. 2008.

20 Mazrui, Ali A: Aesthetic Dualism and Creative Literature in East Africa. In Andrew Gurr and Pio Zirimu (eds.) *Black Aesthetics: Papers from a Colloquium Held at the University of Nairobi, June 1971.* Nairobi, Kampala, Dar es Salaam: East African Literature Bureau, pp 32-51.

21 This author saw him several times while passing through Nairobi with the Agatha Christie detective fiction centered on the morbid British predilection for murder stories.

22 Personal communication, Istanbul, May, 2013.

23 Two particular books contributed to the debate about the role of English in Africa and its relationship to indigenous African languages. These are *The Political Sociology of Language. An African Perspective. Contribution to the Sociology of the Language;* and Ali A. Mazrui and Alamin Mazrui : *The Power of Babel. Language and Governance in the African Experience.* The University of Chicago Press. 1998.

24 The widely publicized Wole Soyinka| Ali Mazrui spate is an example of this criticism tinged with religious malice. Soyinka is a critic of world's major religions and defender of indigenous naturalistic religions like primordial African belief systems and Shintoism and Hinduism.

25 Thomas Hodgkin: The Islamic Literary Tradition in Ghana. In I.M. Lewis (editor): *Islam In Tropical Africa. Studies Presented and Discussed at the Fifth International African Seminar, Ahmadu Bello University, Zaria. 1964.* Published for International African Institute, by the Oxford University Press. 1966.

26 On this issue, see Stanislav Andreski's controversial book: *Social Science as Sorcery.* Andre Deutsch. 1972.

27 Joshua Kurlantzick: A review of *A Life Beyond Boundaries* by Benedict Anderson – How to understand nationalism. *The Guardian.* 30, June, 2016.

28 Ali A. Mazrui: Africa and Egypt's Four Circles. In *African Affairs.* London *1964. 63 (251),* pp. 129-141.

29 Ali A. Mazrui: Islamic and Western Values. *Foreign Affairs.* September/ October 1997 Issue.

30 Ali Mazrui and Teshome Wagaw: *Towards Decolonising Modernity: Education and Culture*

Conflict in East Africa. Symposium on the Educational Process and Historiography in Africa; Dakar; 1982; Ali A. Mazrui: Africa Between the Meiji Restoration and the Legacy of Ataturk. Comparative Dilemmas of Modernisation. 1981. In: Ricardo Rene Laremont & Fouad Kalouche: *Africa and Other Civilisations.* 2002.

[31] For example, see the work of Charles Taylor: *Multiculturalism and the Politics of Recognition.* Princeton University Press.1992. Kwame Anthony Appiah: *The Ethics of Identity*, Princeton University Press. 2005. Will Kymlicka: *Multiculturalism and Citizenship. A Liberal Theory of Minority Rights.* Oxford University Press.1992.Tariq Modood: *Multiculturalism.* Polity. Second Edition. 2013. Ernest Gellner: *Nations and Nationalism.* Cornell University Press Second Edition.2009. Miroslav Hroch: *European Nations. Explaining Their Formation.* Verso. 2015; Benedict Anderson: *Imagined Communities.* Verso.1983.

[32] Bernard Lewis: *The Emergence of Modern Turkey.* Oxford University Press. 3rd Edition. 2001.

[33] *See* Steven Runciman: *The Decline and Fall of Constantinople.* Canto. 2014.

[34] *See* for example Yesim Bedlek: Imagined Communities in Greece and Turkey. Trauma and Population Exchanges Under Ataturk. I. B. Taurus. 2015;

[35] Kerem Oktem: *Angry Nation.* p.1. Zed Books. 2011. *See also* Serif Mardin: *Religion, Society, and Modernity in Turkey.* Syracuse University Press. 2006.

[36] Ali A. Mazrui: *Nkrumah, the Leninist Czar.* Transition 75/76. The Anniversary Issue. 1961-1976. p. 106-126.

[37] Ali A. Mazrui: *Tanzaphilia.* Transition. No. 31. (Jun. – Jul; 1967.

[38] Ali A. Mazrui: Monarchical Tendency in African Political Culture. *The British Journal of Sociology.* Vol. 18, 1967, pp. 231-250.

References

Achebe, C. (1977). *Morning Yet on Creation Day.* Heinemann Educational Books.

Anderson, B. (1983). *Imagined Communities.* Verso.

_____. (2016). *A Life Beyond Boundaries.* Verso.

Andreski, S. Social Science as Sorcery.

Appiah, K. A. (2005). *The Ethics of Identity.* Princeton University Press.

Bedlek, E. Yesim. (2015). *Imagined Communities in Greece and Turkey. Trauma and Population Exchanges Under Ataturk.* Ib. Taurus.

Boccaccio, D. (2003). Penguin Classics.

Boswell, J. (1992). *The Life of Samuel Johnson.* Everyman's Library.

Brady, C. (2013). *James Anthony Froude: An Intellectual Biography of A Victorian Prophet*. Oxford University Press.

Bragg, M. (2011). *The Book of Books. The Radical Impact of King James Bible 1611-2011*. Hodder and Stoughton.

Burke, E. (2009). *Reflections on the Revolution in France. Oxford World's Classics*. Oxford University Press.

Carlyle, T. (2012). *On Heroes, Hero-Worship, and the Heroic in History*. Forgotten Books.

Currey, J. (2008). "The Novel as Political Science." In Currey, J. *African Writers Write Back*. James Currey, Oxford.

Dante, A. *Divine Comedy*. Everyman's Library.

Gellner, E. (2009). *Nations and Nationalism*. Cornell University Press. Second Edition.

Gibbon, E. (1910). *The Decline and Fall of the Roman Empire*. Everyman's Library.

Hazlitt, W. (2009). *Selected Writings. Oxford World's Classics*. Oxford University Press.

Hobsbawm, E. (1996). *Age of Revolutions*. Vintage Books.

_____. (1996). *The Age of Capital 1848-1875*. Vintage Books.

_____. (1989). *The Age of Empire 1875-1914*.Vintage Books.

_____. (1996). *The Age of Extremes 1914- 1991*. Vintage Books.

Hodgkin, T. (1966). "The Islamic Literary Tradition in Ghana." In Lewis, I.M (ed) *Islam in Tropical Africa*. Studies Presented and Discussed at the Fifth International Seminar, Ahmadu Bello University, Zaria, 1964. Published for the International African Institute by Oxford University Press.

Hroch, M. (2015). *European Nations. Explaining their Formation*. Verso.

Kurtantzick, J. (2016). A Review of *a Life Beyond Boundaries*. The memoir of Benedict Anderson. The Guardian. June 30, 2016.

Kymlicka, W. (1992). *Multiculturalism and Citizenship: A Liberal Theory of Minority Rights*. Oxford University Press.

Leavis, F. R. (2011). *The Great Tradition*. Faber and Faber.

Lewis, B. (2001). *The Emergence of Modern Turkey*. Oxford University Press. 3rd Edition.

Mardin, S. (2006). *Religion, Society and Modernity in Turkey*. Syracuse University Press.

Mazrui, Ali, A. (1964). Egypt's Four Circles. *African Affairs*. London.

_____. (1967). Monarchical Tendency in African Political Culture. *The British Journal of Sociology*. Vol. 18, pp. 231-250.

_____. (1967). Tanzaphilia. *Transition* 31. Jan-Jul; 1967.

_____. (1997). Nkrumah the Leninist Czar. *Transition*. 75/76. The Anniversary Issue 1961-1976, pp. 106-126.

_____. (1971). The Trial of Christopher Okigbo. African Writers Series. Heinemann.

_____. (1971). Aesthetic Dualism and Creative Literature in East Africa. In Gurr, Andrew and Calder, Angus (eds) Black Aesthetics. Papers from a Colloquium Held at the University of Nairobi, Kenya. June, 1971.

_____. (1977). The Political Sociology of Language in Africa. Contributions to the Sociology of Language.

_____. (1997). Islamic and Western Values. *Foreign Affairs*. September/October. 1997 Issue.

Mazrui, Ali, A. et.al. (1982). Towards Decolonising Modernity. Education and Culture Conference in East Africa. Symposium on Educational Process and Historiography in Africa. Dakar.

Mazrui, Ali A, et.al. (1998). The Tower of Babel. Language and Governance in the African Experience. University of Chicago Press.

Mazrui, Ali A. (2001). Africa Between the Meiji Restoration and the Legacy of Ataturk.

Mazrui, Al'Amin A. (2002). Comparative Dilemmas of Modernity. In Ricardo Laremont and Fouad Kalouche (eds) Africa and Other Civilizations. Africa World Press. Inc.

Modood, T. (2009). *Multiculturalism*. Polity. Second edition.

Oktem, K. (2011). angray Nation. Zed Books.

Runciman, S. (2014). *The Decline and Fall of Constantinople*. Canto.

Schmitt, C. (2005). *Political Theology*. University of Chicago Press.

Seifudien A. (2002). *Paradigm Lost, Paradigm Regained. The Worldview of Ali A. Mazrui*. Global Scholarly Publications.

Taylor, C. (2005). *Multiculturalism and the Politics of Recognition*. Princeton University Press.

Thiong'o, N. (2010). *In the House of the Interpreter*. Harvill Secker.

Vasari, G. (1996). *Lives of the Painters, Sculptors and Architects*. Everyman's Library.

Watson, P. (2001). *The Modern Mind. An Intellectual History of the Twentieth Century*. Harper Perennial.

Eclecticism as a Theoretical Approach: The pillar of Ali A. Mazrui's Intellectual Legacy

Samuel M. Makinda

Introduction

This chapter is about two interconnected issues: a theoretical or conceptual framework called "eclecticism" and Ali A. Mazrui's contribution to it. I examine eclecticism as an innovative and dynamic intellectual tool and what role Mazrui played in its construction and subsequent growth. I argue that while Ali Mazrui's intellectual achievements have been celebrated, analyzed and critiqued widely by both his detractors and admirers, one of his outstanding contributions, that is, eclecticism, has not been closely associated with him. My argument is based on three claims. The first is that from the 1970s, Mazrui's enormous intellectual output was animated by an inclination towards eclecticism. His publications revolved around the synthesis of various traditions and norms, including a variety of African traditional values, Islamic culture, and Western political thought. This synthesis, which establishes connections among various developments that have been taking place at societal level for many years, falls within eclecticism.

The second claim is that while Mazrui defined eclecticism in an article entitled, "Eclecticism as an ideological alternative: an African perspective" (Mazrui 1976), he did not elaborate on this concept in his subsequent publications. Instead, Mazrui adopted the concept of a "triple heritage" to describe an agenda that he had previously treated under the label "creative eclecticism" in 1976. It is not clear whether he found the term eclecticism unattractive or he was simply more fascinated by the label triple heritage. Whatever the reason, Mazrui failed to nurture eclecticism as an intellectual approach to the point where it would have universal application. Moreover, it is puzzling that Mazrui appears not to have cited the 1976 article in any of his work. A more accurate way of reporting this is that I was unable to find any publication in which he cited this article, but it is possible he cited it in a publication that has not come to my attention.

The third claim is that if Mazrui's post-1970s publications were stripped of eclecticism, they would appear as isolated pieces of works that lack a coherent intellectual framework. The fulcrum of his research during this period was the synthesis of insights, values and narratives from different traditions. For example, works such as, *The Africans: A triple heritage* (Mazrui 1986) and *The African Condition* (1980), both of which were initially produced for the British Broadcasting Corporation (BBC), can best be explained largely within the framework of Africa's "triple heritage of values", which is itself a proxy for eclecticism. As of October 2016, the Google Scholar citation count indicated that Mazrui's 1976 article on eclecticism had been cited 10 times, whereas *The Africans: A triple heritage* had been cited 740 times and *The African Condition* had been cited 295 times.

Beyond the above claims, this chapter aims at addressing two interrelated questions. Why is eclecticism considered important? And, how significant was Mazrui's contribution to understanding eclecticism? To tackle these questions, the remaining part of this chapter is divided into three sections. The first section provides the meanings, significance and history of eclecticism. The second section discusses Mazrui's contribution to eclecticism through his 1976 article and subsequent publications, most of which were based on the "triple heritage". In the third and final section, I conclude that although Mazrui appears not to have been interested in promoting and elaborating on the concept of eclecticism after his 1976 article, an eclectic epistemology remains the pillar of his intellectual legacy.

Meanings, significance and history of eclecticism

Like all social science concepts that have a history, eclecticism does not have a clinical or universally accepted definition. However, in most writings, it is regarded as a process through which scholars combine insights from different research traditions to analyze a given problem. It is an ethic of pluralism, which is basically a defiance of the socio-mental boundaries that have been established by paradigms in our disciplines. For this reason, eclecticism cannot be rigid. It is a dynamic process through which researchers search paradigms for insights to illuminate the issues they intend to investigate. Some scholars refer to "creative" or "analytic" or "principled" eclecticism. Other scholars, such as Kenneth N. Waltz (1959), Michael W. Doyle (1997) and Alexander Wendt (1999), have self-consciously employed an eclectic epistemology without proclaiming it.

The common characteristic of scholars who employ eclecticism, especially in the field of International Relations that I am most familiar with, is their determination to go beyond the boundaries and other constrictions that have been imposed by various research traditions. They believe that social science research traditions are too restrictive and often work to hinder progress in their disciplines. For example, Peter Katzenstein and Rudra Sil (2008: 110-111) argue: "What we refer to as analytic eclecticism is distinguished by the fact that *features of analyses in theories initially embedded in separate research traditions can be separated from their respective foundations, translated meaningfully, and recombined as part of an original permutation of concepts, methods, analytics, and empirics*." (Emphasis in the original). They believe that eclectic scholarship "can be analytically coherent, intellectually interesting, and responsive to normative concerns and policy debates" (Katzenstein and Sil 2008: 111). I shall discuss Sil and Katzenstein's contribution to eclecticism later in this section.

In most social science disciplines, supporters of particular research traditions or paradigms and their challengers have one thing in common: they are primarily interested in establishing intellectual hegemony. They often ignore aspects of a phenomenon if it does not fit into their intellectual frameworks. In some cases, they ignore particular subjects because such subjects do not fall within the predetermined theoretical boundaries. However, exponents of eclecticism recognize that the complexity of social, political, and economic issues and phenomena require more than one research tradition. For example, in International Relations, promoters of eclecticism argue that world politics requires more than one research tradition to guide scholars and policy makers, alike. Put differently, eclecticism promotes the view that the intellectual hegemony of one research tradition could be counter-productive because it might result in the poverty of knowledge. Eclecticism also exposes the myth, inaccurately attributed to Thomas

Kuhn, that paradigms in social sciences, or International Relations, are incommensurable.

I call the claim of incommensurability in social sciences a myth for several reasons. First, while Kuhn (1962) claimed in his book, *The Structure of Scientific Revolutions*, that paradigms in "normal" science (meaning natural sciences) were incommensurable, he did not expect this term to apply to research traditions in social sciences. Indeed, Kuhn (1962: 15) appeared hesitant to apply the term "paradigm" to social science research traditions when he stated: "it remains an open question what parts of social science have yet acquired such paradigms at all". To the extent that Kuhn expressed skepticism about the existence of paradigms in social sciences, it is reasonable to conclude that he did not intend the idea of incommensurability to be applied to the research traditions in social sciences. Second, Kuhn clarified the meaning of commensurability in an essay entitled, "Commensurability, Comparability, Communicability", in 1982, when he argued that the term incommensurability simply meant that there was no common language between two or more theories. He posited: "The claim that two theories are incommensurable is then the claim that there is no language, neutral or otherwise, into which both theories, conceived as sets of sentences, can be translated without residue or loss" (Kuhn, 1996: 36). Kuhn (1996: 36) further argued: "No more in its metaphorical than its literal form does incommensurability imply incomparability". By so arguing, Kuhn left the space open for eclecticism.

Despite Kuhn's explanations, there are social scientists who may not have read *The Structure of Scientific Revolutions* correctly. Some of these scholars insist that social science, or International Relations, research traditions are incommensurable and, therefore, insights from them should not be combined. Indeed, almost every year I receive referee reports on my articles or research proposals that are strongly opposed to my decision to combine perspectives from different paradigms. While it is difficult to explain why some senior scholars are opposed to eclecticism, it is plausible to argue that they are driven by a sense of fear and insecurity. The way social sciences are taught in some institutions, and the manner in which some senior scholars seek to establish a community of compliant admirers, may hinder junior scholars from adopting eclecticism. The actions of such scholars might stem from a sense of insecurity on the part of both senior and junior researchers. What is needed to alter the thinking of such scholars is an opportunity for them to view eclecticism as a possible alternative to creating knowledge. The only things such scholars will lose are their insecurity and the attendant mental constrictions.

In social sciences, most research traditions have a common language and overlapping epistemological and methodological boundaries. The main differences between these research traditions are based on social, political and normative objectives, which, under favorable circumstances, can be mediated. Indeed, one of the benefits of eclecticism is that it can provide a platform for mediating the competing social and political agendas that underpin social science paradigms.

Interestingly, the first scholar in the field of International Relations to apply eclecticism, Kenneth Waltz, did so before the publication of Kuhn's book. Waltz (1959), in *Man, the State and War: a theoretical analysis*, applied eclecticism, but he did not describe his approach as eclectic. In this book, he set out to demonstrate that a more satisfactory approach to understanding world politics was to adopt what he called "three images". The first image focused on how human behavior, particularly the character of key decision-makers, could impact on world politics. The second image looked at how the internal structures of key states, especially major powers, could affect the course of world politics. And the third image analyzed how the character of the international system, particularly anarchy in the international system, could influence the nature of world politics. After applying these three images to provide a richer and more nuanced picture of world politics, Waltz (1959: 230) concluded:

> The prescriptions directly derived from a single image are incomplete because they are based upon partial analyses. The partial quality of each image sets up a tension that drives one toward inclusion of the others… One is led to search for the more inclusive nexus of causes...

In the above quotation, Waltz appears to have been frustrated by the boundaries established by research traditions or paradigms and sought to operate above these boundaries. He recognized the limited capacity of any one research tradition or paradigm to explain world politics adequately. Although he did not use the term "eclecticism", he engaged in a process, which could be described as self-conscious or principled eclecticism.

While Waltz applied self-conscious eclecticism without naming it, Ali Mazrui (1976) was possibly the first social science scholar to define eclecticism and apply it to the African socio-political landscape. He coined the term "creative eclecticism", which he explained in terms of synthesizing and utilizing values from different traditions. Mazrui described eclecticism as "a genius for selectivity, for synthesizing disparate elements, and for ultimate independent growth in the intellectual field" (Mazrui 1976: 465). Unlike Waltz who viewed his approach in terms of the limited capacity of one image to explain the world, Mazrui saw eclecticism primarily in terms of recognizing the various cultural, ideological and religious forces that shaped the history and experience of Africa. Mazrui also believed that creative eclecticism was "the only ideological alternative compatible with African autonomy in modern conditions". In this sense, he viewed eclecticism as a set of ideas that would lead to particular material benefits. There will be a further discussion of Mazrui's contribution in the next section.

Another contemporary of Ali Mazrui who defined eclecticism and sought to promote it in the analysis of world politics was Susan Strange (1991). While Mazrui explicated eclecticism in relation to the values that shaped Africa's history and experience, Strange (1991) sought to promote eclecticism as a way of enhancing the newly-formed sub-field of International Relations called International Political Economy (IPE). By the late 1980s, Strange was frustrated by the failure of scholars to transcend the three major paradigms in International Relations at the time: realism, liberalism/idealism, and Marxism. Realists were keen to pursue the mercantilist traditions and often emphasized the need for states to control the markets, while liberals promoted the "free" market and competition as a way of enhancing global welfare. On the other hand, Marxists, who were opposed to the free market, saw capitalism as an exploitative system.

In her book, *States and Markets: An introduction to international political economy*, Strange (1988: 16) compared the competing research traditions to "three toy trains on separate tracks, travelling from different starting-points and ending at different (predetermined) destinations, and never crossing each other's paths". Consequently, she sought not only to open the field to the concerns and insights of a variety of disciplines and professions, but also to develop "a truly eclectic approach to international political economy" (Strange 1991: 33). In a chapter entitled "An Eclectic Approach", Strange (1991) argued that the "conventional" way of explaining the International Political Economy through three research traditions was not satisfactory.

Strange (1991: 34) explains that she had three other reasons for taking the eclectic route. The first was that defining "the subject in the conventional way too often meant limiting it, consciously or unconsciously" (Strange 1991: 34). Her second "reason was to introduce into the field a serious discussion of" the ends and means. And the third reason was the need "for some analytical framework that would end the mutual isolation of the three standard paradigms of international relations, which so far had produced only a dialogue of the deaf". She felt that the field of International Political Economy needed such a formula through which scholars could explain and understand four types of structural power: production structure, financial structure, , and knowledge structure. As with other exponents of eclecticism, Strange's move towards eclecticism was driven by the failure of any one of the then existing paradigms to provide a broader picture of the international political economy. She sought to transcend the boundaries of the existing paradigms.

It was partly against this background that Michael Doyle (1997), a liberal scholar, embraced epistemological pluralism by analyzing conceptions of war and peace from the perspectives of realism, liberalism and socialism. Similarly, Stephen M. Walt (1998), a realist, declared he recognized the limitations of current research traditions as he claimed: "No single approach can capture all the complexity of contemporary world politics". He then offered support for eclecticism when he argued: "The 'compleat' diplomat of the future should remain cognizant of realism's emphasis on the inescapable role of power, keep liberalism's awareness of domestic forces in mind, and occasionally reflect on constructivism's vision for change". At about the same time, Alexander Wendt published *Social Theory of International Politics* (1999), which was described as "a great work of self-conscious eclecticism" (Makinda 2000a). Wendt used neo-realism, neo-liberalism and constructivism to construct a social theory of international politics. Thus, by the late 1990s, a good number of scholars in the field of International Relations were in agreement that while the proliferation of paradigms had opened up the field to many perspectives, there was a need for reflection, evaluation, and integration. This recognition of the need for cross-paradigm fertilization helped open space for a more bold advocacy for eclecticism. The earliest scholars to explore this space were Rudra Sil, Peter Katzenstein and myself. In the remaining part of this section, I will discuss Sil and Katzenstein's approach to eclecticism before explaining mine.

Sil and Katzenstein have done more work than anyone else since 2000 to promote, and put in practice, what they have described as "analytic eclecticism". They call for "the accommodation of eclectic modes of scholarship that trespass deliberately and liberally across competing research traditions with the intention of defining and exploring substantive problems in original, creative ways, selectively drawing upon a variety of existing and emerging research traditions" (Katzenstein and Sil 2008: 110). They emphasise that the goal of eclecticism is not to "subsume or replace" paradigms. Its goal is "to demonstrate the practical relevance of, and substantive connections among, theories and narratives constructed within seemingly discrete and irreconcilable approaches" (Sil and Katzenstein 2010: 3).

The approach that Sil and Katzenstein have taken highlights at least three important features. The first is the capacity to operate across, or to trespass, paradigmatic boundaries. The second is the emphasis on the need to shift from paradigm-driven to problem-driven research or scholarship. And the third relates to the need to open a dialogue or conversation between academia and the public policy community. Thus, they believe eclecticism will enable scholars to communicate more effectively with the policymakers. Sil and Katzenstein's (210: 20) views on eclecticism are encapsulated in the following quotation:

> Analytic eclecticism ... does not exist in direct competition with research traditions... Its value-added lies instead in expanding the scope and complexity of questions so as to facilitate a more open-ended analysis that can incorporate the insights of different paradigm-bound theories and relate them to the concerns of policymakers and ordinary actors.

Having shown the evolution of thinking on eclecticism from the 1950s to 2010s, let me describe briefly my own perspectives before I wind up this section. As there are many similarities between Sil and Katzenstein's views, on one side, and my own views, on the other, I have no need to repeat what I have attributed to them. Suffice it to say that I have previously defined eclecticism in the International Relations field "as a process through which a theorist constructs a coherent analytical approach by utilizing, synthesizing and reflecting on insights from disparate paradigms" (Makinda 2000b: 398). I called this type of approach "principled" or "self-conscious" eclecticism. I stressed that theorists who seek to explore and employ an eclectic epistemology would need to meet some conditions. "First, they would need to recognize, but at the same time refuse to be confined by, paradigmatic horizons" (Makinda 2000b: 400). I argued that refusal "to be bound by paradigmatic boundaries requires acknowledgement that these socio-mental constructions are not fixed, but contingent" (Makinda 2000b: 4000). I also posited that such theorists need to recognize that balanced growth in the discipline is partly dependent on meta-theoretical reflections, which is the process of evaluation and theorizing that takes place above, not within, the discipline's major paradigms (Makinda 2000a).

It is important at this stage to point out that there could be "genuine" and "false" eclecticists. Genuine eclecticists seriously engage the existing and emerging research traditions before selecting insights from them to apply to the problem they intend to study. False eclecticists, on the other hand, include people who simply declare that they are using eclecticism without first demonstrating that they have engaged existing paradigms and derived particular insights from them.

In recent years, I have gone beyond the Euro-centric research traditions and argued that eclecticism would provide an opportunity for "the incorporation of non-Western traditions into [International Relations] debates" (Makinda 2000b: 399). If we regard eclecticism as an ethic of pluralism, "we should explore the possibilities of pursuing an IR discipline that takes account of the perceptions of us/them, self/other and inside/outside in non-European traditions" (Makinda 2000b: 399). This is part of what Ali Mazrui (1976: 484) described as "vertical cultural integration". In a field like International Relations, the incorporation of African, Asian and other non-European perspectives is all the more important because the dominant paradigms and their challengers are American, British or European, and they often seek hegemony or domination. For scholars from Africa, Asia or the Middle East, the struggle between the older paradigms and the new ones might appear like a family dispute within the Western dominated discipline. In such a situation, the contenders simply seek to dominate the discourse and academic tools through which the rest of the world should define its identity and interests. Eclecticism, if properly constructed, should provide an opportunity for non-European, including African, perspectives to play a role in shaping the production of knowledge.

Finally, I regard eclecticism as a part of the critical investigation project. One of the primary purposes of the critical investigation project, going back into history, is to challenge hegemony, domination, alienation, and marginalization. The critical investigation project also seeks to facilitate justice, emancipation and the dismantling of all lines of exclusion. Critical theory, associated with the Frankfurt School and other neo-Marxist traditions, emerged from the critical investigation project. However, once critical theory established itself as one of the competing paradigms with its own boundaries and discourse, it acquired the features of other paradigms, including exclusive practices and hegemonic ambitions. Eclecticism, on the other hand, remains dynamic, inclusive, and emancipatory. Part of its purpose is to point to the limitations of all paradigms, including critical theory. This is why in 2000 I made the following proclamation: "To all IR practitioners I suggest: rise up and embrace eclecticism; you have nothing to lose but your paradigmatic constrictions!" (Makinda 2000b: 400). From this perspective, I regard the version of eclecticism that I subscribe to as the legitimate heir to the critical investigation project. By taking eclecticism in this direction, I believe I have made use of Ali Mazrui's (1976: 465) claim that eclecticism is a genius "for ultimate independent growth in the intellectual field".

Mazrui, eclecticism and Africa's triple heritage

Ali Mazrui adopted eclecticism partly with a view to explaining the multiplicity of influences on Africa's history and experience. It was to demonstrate that one could not explain the identity of Africans from a single perspective. Mazrui adopted eclecticism also partly to suggest that Africans did not have to choose one particular path to development. It was intended to illustrate that several ideological approaches were available and Africans were at liberty to derive insights from these ideologies to shape their own future. In doing so, Mazrui sought to remind his fellow Africans of the nature of imperialism and colonialism. In "Eclecticism as an ideological alternative: An African perspective", Mazrui (1976: 466) claimed that a "critical point to grasp [was] that colonialism was based on both a structure of domination and a structure of damnation". The structure of domination comprised the entire machinery of colonial control, while the structure of damnation "utilized the sanctions of religious experience as part of the process of obtaining obedience and submission" (Mazrui 1976: 466). Eclecticism was designed to provide a framework to deal with the consequences of these two structures.

Due to my continuing interactions with Mazrui when I was an undergraduate at the University of Nairobi, I had the benefit of receiving from him a draft copy of his article on eclecticism in March 1976. By this time, the article had been accepted for publication by the newly-launched journal, *Alternatives*. The article focused on what Mazrui termed "four systems of thought which … profoundly influenced Africa" in the 20th century (Mazrui 1976: pp. 483-484). These were "the liberal-capitalist system, the complex of nationalism and race consciousness, socialism with special reference to the Marxist tradition, and the resilient forces of traditionalism and primordial values" (Mazrui 1976: p. 484). In the face of these influences, Mazrui (1976: 465) claimed that ideological eclecticism was "the only ideological alternative compatible with African autonomy in modern conditions". He also suggested other measures, which included "a process of fusion of the multiplicity of domestic subcultures into larger complexes of national and regional cultures" (Mazrui 1976: 484). He also suggested "a new basis of interaction between indigenous cultures and the heritage imported from the outside world" (Mazrui 1976: 484). This would constitute what Mazrui (1976: 484) termed "vertical cultural integration, implying a mobility of African values into world culture as well as an African receptivity to the influence of the global heritage". Mazrui (1976: 484-5) proclaimed: "Vertical cultural integration implies not merely a relationship between Africa and western civilization, but a relationship between Africa and all major external civilizations – Chinese, Indian, Islamic, and others". Thus, he conceived eclecticism within the universe of values, norms, cultures, and traditions.

From the late 1970s, Mazrui continued to explore the range of cultures and values that shaped Africa's past and future, but he appears to have abandoned the concept of eclecticism. In other publications, including *The African Condition* (1980), which was conceived as part of the prestigious British Broadcasting Corporation "Reith Lectures", Mazrui emphasized Africa's triple heritage of values. This theme culminated in his British Broadcasting Corporation documentary, "The Africans", which resulted in a book, *The Africans: A Triple Heritage* (Mazrui 1986), in which Mazrui described these influences as the three interacting heritages: African traditions, Islamic influence, and Western values. The concept of the triple heritage added enormously to Mazrui's international reputation, but it also earned him some enemies (Makinda 2005). As Mazrui focused on the triple heritage, he appeared to have collapsed the liberal-capitalist system and the Marxist tradition into one category termed Western or European influences. He also appeared to have collapsed nationalism and race consciousness as well as traditionalism and primordial values into one category of African traditional values.

Mazrui (1976: p. 481) argued that traditionalism "as a system of values is by definition the most African. It mainly implies a continuity with the pre-colonial past, and asserts the primacy of roots". While many African traditions had experienced the stifling weight of foreign dominance, some of them were resilient and durable. Western influences came through ideas, especially education and Christianity, but they also had a material base, including military technology. In reference to Africa's rulers who were either well-educated and spoke the European languages fluently or acquired power through military coups, Mazrui (1976: p. 469) observed that "the eligibility as ruler in post-colonial Africa [was] directly dependent on competence in either Europe's heritage of words or Europe's heritage of weapons". The article on eclecticism did not say much about the Islamic heritage, but Mazrui's subsequent publications on the triple heritage emphasized the role of Islam as the third element in the socio-political trilogy.

At a personal level, Mazrui regarded himself as a product of these three influences. Like any other African Muslim growing up in Mombasa, Kenya, the young Mazrui absorbed both African and Islamic values. Moreover, Mazrui's father, Sheikh al-Amin bin Ali al-Mazrui (1891-1947), was the leading Muslim intellectual in East Africa at one time. Yet, Ali Mazrui also received education at some of the leading Western institutions of learning, including the University of Oxford in the UK and Columbia University in the USA. His focus on the triple heritage was part of the continuing process of self-understanding.

It is this self-understanding that, in part, led to his theorizing about both eclecticism and the triple heritage. In theorizing about eclecticism and the triple heritage, Mazrui saw both material and ideational forces at work. Although I had several opportunities to ask Mazrui why he abandoned the term eclecticism in apparent preference for the concept of a triple heritage, I never raised the question. It is a question for which we might never get a full answer.

Conclusion

Although Ali Mazrui was possibly the first political scientist to define and utilize eclecticism, he did not adequately promote this concept. Here I would like to distinguish the "concept" of eclecticism from the "processes" that constitute it. Thus, while he may have failed to promote the "term" eclecticism, he did not abandon the "process" that eclecticism represents. Most of Mazrui's publications from the late 1970s applied an eclectic epistemology. In the majority of cases, Mazrui used the term "triple heritage", which, in my view, served as a proxy for eclecticism.

Eclecticism, as defined by Mazrui, need not be limited to ideological engineering or African conditions. To the extent that Mazrui raised issues about domination and damnation, about aggressive dependency and submissive dependency, and about vertical cultural integration as well as horizontal cultural integration in the 1976 article, his view of eclecticism has the potential for universal application. Most of Mazrui's major intellectual output in the last 40 years of his life was based on the synthesis of ideas, values and insights derived from disparate sources. This is why I regard eclecticism as the pillar of Mazrui's intellectual legacy.

In a debate that I had with Ali Mazrui in September 2002 entitled "Between Makinda and Mazrui: A reciprocal critique", which was in relation to a chapter I (Makinda 2003) was preparing to publish on him, he argued: "Authors who write a lot run the risk of fluctuating between the profound and the shallow". He further observed that "if the balance between the shallow and the sharp is ultimately on the positive, such an author may be in the tradition of Karl Marx and V. I. Lenin on the Left and Edmund Burke on the Right". In his view, Marx, Lenin and Burke "combined the power of the moment and the profundity of the eternal".

Ali Mazrui's article on eclecticism combined the power of the moment and the profundity of the eternal. It has already been used to explore the possibility of operating above paradigms in International Relations (Makinda 2000a and Makinda 2000b) and other areas of political science. Indeed, eclecticism has the potential to foster a dialogue between Western-centric perspectives and non-Western contributions to social sciences, something that Mazrui would have applauded.

References

Doyle, M. (1997). *Ways of War and Peace: Realism, Liberalism, and Socialism*. New York W. W. Norton & Co.

Katzenstein, P. and Sil, R. (2008). "Eclectic Theorising in the Study and Practice of International Relations", In C. Reus-Smit and D. Snidal, eds, *The Oxford Handbook of International Relations*, pp. 109-130.

Kuhn, T. S. (1962). *The Structure of Scientific Revolutions*. Chicago: University of Chicago Press.

Kuhn, T. S. (1996). *The Road Since Structure*. Chicago: University of Chicago Press.

Makinda, S. (2000a). "International Society and Eclecticism in International Relations Theory", *Cooperation and Conflict*, 35(2), pp. 205-216.

Makinda, S. (2000b). "Reading and Writing International Relations", *Australian Journal of International Affairs*, 54(3), pp. 389-401.

Makinda, S. (2003). "Epilogue: Ali Mazrui and his works" in Alamin Mazrui and W. Mutunga, eds, *Governance and Leadership: Debating the African condition*, Mazrui and his critics, Vol. 2. Trenton, NJ: Africa World Press Inc, pp. 431-453.

Makinda, S. (2005). "The Triple Heritage and Global Governance" in Bemath, A. ed., *The Mazruiana Collection Revisited: Ali A. Mazrui debating the African condition*, Pretoria: Africa Institute of South Africa; and Berkshire, UK: New Dawn Press, Inc, pp. 354-362.

Mazrui, A. (1976). "Eclecticism as an ideological alternative: An African perspective", *Alternatives*, 1(4), pp. 465-486.

Mazrui, A. (1980). *The African Condition: A Political Diagnosis*, Cambridge: Cambridge University Press.

Mazrui, A. (1986). *The Africans: A triple heritage,* New York: Little Brown & Co; and London: British Broadcasting Corporation.

Sil, R. and Katzenstein, P. (2010). *Beyond Paradigms: Analytic eclecticism in the study of world politics,* Basingstoke: Palgrave Macmillan.

Strange, S. (1988). *States and Markets: An introduction to international political economy*, London: Pinter.

Strange, S. (1991). "An Eclectic Approach" in C. Murphy and R. Tooze, ed., *The New International Political Economy*. Boulder, CO: Lynne Rienner, pp. 33-49.

Walt, S. (1998). "International Relations: One World, Many Theories". *Foreign Policy*, No. 110, pp. 29-46.

Waltz, K. 1959. *Man, the State and War: a theoretical analysis*, New York: Columbia University Press.

Wendt, A. (1999). *Social Theory of International Politics*, Cambridge: Cambridge University Press.

Mazrui and the Whig Interpretation of African Nationalism

P. Anyang' Nyong'o

Introduction

After almost a year of coming to terms that Ali Mazrui is no longer with us, time has come to soberly reflect on his intellectual works and discuss them dispassionately and objectively. The period of mourning is over: the dawn of reflection has arrived. And this, perhaps, is the significance of this symposium. Let us take a leap into the past and reflect on what Mazrui did, the intellectual heritage he left behind and our take on this heritage.

In the early 1960s, as early Mazrui graduated from Nuffield College, Oxford, with a doctorate in philosophy in the area of political science, he was immediately hired in Makerere University College as a lecturer, climbing very quickly to full-time professorship in the mid-sixties. While at Oxford, Mazrui's main area of concern in research and writing was on African nationalism and Pan-Africanism, not to mention his wider interest in political theory having been a student of John Plamenatz. Mazrui was on an intense lecture circuit locally and abroad; he was under great pressure to constantly share his thoughts with the public.

The three books that he published first were products of his work at Oxford. These were *The Anglo-African Commonwealth* (Oxford: Pergamon Press 1967); *On Heroes and Uhuru Worship* (London: Longmans 1967) and *Towards a Pax Africana* (London: Weidenfield and Nicolson 1967).

These early writings, along with his numerous journal articles, which concentrated more or less on the same topics, attracted substantial reviews and critics from scholars. Writing in *The Journal of Modern African Studies* (Vol. 1. No. 3 of October 1968: 389-409), Jitendra Mohan contended that Mazrui was more of a publicist in his writings than a political scientist. Jitendra went even further: he accused Mazrui of having "*A whig interpretation of African nationalism and Pan-Africanism.*"

This critique by Mohan, widely read and shared, influenced subsequent criticisms beyond the three publications that Mohan focused on. No doubt Mazrui remained the most influential African political scientist, at home and abroad, later moving out of his focus on Africa to what he described as *global studies.* These studies ranged from a focus on Islamic affairs, cultural studies, the role of language in politics and pure international relations. In his later works, therefore, having gone beyond African politics, Mazrui might have outgrown the 'Whig interpretation of politics' to be much more concerned with global issues of culture and trans-cultural relations. With a liberal approach to the analysis of social, political and economic affairs, Mazrui's scholarship occupied a class of its own. At times he was a gadfly, at others, he was an activist of a liberal persuasion seeking to intervene on what he regarded as illiberal behavior of governments in Africa and elsewhere.[1] Indeed his whig interpretation of African politics and Pan-Africanism came more or less to an end when he crossed the Atlantic and settled in the USA to pursue his intellectual career outside his motherland. Mazrui now concentrated his focus on the role of culture, language and religion on politics, very often seen by his colleagues in the west as somehow anti-western, a stigma he had to endure when he did his BBC documentary *The Africans: A Triple Heritage.*

This address will, however, seek to revisit Mohan's criticism in the context of the enormous publications that Mazrui had in the first decade of his half-century intellectual work. I cannot, in any way, attempt to comment on all of Mazrui's works, hence we shall confine ourselves to two important issues in his early writings: African nationalism and Pan-Africanism. Why did Mohan argue that Ali dissected and commented on African nationalism and Pan-Africanism from the point of departure "of intellectual whiggism," and what did this really mean? What is the importance of drawing the English whigs into Mazrui's scholarship?

What is Intellectual Whigism?

In 1931, a young history don at Cambridge University called Herbert Butterfield, wrote a slender book which he called *The Whig*

Interpretation of History. As William Cronon commented almost 80 years later in a publication of the American Historical Association called *Perspectives on History* (September 2012), very few scholars paid attention to Butterfield's book when it came out. Many years later, however, his subject matter could not be ignored. And this subject matter could be framed in terms of a question: *how do historians do their research and to what extent is their interpretation of what they view as history influenced by the present and the rather idiosyncratic style that some adopt regarding what might have gone on in the past?* As Cronon observed, Butterfield's chief concern was with *oversimplified narratives*—he called them "abridgements"— that achieve drama and apparent moral clarity by interpreting past events in light of present politics. This, in deed, is what prompted Mohan to associate Ali Mazrui's writings on African nationalism and Pan-Africanism with intellectual whiggism.

Ali Mazrui as a whig scholar

In that regard, Mohan, consciously or unconsciously, was reading from the same page with yet another academic, Rupert Emerson, who had called Mazrui an "intellectual gadfly". Writing in *Mawazo*, Makerere University Department of Political Science Journal, Emerson commented:

> Nothing pleases Ali Mazrui better than to seize upon an idea, a slogan, an event, and worry it, toss it up in the air and watch it come spinning down, stand it on its head, turn it inside out, and adroitly dissect it piece by piece. Nor is there anyone who indulges in such a sport with greater wit and skill. Although occasionally so fine-spun and intricately woven as to seem somehow insubstantial, his analysis is always enriching as well as entertaining, and often cuts to the heart of the matter.[2]

In the preface to his book, Butterfield argued that a whig interpretation of history tends to simplify history, to see causal relationships among past phenomena from the point of view of current relationships and experiences and hence to replace "historical research from general history." This, argued Butterfield, would perhaps be excusable in journalism; but it cannot be useful in a scholarship that seeks to explain and not simply to praise or condemn. It is not always the case that historical happenings are logical, nor can we argue that "progress has certain immutable principles" which are deterministic. This should not, however, lead us to rely on iconoclasts as the only true historians; it should, on the other hand, lead us more to painstaking research as the only way to discover how events follow each other in history, and whether we can discover certain patterns that lead to correlations (or explanations) in the past. The whig historian, however, *stands in the summit of the 20th century, and organizes his scheme of history from the point of view of his own day,* quite often simplifying complex relationships into "either/or" assertions. *The fallacy of the whig historian is the way in which he takes his short cut through the complexity of history.*

Mohan felt very strongly that Mazrui was very much like a whig historian, particularly in writing on African nationalism and Pan-Africanism in his first three volumes. Perhaps as a result of the pressure "to publish or perish", *there is much repetition in the three volumes, sometimes tiresome, in the development and presentation, and frequently in the actual wording, of his arguments.* Rather than delve into the complexity of the genesis and evolution of both African nationalism and Pan-Africanism, Mazrui, according to Mohan, is much more indulgent *in the colorful phrase, the striking metaphor, the novel comparison, the bold hypothesis, the dashing generalization:* all of which *give his writings an air of fluency and readability.*

No doubt that is why Mazrui was so successful with the general public: his writings were enjoyable and readable. But therein lay the danger: *complex problems do not require simple explanations to get understood.* With broad generalizations, certain things are likely to be obscured while others are taken for granted as "explanations" by the reader or listener who is neither conversant with the situation being described or written on, nor has the patience to read other works which could contradict or shed more light on what may be received as "the truth". Because of his enormous influence as a specialist on African affairs in the global scene, Mazrui's works were quite frequently received as *ex cathedra* exposes. Herein, argued Mohan — and in very strong terms - lay the danger in his works: *his approach is abstract, his method unsociological, and his perspective parochial and static,* asserted Mohan.

Ali Mazrui's Rendition of African Nationalism

What did phrases — or shall we say concepts — like *pigmentational self-determination, racial sovereignty, multi-pigmentationalism, pan-pigmentationalism,* really mean in the history and study of African nationalism? Within a closed body of language called "Mazruiana" they could very well be understood by the sect, which spoke that language. But Mohan contended that these concepts did not even help Mazrui in developing a thorough and systematic analysis of African nationalism. African nationalism remained simply an intellectual exercise, not an exercise in studying a social phenomenon, which deeply affected lives of people, and in which more than the elites were involved.

Granted that nationalism was spearheaded mostly by the educated elite, one cannot ignore the fact that they played their role within a social fabric "with others" whose interests were expressed in the ideology of nationalism, and "others" without who the elites would not have had the material or context for their political work. Quite often these "others", like the "returned soldiers" with little or no education, were as conscious as the elites about the evils of colonialism, and perhaps even more enraged against it, than the elites. Yet, according to Mazrui, history seems to have been shaped by the elite, unencumbered by the complicated class struggles and cultural diversities that differentiated the dynamics of nationalism from one region to the other, one type of colonial political economy from the other.

Thus, concluded Mohan, *Mazrui's mode, or rather want, of analysis prevents him from recognizing the variety of nationalism in Africa. It prevents him indeed from making even that comparative analysis which, as a political scientist avowedly interested in comparative politics, he might reasonably be expected to offer.* Granted that nationalists— and great historical individuals—shaped the history of Africa at the dawn of independence, what explained the difference between Kwame Nkrumah of Ghana and Hastings Banda of Malawi? Mazrui would perhaps quickly reply: the former was a Leninist Czar[3] while the latter was just Banda, a conservative African chief of a Czar!

Mazrui on Pan-Africanism and Non-alignment

To Mazrui, Pan-Africanism was simply *an allegiance to the African continent,* pure and simple. The complicated issues that Ann Seidman and Reginald H. Green developed in their book, *Unity or Poverty: the Economics and Politics of Pan-Africanism,*[4] published in the same year as Mazrui's triology, scarcely featured in Mazrui's essays on Pan-Africanism. If anything, the *politics of Pan-Africanism* was reduced to a study of *the style of leadership—or preferences* - of African statesmen. Some opt for this while others opt for that. Some prefer to approach

African unity through regional integration while others prefer radical unification at the continental level without much delay. Why these "preferences" are chosen is not very clear. Quite often it is resolved with reference to the "ambitions" of the individual leader. What a Leninist Czar would prefer is quite different from what an African chief Czar would opt for. What Mazrui did not have the patience for was the need to study the effect of national politics on Pan-Africanism so as to establish how "national and regional interests" shaped and impacted on Pan-Africanism. Mazrui got very close to doing this in the case of the impact the Union between Tanganyika and Zanzibar had on prospects for East African integration in 1964. But he missed the point when he saw this much more in terms of "the politics of non-alignment" rather than in terms of the contradictions between imperialist interests and class struggles on the island of Zanzibar itself.[5]

But let us credit Mazrui with one important insight. His analysis of the capacity of African states to be non-aligned while they do not have the military capacity to defend themselves against external aggression is important. Indeed, in the world in which Mazrui wrote in the 1960s, with cold war politics and the cut-throat competition by external powers to control the future of Africa, the balkanized states made leaders extremely vulnerable to external manipulation. In this regard Nkrumah was right: without continental political unity little else would be achieved in terms of economic development and social transformation. But Nkrumah added a rider: all this would not happen without a revolutionary ideology.

But what, we may want to conclude, is *Pax Africana* in Mazrui's political thought, and what bearing does it have on Pan-Africanism and Non-Alignment?

Essentially, Pax Africana means that *the peace of Africa is to be assured by the exertions of Africans themselves.*[6] Pax Africana postulates 'a triumph of continental jurisdiction, and perhaps of racial sovereignty. By continental jurisdiction Mazrui means that *there are certain African problems which should only be solved by Africans themselves.*[7] How this is to happen is nowhere discussed in *Towards a Pax Africana,* yet Nkrumah had spoken and written extensively on the need for an African High Command, a proposal which proved very unpopular with western imperialist powers and their local surrogates in Africa. Subsequently, with regard to the wars on national liberation in Southern Africa, the then Organization of African Union (OAU) –

present African Union - established the Liberation Committee based in Dar es Salaam which militarily supported and coordinated the liberation movements. This stands out as the most successful OAU project, and perhaps a much better example of *Pax Africana* than any that Mazrui could have alluded to.

Conclusion

In conclusion, the three books that Mazrui wrote, essentially compilations of his essays published over time after his graduation from Oxford, were useful reading at a time when there was very little published by African scholars on African politics and international relations. Their impact and influence was to be expected. But their durability as more scholars came into the field with better researched work soon became dubitable. Mazrui was perhaps conscious of this; hence his intellectual migration into other areas of concern like global cultural studies,[8] and his concentration on the role of culture and religion on politics and global affairs.[9] But one must not forget the BBC Reith Lectures which were televised and produced as *The Africans: A Triple Heritage.* This saw Mazrui at his best, perhaps reunited with his first love: journalism. Mazrui was a scholar from three academic persuasions: a political theorist, a novelist *(The Trials of Christopher Okigbo)* and a journalist. And in each of these fields, there were influences from the other fields: it was a triple communion.

It was after his Reith lectures that Mazrui came to the conclusion that *Pax Africana* could only be achieved were Africa to have access to nuclear weapons so as to provide a power balance between *Pax Occidentalis* and *Pax Orientalis.* Libya, according to Mazrui, would be the most likely candidate to spearhead this acquisition of nuclear power. Eventually an independent black ruled South Africa would follow suit. Nkrumah must have danced in his grave on hearing his Africa High Command proposal elevated to the level nuclear power in Africa by Mazrui. But the West was not amused by Mazrui. It is no wonder that the Public Broadcasting Service (PBS) in the US was denying funding by the US government once it aired *A Triple Heritage.*

As he entered the last three decades of his intellectual career, Mazrui's contribution to Islamic studies needs to be appreciated in the extent to which he employed his wide grasp of history, theology and Muslim societies to analyze the theological, historical and political influences on Muslim identity. In his last book, *Resurgent Islam and the Politics of Identity,*[10] a collection of essays under this theme, he used comparative examples from Africa, the Middle East, South Asia and Muslim communities in the West to delve into the complexities of Muslim identity and social stratification, and to provide contributions to key debates on modern Islamic political ideology. Mazrui had at last liberated himself from the grasp of a whig approach to analyzing social phenomena. Accusing his western detractors of a poor understanding of Islam, he sought to demonstrate that Islam was compatible with both liberalism and modernity. Mazrui was no longer excited simply with playing with words in his writings. He once defined an intellectual as "a person who has the capacity to be fascinated by ideas, and has acquired the skill to handle some of those ideas effectively."[11]

By the sunset of his life Mazrui had settled on handling key issues, not just ideas, which he thought were significant in shaping the politics and affairs of Africa and the modern world, and Islam was prominent among these issues. Few intellectuals on the African continent had risen to the pedestal of international recognition and respect as had Ali Mazrui. One could disagree with Mazrui genuinely in some of the intellectual and political positions he took; and many did. This was, indeed, his value to the global intellectual and academic environment: always ready to express his opinions, never shying away from controversy, and prepared until the last moment of his life to defend what he believed in.

Endnotes

[1]   See, for example, the collection of essays by various scholars on the works of Ali Mazrui in Omari H. Kokole (ed.), *The Global African: A Portrait of Ali A. Mazrui,* (Africa World Press: Trenton New Jersey, 1998).

[2]   Rupert Emerson, "Book Review: *Towards a Pax Africana,"* *Mawazo,* Vol.1, No. 1, (June 1967): 56-57.

[3]   See Ali Mazrui, "Nkrumah; The Leninist Czar," *Transition* (Kampala), Vol. 6, No. 26 (March 1966): 9-17. Also published in his book *On Heroes and Uhuru Worship,* pp. 112-133.

[4]   (Harmondsworth: Penguin, 1967).

[5]   Mazrui, *On Heroes and Uhuru-Worship,* p.93; *I Saw the Future and It Works*

[6]   *Towards a Pax Africana,* p. 203.

[7]   *Ibid.* p. 118.

[8]   See for example, Ali Mazrui, *Cultural Forces in World Politics* (Nairobi: East African Educational Publishers, 2005).

9   Hence the name of the Institute that he founded at the State University of New York in Binghampton: *The Institute of Global and Cultural Studies* in 1991.

10   Ali Mazrui, (Edited by Ramzi Badran and Thomas Uthup) *Resurgent Islam and the Politics of Identity* (Cambridge: Cambridge Scholars Publishing, 2014).

11   In a debate with Akena Adoko, Main Hall, Makerere University, Kampala, in 1968. But also see *The Annual Mazrui Newsletter, No. 30* (Spring 2006).

Ali A. Mazrui: An Anecdotal Essay[1]

Abdul Samed Bemath

The Africans Television Series

"*So you are in Africa after all!*" That is what Ali Mazrui said when the phone got cut off during his stay at a Johannesburg hotel, when he came to deliver the 1990 Sixth Desmond Tutu Peace Lecture. He said that South Africa is not exceptional and is part of Africa as he narrates in his nine-part television series *The Africans* in a scene where he opens the water tap in a West African hotel and no hot water flows as the pipe has not been connected. He calls the receptionist to complain - and the phone is not working! This is one of my vivid memories of Ali Mazrui.

Illustrating his "Africa's Triple Heritage" at this same Desmond Tutu lecture, prayers were read in the Abrahamic faiths (Islam, Christianity, and Judaism) and the Hindu religion. Mazrui opened his lecture by asking, "What about prayers from the indigenous faith?" This observation was appropriate as the lecture title was *Africa's Pro-Democracy Movement: Indigenous, Islamic, and Christian Tendencies* - looking at the impact of "Africa's Triple Heritage"- the interplay of indigenous African culture, Islam, and Christianity, accompanied with Western culture on Africa, and its contribution to pro-democracy in South Africa. I asked him several days after the lecture what answer he received and he replied: "Just some vague excuse!"

"The Africans" captured the imagination of South Africans, especially its Black majority. For me this was a different form of exposure to Mazrui; a visual one, encapsulating his perspectives of Africa in a television documentary series, and further reinforced my interest in him and in purchasing his book, *The Africans: A Triple Heritage. The Africans* was shown very frequently on the apartheid government's homelands Bophuthatswana BOP TV station during the nineties. BOP TV was also beamed over the Black Soweto Township near Johannesburg and spilled over to the Indian residential area of Lenasia near Soweto where I reside. To my knowledge, it was not shown during that period by the South African Broadcasting Corporation (SABC) television covering South Africa. How unfortunate for White South Africans and fortunate for Bophutatswana's White citizens!

I enquired from BOP TV presenter why "The Africans" was shown so frequently over BOP TV. He explained that the local public was fascinated by these series and that South Africa at that time was undergoing rapid political and social transformation. In Mazrui's series they saw a positive picture of Africa, the pitfalls that the future Black-ruled South Africa should avoid, and lessons learned from the African experience. That, in Mazrui, they saw a visionary and precursor of the African Renaissance. An African friend of mine was praising the western-trained intellectual Mazrui for his belief in the spirit of the African ancestors when he visited a Sangoma (traditional faith healer) in Soweto, and her predicting his future. Mazrui at his "Triple Heritage" best! Many Muslim students in South Africa have been drawn to him over the years because of the Islamic perspective of his Africa's "Triple Heritage." During the Salman Rushdie affair over his book, *The Satanic Verses*, South African Muslims relied on Mazrui's thoughts in their criticism of Rushdie's book.

Mazrui and Aca-Media

Mazrui coined the phrase 'aca-media' at the launch of *The Mazruiana Collection* bibliography at the Zimbabwe International Book Fair in 1998. Aca-Media means linking the world of scholars and the media. At this launch, Professor Mazrui called for an "African Best Books of the Century" similar to the "100 Best Novels published in the English language." The media have had a powerful impact on Mazrui from his youthful days writing the Arab Page for the *Mombasa Times*, and as a radio station broadcaster in Mombasa. I asked him as a Swahili speaker, how he came to have such a command of the English language –both spoken and written– and he put this down to writing for the *Mombasa Times*. Muhammed Rajah, Mazrui's, Manchester University contemporary, told me that Mazrui wrote a piece for the university periodical in impeccable English. Professor Mazrui pointed out to me that the *The Mazruiana Collection* does not list his *1979 Reith Lectures* under section, Radio, Television and Video Recordings. This made me realize the importance the media play in his life and made sure these Reith Lectures were listed in *The Mazruiana Collection Revisited* (2005).

As his Bibliographer

Being associated with him as bibliographer of his works, *The Mazruiana Collection* (Sterling 1998) and *The Mazruiana Collection Revisited* (New Dawn Press and Africa Institute of South Africa, 2005) brings out differing responses from people. Let me elaborate. Garth Le Pere, at that time Director of the Foundation for Global Dialogue, introduced me to one of the University of Zimbabwe Vice-Chancellors at a conference. On telling him that I compiled a bibliography of Professor Mazrui's works, his attitude towards me changed to that of respect. Unlike a Mazruiphobic response on showing my bibliography to a participant at a conference in Johannesburg - he threw my bibliography in disgust to the ground– which is understandable as it is difficult to hold a book with 514 entries, let alone 24 books. A heavy load to carry in both hands! The Foundation for Global Dialogue is one of the seven co-publishers of *The Mazruiana Collection*, in which Bellagio Publishing Network states in its newsletter: "Although this book is not directly concerned with publishing, we list it as an example of good co-publishing arrangements," illustrating the impact Mazrui has on publishers, radio and television stations in search for his views.

My essay, "In Search of Mazruiana: Tracing the Writings of Ali A. Mazrui, 1962-2003," to be published in *Public Intellectuals and the Politics of Global Africa* edited by Seifudein Adem (Adonis and Abbey 2011) traces my worldwide search for Mazruiana. Compiling these bibliographies has connected me to libraries, librarians, academics and institutes worldwide. Most helpful at all times was David Easterbrook, Africana Librarian at Northwestern University in the United States. Dr. Easterbrook facilitated a copy of Professor Mazrui's Columbia University M. A. dissertation for both of us as Professor Mazrui did not have a copy. And, I had a copy deposited in the South Africa-based Africa Institute of South Africa Library. I inquired from Cambridge (UK)-based Terry Barringer, *African Affairs* Journal Bibliographer and Editor of *African Research and Documentation*, whether she could obtain a copy for me of Professor Mazrui's Ph.D. from Oxford University. She suggested that I contact the British Library and I purchased a copy from the British Library's British Thesis Service.

I purchased his entire book via online Amazon.com, ABEBOOKS and other online bookshops I also have *"The Africans"* nine-part television series. I am now the proud owner of *The Trial of Christopher Okigbo* signed: "To Peter and Frances and family from Ali and Molly. With warm greetings for 1973." His essays in these books, roughly about 300, can be compiled into a bibliography on its own, independent of my Mazruiana Collections!

The Mazruiana Collection Revisited has two essays touching on Professor Mazrui's *Triple Heritage*. Dr. Zine Magubane's "Mazrui as Debater: Passion, Power and Polemic in Africanist Scholarship" focuses on three themes in her essay. These are the Mazrui-Wole Soyinka documentary debates on *"The Africans"* and Henry Louis Gates 1999 - *Wonders of the African World* documentary. Dr Magubane also touches in her essay on the acrimonious Mazrui-Archie Mafeje debate on benign colonialism and the Mazrui-William Ochieng debate on the future of African universities. The other essay is Dr Sam Makinda's *The Triple Heritage and Global Governance.*

Associating with Professor Mazrui has taken me to countries abroad and meeting distinguished people. The Institute of Muslim Minority Affairs edition of *The Mazruiana Collection* was jointly launched with the London-based Africa Centre at its African Renaissance Conference in London, November 1999. Lord Ahmed of Rotherham invited me to a special tribute to Professor Mazrui at the House of Lords in 2000. Chief Emeka Anyaoku, former Commonwealth Secretary-General, delivered the keynote address and also wrote a Foreword for *The Mazruiana Collection Revisited*. I also presented a paper at a symposium in his honor for his 70th birthday, in Binghamton, New York in 2003.

I saw a picture, an Internet picture, of Professor Mazrui using a laptop and a group of university students looking on. I was not computer literate and my compilation of his bibliographies prompted me to purchase a computer and become computer literate. Professor Mazrui is referred to as a "knowledge machine" and as his secretary at Makerere University so aptly put it about his prolific literary output to Colin Leys: "I don't know he writes; faster than I can type!" (*Q News Magazine*, July 2000: 25)

How fortunate for him to have such dedicated administrative staff from his Makerere University days. I recall the late Nancy Levis working under great pressure to facilitate *Mazruiana* for me. So have Barbara Tierno with her yellow tab notes to me -'Abdul this book and publication is for you', so was Ravenna Narizzano-Bronson his Administrative Assistant, Anna Maria Palombaro, and recently Jennifer Winans who e-mailed to me his publications for the 2003-2016 *Mazruiana* Annotated Bibliography that will appear as a chapter in Seifudein Adem's edited book titled: *Global African and Universal Muslim. Essays in Memory of Ali A. Mazrui,* to be published by Ayebia Publishing House.

Seifudein Adem asked me, "How do I approach such a great scholar as Professor Mazrui?" I told him just write to him. And Seifudein is now IGCS Associate Director! So our fate has been sealed in many differing ways with Professor Mazrui!

Postscript: A brief Biography

Ali Al'Amin Mazrui (1933-2014) was born in Mombasa, Kenya, and worked as a warden at the Mombasa Institute of Muslim Education (MIOME) and had a low grade Cambridge school certificate and Makerere University in Uganda would not accept him.

He mentioned to the Kenyan colonial authorities his interest in law and journalism. They told him that law was out of the question as colonial lawyers tended to be political agitators. He gave a talk on the Prophet Mohammed (PBUH). An impressed Governor of Kenya Philip Mitchell, who established MIOME, arranged funding for him to do his A Levels at Huddersfield College in the UK. On completion, he went to Manchester University passing with distinction in Governance (1960). He completed his M.A. at Columbia University in 1961 and his dissertation titled: *'The Congo: capacity for self-government and some problems of legitimacy.'* He completed his Ph.D at Oxford University in 1966 and his thesis was published as a book titled: *'Towards a Pax Africana: A study of ideology and ambition* (Weidenfield and Nicholson and Chicago University Press 1967). The book focuses on who should keep the peace in post-colonial Africa.

In 1963 he joined Makerere University as a lecturer in the Department of Political Science and Political Science and became Dean of the Faculty of Social Sciences. He was instrumental in advancing its Law School, a passion to become a lawyer was always with him and influenced by his father Shaykh Al-Amin Bin Ali Al Mazrui, who was the Chief Qadhi -Islamic Jurist of Kenya. The supreme irony is that the same Makerere that would not accept him as a student because of his low level Cambridge school certificate would later appoint him a Dean.

Falling out with the Idi Amin and Milton Obote governments, he joined Michigan University in the USA (1974-1991) as Professor of Political Science and Afro-American Studies and Director of the Center for Afro-American and African Studies. In 1991, he moved to the State University of New York in Binghamton as Albert Schweitzer Professor in the Humanities and established the Institute of Global Cultural Studies.

In 2010 Professor Mazrui approved the establishment of the Ali Mazrui Foundation (AMF) as a method and vehicle of mobilizing resources and energizing his works. In 2009, Makerere University launched the Ali Mazrui Chair and Scholarship Endowment and the Mazrui Centre of Global Studies (MCGS). The two constitute the Makerere-Mazruiana Projects (MMP). The Mazrui Chair at Makerere was in honor of the exemplary record of his accomplishments that began in 1963. Professor Mazrui proposed the agenda of his Chair at Makerere to focus on *Africa's Triple Heritage and the Mazrui* Chair is intended to attract future scholars of exceptional distinction in the objective that any new holder would repeat Professor Mazrui's illustrious record of the past. The Chair will support nationally and internationally credentialed research professors and lecturers in teaching, research, new innovations and knowledge management and exchange plus those engaged in writing and publishing. In 2016, the University of Johannesburg (UJ) in South Africa established the Ali A. Mazrui Chair of Higher Education.

The term public intellectual is in vogue presently but Professor Mazrui was a public intellectual from his Makerere days as Mahmood Mamdani stated at this Mazrui Symposium, that "he (Mazrui) was a public intellectual in the finest sense of the word" and his debates with Ugandan government Minister Akene Adoko on the role of public intellectuals in the Makerere Town Hall in 1969. A student asked Mazrui for one of his papers and returned with notes in the margin by Milton Obote and the latter called him to the Ugandan Parliament and gave him a dressing down. Ironically, after Mazrui's passing on, the same Ugandan Parliament established the Ali A. Mazrui Corner exhibiting his publications!

Professor Ali Mazrui and I had a lovely lunch in London and on returning to his hotel he mentioned to me, on entering the lift, "his search for immortality." I have often wondered over the years what he meant. Seifudein Adem answers this and I quote him. "I've put in so many enigmas and puzzles in my writings that it will keep the professors busy for centuries arguing over what I meant and that's the only way of insuring one's immortality." Those lines are from James Joyce, the great Irish writer, not from Ali Mazrui. But I would not be surprised in the least if Mazrui had similar thoughts. Whatever the case, the "enigmas and puzzles" in Mazrui's scholarship (and there are many of them) will, I believe, continue to fascinate us. And that, to me, is also an important aspect of his lasting intellectual legacy (*African Studies Review*, 57(1), April 2014: 133).

As Mazrui put it: "Many people disagree with me. My life is one long debate." The 2016 Nairobi Ali Mazrui Symposium continued this debate on him and his works. This publication advances it. The debate continues further in a tribute book, titled: *A Giant Tree has Fallen. Tributes to Ali Al'Amin Mazrui.* Edited by Seifudein Adem, Jideofor Adibe, Abdul Karim Bangura and Abdul Samed Bemath. Johannesburg, South Africa: African Perspectives, 2016. An expansive book memorializing the life and work of Mazrui, containing more than 130 tributes written by people ranging from heads of states to journalists.

My last meeting with him and Pauline was in November 2012 at the University of Pretoria and he wrote the following dedication to me on his paper delivered at this Seminar: "To Abdul, With high esteem and affectionate regard. Ali Mazrui." Such a treasured dedication to me! In the audience were law professors. He remarked to me, "Abdul, note all these professors of law." Deep down he was always a man of law and contributed to the development of Makerere University's Law Faculty. I last spoke to him on his 80th birthday, wishing him well. And he remarked, "Abdul you have e-mailed to me an article which I am still to read." This was a review of *The Mazruiana Collection Revisited* in Russian!

Endnotes

[1] This tribute was first published in the *Newsletter of the Institute of Global Cultural Studies* IGCS), volume 9, 2012. I have added additional information to the original tribute.

Was Mazrui Ahead of His Time?

Seifudein Adem

Introduction

Ali Mazrui loved many things. He loved debates, for instance; he loved controversy; and he loved prediction. But his love of prediction was perhaps one aspect of his scholarship which had been remarked upon the least, if at all. I wish to take a small step in this chapter towards filling that gap.

Mazrui was not a great fan of the scientific method. He never aspired nor claimed to be its practitioner. In fact, he was critical of it. He also viewed the whole enterprise of scientific prediction with a good deal of skepticism. Indeed, Mazrui (1969: 172) once said: "...only a thin dividing line separates scientific prediction from fortune telling." He said this at least 20 years before his scientifically-oriented colleagues, with their sophisticated game theories, large data sets and complex statistical methods were humbled by their inability to correctly predict two major international events of our time: the sudden collapse of communism and the rise of China as an aspiring global hegemon. Some of Mazrui's "empirical" colleagues later suggested, directly (Singer 2008: 256), or indirectly (Jervis 1998: 974), that in some areas Mazrui was ahead of his time.

Despite what he said about the fine line between fortune-telling and prediction, Mazrui sometimes wrote as a fortune-teller for whom persuasion was also the ultimate goal. He had also anticipated some of what have come to pass in social theory, African politics and international relations. Mazrui's observations in this regard could be classified into two broad categories, those pertaining to ideas (which include theories, methodologies and concepts) and events. We will sample a random selection of both of them in this chapter.

For at least two reasons, scrutinizing the events Mazrui had predicted is easier and intellectually more profitable than trying to analyze the social theories, method and concepts he had anticipated. Firstly, whenever a claim is made that someone had anticipated a social theory or a concept, interpretive issues are always involved. By definition this means that those claims are legitimately more contestable. Secondly, it is a more straightforward task to verify whether or not a predicted event had occurred since after all what is at issue becomes a factual claim. A focus on events will thus enable us to be more objective in our assessment of Mazrui. In spite of these challenges, or because of them, let us in any case begin with Mazrui's ideas.

Ideas

Culture and Identity Formation: Mazrui's (1963: 88-97) first major academic article was about the notion of culture and collective identity formation in the African context, written decades before this theme began to capture the attention of many political scientists. There is currently a proliferation of literature about collective identity formation, and the "return of culture" is now widely recognized (Wendt 1994: 384-396; Lapid 1996: 3-20; Lebow 2009).

Mazrui had articulated (or anticipated) some of the major social constructivist postulates in a language strikingly similar to that of social constructivists. These postulates, too, centered especially on culture and identity formation (*see*, for instance Hurd 2008: 301; also *see* Jervis 1998: 974). The question thus becomes: was Mazrui a social constructivist before social constructivism was accepted as a major paradigm in the study of international relations? Relatedly, Mazrui (1968: 69-83) was one of the first to draw attention to the deterministic nature of modernization theories, suggesting also that such orientation was in the tradition of Darwinism.

Dependency and Neo-dependency: Mazrui (1967) invented the term neo-dependency in his doctoral dissertation, later converted into a book. This was long before dependency theory became popular among leftist African intellectuals. In the past half a century, two views have dominated the development debate. On the one hand, there was the view held by Marxist and neo-Marxist intellectuals such as Amin (1977) that global capitalism has the propensity to under-develop Africa and that the solution was for Africa to disengage itself from world capitalist system through the adoption of inward-looking policies. This view is also sometimes known as Dependency Theory.

On the other hand, right-leaning intellectuals saw the process of economic exchange between Africa and the West as a positive-sum game, beneficial to both sides, even if the benefit was never equal. In a variant - or distant relative - of this paradigm, what some would call "African liberalism", Mazrui (1980a: 5) maintained that it was just too late to disengage from global capitalism; he suggested, instead, that Africa should counter-penetrate global capitalism. A prominent articulator of Dependency Theory, Andre Gunder Frank, conceded in 1991 that the call for disengagement was perhaps no longer a realistic strategy for developing countries (mentioned in Leys 2009: 32). Following China's return to Africa as an aspiring global hegemon, left-leaning intellectuals, too, seem to be reversing their position by advocating Africa's deeper engagement with China and by suggesting that this could accelerate Africa's own development.

Guns, Germs and Steel: On the role of technology in widening the gap between the Global North and Global South, Mazrui had anticipated an argument which Jared Diamond (1999; 2008: 83-90) articulated more recently in his ground-breaking book, *Guns, Germs and Steel: The Fates of Human Societies.* For Mazrui (1980b: 63-79) it was three types of technology which were particularly important for the rise of the West to global preeminence: technology of violence, technology of production and technology of communication. According to both Mazrui and Diamond, these technologies increased the destructive, productive and inventive capabilities of the West.

Political Economy Approach: Mazrui was perhaps ahead of his time also in calling for an international political economy approach to world affairs. Mazrui (1972a: 293) wrote:

> ...the Political Economy of World Order cannot be adequately understood purely on the basis of inter-hemispheric or even inter-state relations. Domestic and diplomatic issues are inextricably intertwined. How quickly the poor nations can cease to be poor is a question which touches both the potentialities of internal development in a given poor country and the prospects for a favorable international climate. Whether the rich nations embark on more imaginative policies in economic diplomacy is also an issue which pertains both to inter-state relations and to prospects for a favorable domestic climate within the rich nations in relation to those imaginative policies.

Mazrui was challenging above the foreign/domestic dichotomy long before it was fashionable to do so.

On international political economy, a field of study which Susan Strange single-handedly invented in the 1980s, did Mazrui also anticipate elements of her theory of structural power? In her brilliant book, *States and Markets*, Strange (1988: 119) introduced the four structures of power in global political economy, namely; the security structure, the production structure, the financial structure, and the knowledge structure, which she defined respectively as:

> ...the framework of power created by the provision of security by some human beings for others; the sum of all the arrangements determining what is produced, by whom and for whom, by what method and on what terms; the sum of all the arrangements governing the availability of credit plus all the factors determining the terms on which currencies are exchanged for one another; what is believed (and the moral implications and principles derived from those beliefs); what is known and perceived as understood; and the channels by which beliefs, ideas and knowledge are communicated -including some people and excluding others.

In 1985, Mazrui (181-183) laid down the elements of the theory of what he called structural dependency, making a distinction between the five elements of power: production, consumption, currency or liquidity, technology and (the English) language.

> ...structural dependency concerns the organizational aspects of political, economic and technological imbalance. A lack of symmetry in power relations, captured in institutional framework, lies at the heart of structural dependency. The phenomenon of multinational corporations constitutes one of the latest structures of dominance emanating from the Western world and operating elsewhere. Financial institutions, certain types of technological transfers, as well as large-scale military alliances involving major powers, are all forms of dependency structurally defined...A final language available to the United States is, quite simply, the English language, the most widely understood tongue in history. It is America's power that gives prestige to present-day English. Unfortunately, the United States is better at using English for transmitting its message than it is at using the language to listen to the whispers of the rest of humanity.

Mazrui's and Strange's theories are not identical, of course; nor are they closely related. It is clear that Mazrui's frame of reference was narrower than Strange's since he was concerned more with North-South relations or, more specifically, with the relationship between the United

States and the Third World. But it cannot also be denied that there is some convergence between Mazrui's and Strange's perspectives on how those issues should be conceptualized and framed.

Global International Relations: The distinguished scholar of international relations Amitav Acharya (2016: 4-15) had observed:

> The encounter among civilizations is another major theme of a Global IR research agenda. Huntington's popular thesis about the clash of civilizations has all the ingredients of traditional IR; it defines a major issue of the day from predominantly Western, especially American, vantage point. In essence, it captures the West's fear of Islam (and Confucianism) rather than Islam's fear of the West.

Indeed, Mazrui (1997: 131) wrote a response to Huntington about Islam's fear of the West pointing out, among other things, that:

> Western liberal democracy has enabled societies to enjoy openness, government accountability, popular participation, and high economic productivity, but Western pluralism has also been a breeding ground for racism, fascism, exploitation, and genocide.

If so, was Mazrui practicing Global IR before Amitav Acharya theorized about it?

Analytical Eclecticism vs. Ideological Eclecticism: Mazrui (1975a: 468-486) advocated what he called eclecticism as an ideological alternative, defining it as selectivity for synthesizing disparate elements, and for ultimate independent growth in the intellectual field. This was at least a quarter of a century before such prominent scholars as Peter Katzenstein and Rudra Sil (2010: 411-431) floated a roughly similar idea. Did Mazrui's call for "ideological eclecticism" also predate the maxim later popularized by Deng Xiaoping of China that "it doesn't matter whether a cat is white or black, as long as it catches mice"?

Mature Interdependence vs. Complex Interdependence: Does Mazrui's (1980b) theory of "mature interdependence" have an affinity with what international relations scholars Robert Keohane and Joseph Nye (1989) had called the theory of "complex interdependence"? Mazrui defined "mature interdependence" as "a form of interdependence (between groups), combining sophistication with symmetry. The sophistication comes from enhanced technological capabilities and expanded intellectual awareness; the symmetry emerges out of a few egalitarian morality and a more balanced capacity for mutual harm (reciprocal vulnerability)." The other forms of interdependence in

Mazrui's (1980d: 63-79) categories of classification are "primitive interdependence" and "feudo-imperial interdependence".

The End of History? Mazrui (1984: 303) wrote:

> [G]lobal capitalism is much more obstinate and resilient than its critics assume. Even the largest of the Communist countries - the Soviet Union and the People's Republic of China - are sensing a growing dependency on the world market, which in turn is dominated by capitalism and its methods.

These words were written long before there was any clear sign that Soviet Communism was about to collapse and about 10 years before Francis Fukuyama (1993) popularized his idea of the end of history.

Mazrui (1985: 184) also wrote:

> Capitalism may be thought of as the doctrine of competitive economics, resulting in market forces. Liberal democracy may be thought of as the doctrine of competitive politics, resulting in political pluralism. On balance, the United States has been much more successful in transmitting capitalism than in transmitting democracy.

Mazrui's prescience here was affirmed by what have been taking place in places ranging from China, where market socialism or authoritarian capitalism has triumphed, to Egypt, where the first democratically-elected government was overthrown by the military.

The Rise of BRICS: In 2003, Mazrui (*see* Mazrui and Kaba 2016: 203) observed:

> Brazil is to Portugal what the United States is to Britain: a child that grew too large for the mother. And just as the United States will in time overshadow Great Britain in influence in former British colonies in Africa, so Brazil will one day overshadow Portugal in influence in former Portuguese colonies in Africa.

Again, this was long before the influence of Brazil as a part of the BRICS started to be felt in the former Portuguese colonies in Africa, and beyond.

Confucius Institutes: Also in 2003 (*see* Mazrui and Kaba 2016: 38), before China's Confucius Institutes proliferated in Africa and elsewhere on a wider scale, Mazrui wrote:

> ...there is at most some interest in Mao Tse-tung in political science departments these days [in African universities], but still no interest in

Confucius. Mao's China is relevant not only to ideology and economic organization, but also to intermediate technology, medicine and new methods of agriculture. A conscious effort to learn more about what is done in China since Mao, and an attempt to see how much of it is relevant for African needs could help to add technical richness to cultural pluralism.

Clash of Cultures vs. Clash of Civilizations: Mazrui (1994: 521) rhetorically asked: "Will Islam replace communism as the West's perceived adversary?" This was at about the same time when Samuel Huntington published his famous and ground-breaking article "The Clash of Civilizations?" in 1993 (22-49).

Mazrui (1989b: 168) also wrote:

> Islam in despair could be pushed to a nuclear terrorism as a version of jihad. And a future case of Islamic nuclear terrorism - aimed probably against either Israel or the United States or both - may well be the outcome of the present Israeli-American insensitivity to the sense of honor of Islamic civilization.

Mazrui made the above observation more than a decade before "terrorism" and "clash of civilizations" became the principal categories of discourse in the West. Even earlier, Mazrui (1986) produced a documentary, a portion of which was based on the idea of what he called "clash of cultures." This, too, was before Huntington launched his clash of civilizations thesis.

The Rise of ISIS: Mazrui (1998: 18) wrote:

> While the first industrial revolution of capitalist production and the Christian reformation became allied to the new forces of nationalism in the new Western world, the third industrial revolution and any Islamic reformation will be increasingly hostile to the insularity of nationalism of the state...Islam and the information revolution will be allies in breaking down the barriers of competing national sovereignties. The new technology will give Islam a chance to realize its original aim of transnational universalism.

Mazrui made the above observations more than a decade before a movement was born which was presumably bent on creating a caliphate in the Middle East.

The Obama Doctrine: "Africa does not need strong men; it needs strong institutions." Those were the words of Barack Obama, uttered in Ghana during his first presidential trip to Africa in 2009. At least since he published his "The Monarchical Tendency in African Political Culture" in 1970, Ali Mazrui (1970a: 18-33) had sought to remind us about the pressing need for building strong institutions in Africa. Mazrui was not thus only ahead of Obama in articulating this paradigm but also he was almost prophetic in his appreciation of the associated challenges.

Also consider this: "If nuclear proliferation will not create the necessary sense of urgency, let us pray for a miracle of moral conversion." Mazrui (1981: 2) uttered those words 35 years before President Barack Obama (2016) would say basically the same thing: "The scientific revolution that led to the splitting of an atom requires a moral revolution as well."

Understanding the Arab Spring: Mazrui (1970b: 1185-1196) classified the phenomenon of protest into four groups as follows:

> ...*protests of conservation* (those acts or movements which are aroused by a sense of impending peril to a system of values dear to the participants); *protests of restoration* (nostalgic seeking to restore a past which has already been disrupted or destroyed); *protests of transformation* (a manifestation of a profound disaffection with an existing system of values); and *protests of corrective measures* (an *ad hoc* demand for a particular modification in the system).

A case can be made that if we had applied this theory to the so-called the Arab Spring of 2011, rather than using such a broad concept as reformist movement, to describe it, we could have foreseen that the Arab Spring was indeed an expression of divergent interests which was by definition irreconcilable.

Events

Since Ali Mazrui loved to travel, let us now travel with him in our imagination to different countries and issue areas to see the specific events he was able to predict, sometimes with pinpoint accuracy.

Zimbabwe: Mazrui (1972b: 20) wrote:

> When the hold of the white minority in Rhodesia is one day broken, we will almost certainly have a country called Zimbabwe.

Rhodesia gained independence in 1980 and was renamed Zimbabwe.

China: Mazrui (1973: 154) maintained that:

...before long the question was bound to be asked whether China belonged to the ranks of the weak and underprivileged, or was about to join the ranks of the powerful.

This was at least half a decade before Deng Xiaoping opened up China for business - a process that unleashed it as a rising global power.

But, even earlier, Mazrui (1967: 194) posed the following intriguing question about Sino-African relations:

> In the romance of shared humiliation, the Chinese had once touched the history of Pan-[Africanism] and been at times almost identified with it. But the future of Sino-[African] relations promises to be different in important ways. Latter-day-Garveyites might never again find it easy to confuse or equate the concept of "the [Black] race" with that of "the coloured people".

Czechoslovakia: Mazrui (1975b: 6) once lamented:

> ...we are nowhere near an international police force strong enough to keep the Russians out of another Czechoslovakia.

Apparently, Mazrui was referring to the 1968 Soviet intervention in Czechoslovakia which it sought to crush what was then called the Prague Spring. So, in 1979, Russians invaded Afghanistan.

Global Africa: In a paper titled, "Branches: An African Saga," a tacit reference to Alex Haley's 1976 book or the movie which was based upon it *Roots: The Saga of an American family*, Mazrui (1980c) prophesied:

> In the 21st century two sets of Blacks are likely to exercise significant power in world affairs -Black South Africans and Black Americans. Black South Africans will have inherited the industrial and mineral wealth of their part of the continent - with strategic minerals fundamental to the economic health of the industrial West. Black Americans will have narrowed the gap between themselves and Jewish Americans, their compatriots. Black influence will have become as significant in shaping American policy towards Africa as Jewish influence has been in shaping American policy towards the Middle East.

In the above passage, was Mazrui too optimistic? Perhaps not, since we are still in the opening decades of the 21st century.

South Africa: In his TV series *The Africans* (Programme 5), Mazrui (1986) asserted that South Africa will be free from the white minority rule in the 1990s. In 1994, the white minority rule came to an end in South Africa. In 2013, I asked him what he thought regarding his prediction about South Africa. He said: "I was vindicated about the schedule of the end of Apartheid, but I was wrong about the method or strategy of ending it. I was glad Apartheid ended with less violence than I predicted..."

Pakistan: Mazrui (1989a: 158) predicted:

> If Islam gets nuclearized before the end of the century, two regional rivalries are likely to have played an important part in it. One is the rivalry between India and Pakistan; the other is the rivalry between Israel and the Arabs.

In 1998, Pakistan exploded the nuclear device and joined the nuclear club.

Western Anxiety: Mazrui (2000: 276) wrote:

> Behind the Western fear of the spread of nuclear expertise to Third World countries is the fear of nuclear weapons proliferation. There is anxiety in Western capitals that what begins as the peaceful use of nuclear energy may become something more ominous -thus the repeated attempts by the United States to pull back Russia from any kind of nuclear cooperation (however peaceful) with a country like Iran.

The above passage could have as well been written this year on the opinion pages of *The New York Times* in reference to what was called the Iran nuclear deal.

9-11? Mazrui (2001) said:

> If Americans are going to spend money only to listen to views which they regard as 'balanced', they had better brace themselves for international shocks in the future at least as 'bewildering' as the Iranian and Cuban Revolution!

Three months later, it was September 11, 2001. I was in Japan, teaching political economy at the University of Tsukuba, when I read the above passage in one of Mazrui's papers. When I emailed him in 2005, drawing his attention to the sentence, and asking him whether he had therefore "foreseen" 9-11, his answers came in the form of questions: "Did I write that? Where?" Mazrui never answered my question, I also never asked him again about it.

Barack Obama? Mazrui (2004: 19) also wrote:

> The United States stands the best chance of achieving before the end of the twenty-first century a historic compromise on race, ethnicity, and

religious differences. The struggle for this historic compromise is likely to be led by African Americans, joined by other Americans of good will.

Was Mazrui prophesizing the election of the first African American president of the United States, four years before the event actually took place?

Uhuru Kenyatta: In his "Africa's Modern Pharaohs," Mazrui (2007a: 4):

> In this new millennium some African presidents are seeking immortality by grooming one of their sons to succeed... It seems conceivable that Kenya will have a younger President Kenyatta before very long [Uhuru Kenyatta].

In 2013, six years after Mazrui made the above observations, Uhuru Kenyatta was elected and became the President of Kenya.

Kenya Power-Sharing: Before the election of Uhuru Kenyatta, Mazrui wrote a paper when Kenya appeared to be on the verge of the eruption of political violence. This was after the 2007 presidential election. In order to avert the looming strife, Mazrui (2008) suggested as one option:

> The new Parliament should be sworn in, and called into session. Its first task should be to consider a constitutional amendment creating the post of prime minister answerable to Parliament and not to the Chief Executive (the president). If the constitutional amendment is passed, Parliament would then vote for the first Prime Minister. Considering the balance of political parties voted into the new Parliament, the new prime minister is almost bound to be the Honourable Raila Odinga. Kenya would thereby become something approximating the Fifth Republic of France with both an executive president accountable to the people, directly, and an executive prime minister accountable to the people's legislative representatives, Parliament. As in the case of the French Republic, the President (Mwai Kibaki) and the Prime Minister (Raila Odinga) would have to find ways of working together in the interest of the people of Kenya.

In Kenya, Mazrui's proposal fell on deaf ears. And yet, Ndri T. Assie-Lumumba (2016) observed:

> Had [Mazrui's] proposal been carefully considered, the post-election violence could have been averted...the solution that was [later] proposed by Honorable Kofi Annan and which was accepted in the end, came to [Mazrui's] formula of power sharing.

South Sudan: Mazrui (2007b) wrote:

> There is a possibility that the South of Sudan would secede from the North by the end of this decade.

In January 2011, South Sudan officially seceded, becoming the newest independent state in postcolonial Africa.

The Arab Spring/Egypt: Mazrui wrote in July 2011 (157-158), just after Hosni Mubarak of Egypt resigned, and when the dominant discourse centered on the quite optimistic theme of the "Arab Spring":

> I think because Egypt is a very ancient civilization, it may have to overcome a lot of older traditions, if you like, the pharaonic impediments to democratization. Egypt has had five thousand years of bureaucracy.

Mazrui 2011 (157-158) added:

> I am worried that these ancient tendencies of accepting power at the center which go back in Egypt thousands of years and not just centuries, may themselves prove an impediment to rapid democratization. Egypt's ancient political culture of deference to authority is dying, but not fast enough. *I hope I am wrong.* If Egyptians become democratic within the next fifty years, I hope my children will celebrate, because that will be faster than I was expecting it to happen due to that built-in lethargy of pharaonic traditions. [*Italics mine*].

In July 2013, the Egyptian military overthrew the first democratically elected government of Egypt. To his dismay, Mazrui was proven right - again.

Conclusion

From time to time, Mazrui also wrote about his own predictive power. On this, Mazrui (1980d: 52) had this to say:

> In 1967, in a lecture at Makerere, I predicted that the future of Swahili in Uganda depended on the decline of the Baganda and the rise of the military. The Baganda had been the greatest opponents of Swahili; the soldiers (mainly from Northern Uganda) were the greatest champions of the language. It turned out to be true that one of the very few cultural gains brought about by [Idi] Amin's rule was the greater use of Swahili in national affairs in Uganda.

So, what should we make of Mazrui's predictions? Certainly, Mazrui never said he was a prophet or a fortune-teller. He also rarely commented on meta-theoretical issues such as prediction and explanation. And yet it is remarkable that his approach to scholarship should yield such accurate predictions.

We know that Mazrui's methodology of prediction was not based on the positivist social science. We also know that Mazrui's father Sheikh al Amin Mazrui used to make predictions from time to time. If so, the question which arises is this: did Mazrui's methodology share anything with the methodology that informed his dad's predictions?

Mazrui has proved to be a futurologist; sometimes he also articulated what other would say only decades later but with a unique and inimitable eloquence. As a case in point, let us compare the following observations about postwar Japan.

American analyst and scholar R. Tagart Murphy (2014: 115) observed:

> As the occupation ended, it was a relatively simple matter for the bureaucrats overseeing economic strategy to redeploy the tools at their disposal from military objectives to the goal of capturing as many dollar earnings as possible in export markets.

Mazrui (1978: 7) had shared similar observation in this way:

> Japan as a country has replaced the imperial samurai by the businessman, the battalion with the multinational corporation and the honor-motivated hara-kiri with profit-motivated business.

It is of course important to contextualize Mazrui's predictions. But there is no doubt in my mind that Mazrui was an incisive and insightful observer of African affairs and, indeed, a penetrating interpreter of the drift in international relations. Ali Mazrui was clearly ahead of his time.

References

Amin, S. (1977). *Imperialism and Unequal Development*. Sussex: The Harvester.

Assie-Lumumba, N.T. (2017). Education and Gender as Critical and Cross-Cutting Themes in Ali Mazrui's Scholarship and Activism. In: S. Adem and K. Njogu eds., *Global African and Universal Muslim: Essays in Honor of Ali A. Mazrui*. Trenton, NJ: Africa World Press. Forthcoming.

Diamond, J. (1999). *Guns, Germs, and Steel: The Fates of Human Societies.* New York: W.W. Norton.

_____. (2008). Why Did Human History Unfold Differently on Different Continents for the Last 13,000 Years? In: M.A. Seligson and J.T. Passe-Smith, eds., *Development and Underdevelopment. The Political Economy of Global Inequality.* Boulder & London: Lynne Rienner, 2008, pp. 83-90.

Fukuyama, F. (1993). *The End of History and the Last Man?* London: Penguin.

Huntington, S. (1993). The Clash of Civilizations? *Foreign Affairs,* 72 (3), pp. 22-49.

Hurd, I. (2008). Constructivism. In: C. Reus-Smit and D. Snidal, eds., *The Oxford Handbook of International Relations.* New York: Oxford University Press, pp. 298-316.

Jervis, R. (1998). Realism in the Study of World Politics. *International Organization,* 52(4), pp. 971-991.

Katzenstein, P. and Sil, R. (2010). Analytical Eclectism in the of World Politics: Reconfiguring Problems and Mechanism across Research Traditions, *Perspectives on Politics,* 8(2), pp. 411-431.

Keohane, R.O. and Nye, J.S. (1989). *Power and Interdependence: World Politics in Transition,* 2nd ed. Glenview, Il: Pearson.

Lapid, Y. (1996). Culture's Ship: Returns and Departures in International Relations Theory. In: Y. Lapid and F. Kratochwil eds., *The Return of Culture and Identity in IR Theory.* Bouder: Lynne Rienner, pp. 3-20.

Lebow, R.N. (2009). *A Cultural Theory of International Relations.* New York: Cambridge University Press.

Leys, C. (2009). *The Rise and Fall of Development Theory.* Oxford: Jamese Currey.

Mazrui, Ali A. (1963). On the Concept of 'We are all Africans'. *American Political Science Review* 57(1), pp. 88-97.

_____. (1967). *Towards a Pax Africana: A Study of Ideology and Ambition.* Chicago: University of Chicago Press.

_____. (1969). Political Science and Political Futurology: Problems of Prediction. *Proceedings of the University of East Africa Social Science Council Conference.* Kampala: Makerere University, pp. 172-188.

_____. (1970a). The Monarchical Tendency in African Political Culture. In: M. E. Doro and N. M. Stultz eds., *Governing in Black Africa: Perspectives on New States*. Englewood Cliffs, NJ: Prentice-Hall, pp. 18-33.

_____. (1970b). Toward a Theory of Protest. In: R. I. Rotberg and A. A. Mazrui, eds., *Protest and Power in Black Africa*. New York: Oxford University Press, pp. 1185-1196.

_____. (1972a). The Political Economy of World Order: Modernization and Reform in Africa. In: J. N. Bhagwati, ed., *Economics and World Order*. London: McMillan, pp. 287-319.

_____. (1972b). *Cultural Engineering and Nation-Building in East Africa*. Evanston, Il: Northwestern University Press.

_____. (1973). The Yellow Man's Burden? Race and Revolution in Sino-African Relations. In: I. Wilson, ed., *China and the World Community*. Sydney and London: Angus and Robertson, pp. 152-178.

_____. (1975a). Eclecticism as an Ideological Alternative: An African Perspective. *Alternatives*, 1(4), pp. 468-486.

_____. (1975b). World Culture and the Search for Human Consensus. In: S. H. Mendlovitz, ed., *On the Creation of a Just World Order: Preferred Worlds for 1990's*. New York: The Free Press, pp. 1-38.

_____. (1978). *The Barrel of the Gun and the Barrel of Oil in North-South Equation*. World Orders Model Project. Working Paper. No. 5. New York: Institute for World Orders.

_____. (1980a). *The African Condition*. New York: Cambridge University Press.

_____. (1980b). Technology, International Stratification, and the Politics of Growth. *International Political Science Review*, 1(1), pp. 63-79.

_____. (1980c). Branches. Unpublished Paper. New York: Institute of Global Cultural Studies, Binghamton University.

_____. (1980d). Between Development and Decay: Anarchy, Tyranny and Progress under Idi Amin *Third World Quarterly*, 2(1), pp. 44-58.

_____. (1981). Mazrui Newsletter. Eve of 1981.

_____. (1984). Africa Entrapped: Between the Protestant Ethic and the Legacy of Westphalia. In: H. Bull and A. Watson, eds., *The Expansion of International Society*. Oxford, Clarendon Press, pp. 283-308.

_____. (1985). Uncle Sam's Hearing Aid. In S.J. Ungar, ed., *Estrangement: America and the World*. Oxford: Oxford University Press, pp. 181-183.

_____. (1986). *The Africans: A Triple Heritage*. BBC/PBS TV Documentary.

_____. (1989a). Growing Up in a Shrinking World: A Private Vantage Point. In J. Kruzel and J. Rosenau eds., *Journey through World Politics: Autobiographical Reflections of Thirty-four Academic Travelers*. Lexington: Lexington Books, pp. 469-487.

_____. (1989b). The Political Culture of War and Nuclear Proliferation: A Third World Perspective. In: H. C. Dyer and L. Mangasarian, eds., *The Study of International Relations: The State of the Art*. New York: Palgrave Macmillan, 1989, pp. 155-171.

_____. (1994). Global Apartheid? Race and Religion in the New World Order. In: T. S. Ismael and J. Ismael eds., *The Gulf War and the New World Order International Relations of the Middle East*. Gainsville: University Press of Florida, pp. 521-535.

_____. (1997). Islamic and Western Values. *Foreign Affairs*, 76 (5), pp. 118-132.

_____. (1998). Islam and Afrocentricity: The Triple Heritage School. In: J. C. Hawley ed., *The Postcolonial Crescent*. New York: Peter Lang, pp. 169-184.

_____. (2000). Technological Underdevelopment in the South: The Continuing Cold War. In: P. Wapner and L. E. J. Ruiz eds., *Principled World Politics: The Challenge of Normative International Relations*. Oxford: Rowman and Littlefield Publishers, pp. 275-283.

_____. (2001). The Place of Documentary Films in Africana Studies: The Case of 'The Africans: A Triple Heritage'. Keynote Address at the 4th Annual African Studies Student Research Colloquium. Bowling Green State University, May 23.

_____. (2004). *The African Predicament and the American Experience: A Tale of Two Edens*. Westport, CT and London: Praeger.

_____. (2007a). Africa's Modern Pharaohs: How Mortal are Africa's Presidents? Unpublished Paper. Institute of Global Cultural Studies, Binghamton University.

_____. (2007b). The Cumulative Exceptionalism of the Horn of Africa: From Inter-Faith Contacts to Regional Integration. Keynote Address. UNESCO's Greater Horn Horizon Initiative, Djibouti, November 12-15.

_____. (2008a). *http://www.pambazuka.org/governance/post-election-crisis-kenya-search-solutions.* [Published in 2008; accessed on May 27, 2016.]

_____. (2011). Arab Spring and the Future of Leadership in North Africa. *Transition*, 106 (1), pp. 157-158.

Mazrui, Ali A. and Kaba, A. (2016). *The African Intelligentsia. Domestic Decline and Global Ascent.* Trenton, NJ: Africa World Press.

Murphy, R.T. (2014). *Japan and the Shackles of the Past.* Oxford, UK: Oxford University Press.

Obama, B. (2016). Speech in Hiroshima, Japan. May 27.

Singer, J.D. (2008). Nuclear Proliferation and the Geocultural Divide: The March of Folly. In: R. Reuveny and W. R. Thomson, eds., *North and South in the World Political Economy.* Malden, MA: Blackwell Publishing, pp. 254-265.

Strange, S. (1988). *States and Markets.* London: Pinter Publishers.

Wendt, A. (1994). Collective Identity Formation and the International State. *American Political Science Review*, 88(2), pp. 384-396.

Appendix

Triple Tropes of Triads

Seifudein Adem

Let me begin by acknowledging the presence here of the late Professor Ali A. Mazrui's relatives and family members and thank them for being with us. This is apart from Mazrui's distinguished friends, his colleagues or his former students, groups that include both his critics and his admirers. Of course, an individual could be both a critic and an admirer of Mazrui at the same time or on different occasions. Thank you all for coming.

So, for some reasons, Mazrui used to associate different events and processes, with numbers in general, and number three in particular. Sometimes even the topics of his lectures came in "triads." Mazrui's flagship concept was, of course, the *Triple Heritage*.

In keeping with Mazrui's tradition of using the number three to tell stories, please indulge me also, to make a brief comparative reference to three professors and three universities to tell a story briefly about the relationship between Professor Mazrui and myself. It is an intellectual relationship. Of the three professors, two are Kenyans, Peter Anyang' Nyong'o and Ali A. Mazrui himself, and the other is, Ethiopian, Negussay Ayele. The three universities in question are Makerere, Addis Ababa and Binghamton. Nyong'o was Mazrui's student at Makerere University; I was Nyong'o's student at Addis Ababa University. Nyong'o and I met in my country, Ethiopia. Mazrui and I met neither in my country nor in his. We met in Binghamton, New York, in the United States.

Ayele was Mazrui's colleague at Binghamton University in the 1990s and Nyong'o's colleague at Addis Ababa University in the 1980s. I also happened to be Ayele's and Nyong'o's student at Addis Ababa

University in the 1980s. That Nyong'o, a Kenyan, was teaching an Ethiopian student in Addis Ababa would be, in Mazrui's phraseology, *horizontal inter-penetration*. Ayele's teaching activities in Binghamton represented what Mazrui would call *vertical counter-penetration*.

In Binghamton, New York, Ayele was a scholar turned diplomat turned scholar. He was Ethiopia's ambassador to the Scandinavian countries between his stints at Addis Ababa and Binghamton universities. Is Nyong'o a scholar turned activist turned scholar or, shall we simply say, he combined scholarship with activism?

I am not biologically related to Mazrui, as you know. But could I claim an intellectual lineage to Mazrui not just by virtue of my being the longest-serving associate director of the Institute of Global Cultural Studies which he created at Binghamton University but, and even more importantly, because I was taught by Ayele, Mazrui's former colleague, and by Nyong'o, Mazrui's former student?

On Ayele's side of my family line, I would be Mazrui's intellectual nephew; on the Nyong'o part of my relationship, I would be Mazrui's intellectual grandson. Apart from the mystical relationship between Mazrui and I, which I just outlined, I had also worked with Mazrui like Ayele and studied under him like Nyong'o. Moreover, I coordinated the logistics when, in April 2012, Mazrui invited Nyong'o to give a public lecture in Binghamton. What an amazing and happy convergence of coincidences!

It was in keeping with the Mazrui tradition that I was using the number three in my remarks today, as I already indicated. And also if, in the process, I said more about myself than was probably necessary, please note, that too is consistent with the semi-autobiographical style of Mazrui's discourse.

In addition to his *triple tropes of triads*, Mazrui was known for making penetrating comparison of seemingly unrelated individuals, things, and groups. In this vein, he compared, for instance, Soldier Idi Amin and Boxer Mohammed Ali; the African state and a political refugee; and the Bolsheviks and the Bantu. My own comparison of Professors Negussay Ayele, Peter Anyang Nyong'o and Ali Mazrui is less penetrating for sure, but the comparative exercise itself is in the tradition of Ali Mazrui.

Although Mazrui loved number three in a special way, it is fair to say that he was also a great classifier in general; nothing was unclassifiable for Mazrui whether it was racism, sexism, Africanity or slavery. It is true, too, that his typologies had occasionally brought him into collision course with some of his colleagues who were less impressed by his colorful typologies.

I trust our deliberations in this symposium will critically reflect on Mazrui's numerologies, comparisons, typologies, among other things, also in the spirit of intellectual pluralism and openness.

That said, I wish to welcome everyone, again, to the Ali Mazrui International Symposium in Nairobi, Kenya, and I do so on behalf of Binghamton University and on my own behalf.

Never before have I seen so many experts about Ali Mazrui gathered in the same place at the same time.

Let me close by expressing my appreciation to Professor Kimani Njogu, for his hard work, and others, for their material and moral support. I know it has been quite painstaking and time-consuming to put this together.

Asante Sana!

Index